The Clew

Sylvia Ward

with

Avril Newey

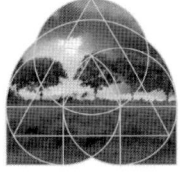

ABEON LTD

The Clew

First published in 2003 by
Abeon Ltd, P.O. Box 3524, Kenilworth CV8 2ZS, UK
www.abeon.co.uk

First Edition 2003

ISBN 0-9546094-0-9

© Abeon Ltd. 2003

All rights reserved. No part of this publication may be reproduced or transmitted in any form or by any means electronic, mechanical including photocopying, recording, or by any information storage or retrieval system, without written permission from the publisher.

Design by John Davies

Printed by Warwick Printing Co. Ltd.
on environmentally friendly paper

The Clew

Dedication

To all our childrens' childrens' children

Our Thanks

To all those who walked, stood, sang, danced … and believed.

* * * * *

For their special help our grateful thanks also go to Janet Ainsworth, Sarah Cohen, Heather Davies, Laurie Heizler, Kris Lee, Margaret Livingstone, Virginia Richards and Jim Ward.

The Clew

Contents

Part 1 – The Story

Prologue vi
Chapter 1 1
Chapter 2 12
Chapter 3 24
Chapter 4 37
Chapter 5 50
Chapter 6 62
Chapter 7 77
Chapter 8 95
Chapter 9 107
Chapter 10 122
Chapter 11 134
Chapter 12 147
Chapter 13 156
Chapter 14 169
Epilogue 184

Part 2 – The Rationale

The Search for Understanding 189
The Astrology of The Clew 197
The Tree of Life and the Turning of the Key 211
The Story Told, The Challenge Made 227
Final Wish 235

Bibiography 236
Acknowledgement 239
Notes 239
The Authors 240

Part One – The Story

The Clew

Prologue

A story so unusual, so evocative, so peculiar and almost unbelievable takes some time to put into perspective. Knowledge forgotten, abilities relearned, relationships remembered, yes, but from which era? And in whose lifetime? During an eight year period an ever-changing and evolving group of individuals are drawn together, by coincidence? By design? They must decide how to respond to requests that they interact with some of Britain's most ancient and sacred sites. Their decision necessitates making personal journeys of discovery into realities they have been unaware of. Making sense of their story, of such unusual requests, unusual energies, unusual realities can become an obsession.

The major source of information for the story, the instructions and inspiration for all the work they undertook, came from an extra-ordinary body of material directed to and received by Avril. Four volumes meticulously record the collected messages. She kept no other actual record of her thoughts, feelings, and experiences during this time. There is no existent diary; the events simply unfolded on a daily basis, in 'real time.'

On one level this is a story of actual situations, events, and interactions which resulted from work the group was mysteriously being directed to do. On another level it recounts interpretations they made of the information available to them. On one level it is a very personal story, unique to the individuals involved. On another level the story speaks a universal message, unique to no one and relevant to all.

Are the realities Avril and members of the group discovered, the experiences, the ways of knowing and remembering, relevant? The messages themselves imply they are not only relevant, but necessary for our survival. Throughout the messages a sense of reverence, appreciation and gratitude to the earth and our human 'mission' is expressed. Early admonitions evolve into gentle guidance and suggestions; suggestions give way to reminders and encouragement; and finally encouragement grows into a more persistent urging: assume responsibility. The story begins with one mystery, and ends with another; unfolds with the solving of one and the discovery of another; begins with the question 'what's going on?' and ends with the question 'where are we going?' And it is, perhaps, that question, 'where are we going?' that feeds the obsession, that necessitates making sense of it all.

Chapter One

Given the nature of the story, it's difficult to know where to begin. In fact, where and when did the journey begin? To each of the players it seems the ending was clear. Even though described as a beginning, still it seemed the ending was recognisable. But the beginning? Was it Avril's 50th birthday, as she sat where the ley lines crossed when the earthquake came? Was the beginning the actual message that came moments later and seemed to make so little sense? Maybe that was the beginning. Or perhaps the beginning was millennia before, in Sumeria or Alexandria, times Avril was repeatedly encouraged to 'remember.' Perhaps the beginning was actually with the sacred sites - standing stones, circles, earthen works, sacred wells, groves, and long forgotten places only sensitives can find. And when did each of the participants actually become a part of the group? When they, whether by coincidence or design, met Avril for the first time? Or centuries before that?

During unexpected moments within the group dynamics, someone could be the self they were in this lifetime, and at the same time be compelled to be someone they had been in some other time and place. At any given moment, the veil between this lifetime and something else could simply dissolve into a space with no past or present. The feelings some members of the group had toward each other could, without warning, erupt into unfinished business from some other shared time long since forgotten. There truly is no time. That was part of the learning. And yet for the story to be told, the words, the events must unfold with some semblance of order. Things must seem to have causes and effects and progress in linear fashion. There must be a beginning, and there must seem to be an end. And so, simply, it must begin.

AVRIL
Entering the Labyrinth

April 2, 1990 : I found out it was an earthquake. I was sitting at the typewriter they had given me and my chair lurched and threw me over the table. My head ached like anything. And I was so confused. It wasn't just the earthquake. I know it wasn't. I'm not absolutely positive what it was, but it was more than the earthquake. I walked around for a while, don't ask me why. I was so confused. And there was this terrible pain in my head. Only it wasn't from hitting anything. I'm not even sure my head hit anything when I went over the table.

Anyway it wasn't that kind of pain. Pain is like the nine years after Joanna died. Children aren't supposed to die before their parents. They're supposed to hang around for our death. When your daughter dies at twenty-one, that's pain. Or maybe pain is knowing you weren't supposed to live in the first place. If you're only three pounds and the doctor casually says "It's dead, don't worry about it," and sort of tosses you aside only to shout a moment or two later, "Good God it's alive!" Maybe that's pain. Maybe living with that for fifty years is pain. Maybe that's why the birthday celebration was so important. Because I've already had fifty years I wasn't supposed to have.

The Clew

But this pain was an urgent thing. Like I had to do something. Absolutely had to, there was no getting around it. Like go to the typewriter and write. Which seems a little strange since that's what I had been about to do anyway. But there was such an urgency to it. Somehow in my confusion I had even wandered outside. I decided to go back in and see what this writing urge was all about. Maybe the headache would go away if I just wrote something. Seemed a little weird to think that, but I turned to go back inside and noticed it right away. There was something wrong with the air in the room. I couldn't get through it. It was too thick. Like rubber. In order to get through the door I had to push through the rubbery air. It seemed strange at the time, but not as strange as it does now looking back on it.

Anyway I did go through it, I did sit down, and I did write. Well I don't actually know if I wrote it, but my fingers hit the keys. One word followed another and then the sentences followed each other and then it stopped. Not just the words. The words did stop, and the sentences stopped. I mean I did stop typing. But something else stopped too. Something had started, and then something just stopped. Unless you call being tipped over a typewriter and having to walk through rubber air and then almost compulsively having to write, unless you call that ceremony, then I would say it began and ended simply, with no ceremony at all. It began, and then it simply ended and was gone. And so was the weird feeling, the rubbery air, the urgency, the headache. Everything was back to normal.

Except that I had this paper with the typed words on it. Words that somehow fit together into sentences that didn't seem to make a lot of sense. Anyway I knew it was finished, so I took the paper out of the typewriter and carried it around on the palm of my hand. It has an energy all it's own, this paper. I don't know quite what to do with it. Or about it. I did finally show it to Warren. He was pretty impressed actually, but he told me I didn't write it. Well I know that. I just don't know who did.

I wish I could say I have no idea what is going on. I wish I could smile and act innocent. But I can't. Partly because, to tell the truth, I'm rather curious. Fascinated, intrigued, and maybe even excited. Carefully so, because I remember the other time. Waking in the night freezing cold and oppressed by the heaviness of it. Knowing something was in the house and knowing it was a something and not a someone. Knowing instinctively I had to protect myself and calling out loudly to my dead grandmother, "Nan, I believe you loved me, prove it now!" The fear and the fright of it, the awful presence. And then the words too big, too challenging, almost too angry to leave my throat, "I know you're here. This is my house and you'll not stay while I have the power to prevent it. If you want a fight, I'm ready." My knees banging together so loudly it could be heard upstairs. The actual physical agony as I felt myself engaged in life and death struggle. For almost an hour the battle of wills until, finally, it left. But only to the garden. No more sleep that night, desperately guarding the house and myself from that awful presence. The next morning practically crawling to the bathroom because I felt like I'd actually been in a physical fight. And looked it too, my husband said. Darkly circled eyes like bruises looking back at me from the mirror. Our housemate, his almost equal terror, the hair on his arms standing straight out even that next morning. Even remembering it I'm surprised by my insistence on seeing that man, that musician he'd been arguing with. And even more surprised to remember my words to him.

"Don't ever let go of that again!"

"But I don't want it."

"You must find some other way. You brought it here you're responsible for it, you take it back!"

Shouting insistently at him, so much fear and pain. And it had left. Left the house anyway. But not the garden. It stayed in the garden. And it took all my energy to protect myself from it. And then someone's mysterious but timely suggestion that I call the cathedral's occult advisor. Oh yes, I was reassured, all dioceses have an occult advisor. I remember the words of my frantic call and his carefully probing answer.

"What do you want of me?"

"I'm in trouble."

"But why me? Why do you want to see me?"

"Because I can't get back."

"I'll be there in 45 minutes."

He believed me. He knew what I had been up against and he believed me. I'd done everything right, he said. Except I hadn't finished it. I hadn't told it where to go. It didn't know and needed to be told. He told it. And it simply evaporated. The lightness of it once it was gone. The incredible lightness of it. I heard singing somewhere off in the distance, didn't know who or what it was as it came closer. Singing. Relief and joy and delight. And the startling thought, 'It's my song.' Off there somewhere, coming toward me, moving back. I was getting back. I remembered my words on the phone, "I can't get back." And then I felt it. I was moving back, into myself, coming back into focus.

Focus. There is something about focus. Like the wardrobe that other time, when I was pregnant with Hugh. Awake from discomfort and thinking the out-of-focus was simply fatigue. I kept trying, but it wouldn't focus. Why did I keep trying? And then the shape moving against the wardrobe. The midwife. But the wrong one, the one at the bottom of the list. She held something aloft. What was it? I couldn't make it out. Then her words, so distinct I repeated them aloud waking my husband. "It's a boy, nine pounds two." Our chuckle at his thinking he must have missed the delivery. We forgot then. The sun rose, the day began, out of focus and untimely words were forgotten. Until the actual sight of it. On the day I delivered Hugh. The wrong midwife, the one at the bottom of the list, the same one I had seen holding something aloft. Spring balances. It was a spring balance she was holding over her head now and had been holding before. I hadn't been able to figure it out before, but in real life there she stood holding them. She washed Hugh, weighed him and smiled my pride. "You've done well, a healthy boy nine pounds two." Hugh's father startled, reminding me finally of that other morning and our chuckle. And then I remembered the story of another midwife, my great great grandmother. An enigma how before the delivery she knew the sex of the baby every time. And another story about her granddaughter, my aunt. "Don't play football today" my aunt had told my uncle, "or you'll never play again." My aunt warned him of the red sweater too. Silly, he said - he always

The Clew

wore a green one. Silly he still said, even when moments before the game they told him to wear the red one instead. And he never did play football again. My great great grandmother. My aunt. And now me?

So perhaps I can't really say I'm a stranger to it. But this is so entirely different. There's such an awesome anticipation to it. I don't know why awesome and I don't know what to anticipate. But the page, the paper with the typed words on it … there's an energy to it. It has it's own energy.

There's something else I've just remembered. At my birthday party. I was ready to cut the cake. Hugh had just made that eloquent speech. Those words as they came out of my mouth. "Well I think I'll start now." Let people think I meant cutting the cake. Only I didn't mean that. I don't know exactly what I meant. I didn't even say the words. Well I said them, but I didn't think them ahead of time. I wasn't even thinking them as I said them. They just came out of my mouth. "Well I think I'll start now." I know it didn't show. How stunned I was, I know no one else knew. What did I think I was starting? I guess I still wonder but in a way I don't because in a way it feels now like it has something to do with this paper with the words on it. Or whatever urged the words onto it. The paper's energy, the urge, the meaning, I can make no sense of it. Things like this :

> *Only good will come from the written word that I write here. The spirit of trees and the green earth surrounds me, on the plain the single tree tells a story that I cannot quite remember … The words are to be unravelled, the story told … Somewhere there is a light which must continue to shine … Hold fast to the truth that walks the Way, follow the paths that lead to the hills, wash in the water over the stones, turn them until the sound is made. There will be power to guide the feet along the tracks, beacons make a line. They will end in the high places for it is the looking down on creation that will preserve all things … look for the ripples - they must be counted. There, feet have made marks and the energy lives, it can be stroked … This is the old way in the hills, the rocks remember where the fires have burned, the men must walk if it is to be saved. Follow the path, the energy must flow again. Take care, carry the rock.* [1]

The rock - at least I know that one. It's the little stone I picked up, the little piece of sandstone I simply couldn't resist in the Dassett Hills last month. That's the rock that must be carried. Take care, carry the rock. It's the knowing that comes with it, that's the strangest part. I simply know some things about some of the words. There's a certain knowing about all of them, but I can't get to it. Can't quite get at the meaning of them. I'll think one moment I almost have it. But I haven't. Trying to focus it, trying to focus and it won't be focused. Curiouser and curiouser.

16th April 1990 : This life of mine is unfolding strangely. Should have been a lark, the palm reader, only she wasn't. Four days exactly. The earthquake and the urgent writing and then four days later the palm reader. "You don't channel by any chance, do you?" Going on about some crescent around the mount of the moon or something and wanting to take a copy of my palm. She probably makes up stories like that for everyone. Well five days ago I would have laughed at her. I wonder if I still wish I could laugh at her. Only I don't think I can. I think the answer is probably yes - I probably did channel. The problem is I just don't know what it means and I don't know what to do with it.

Joy seems to. She didn't miss a beat. Just suggested this man. Fountain International, an earth healing group. Knew about ley lines she said. It's all happening so fast. She'd only just been to his meeting and had Alan's number. Too much of a coincidence to be a coincidence, maybe. I hardly know anything about ley lines and yet, strangely I thought it was referring to them too. These words :

> *There will be power to guide the feet along the tracks, beacons make a line ... There, feet have made marks and the energy lives, it can be stroked ... Follow the path, the energy must flow again.*

What else might they be about? Odd too that Alan would bring Simon along to visit me. Another coincidence? It's so difficult to describe, this sense of knowing I'm beginning to get sometimes. Like when I saw Simon. Immediately. I thought immediately, he's my brother. I remember when I cut the cake and said "I think I'll begin now." It was like that. I don't know where it came from or why I thought it. I don't even have a brother. It still feels true though, in my strange sort of 'knowing' way.

So here's Simon and I've only just met him and he won't sit in the chair I offer him because someone is already sitting there. Of course no one is actually sitting there, but then he describes my first husband's grandmother exactly. There's no way he could have known it was her chair and less what she looked like. All right, so I played along. Or maybe I'm trying to convince myself I was playing along. No, it was more than that. I really did believe him. Really do believe him. Anyway I asked if grandmother was happy and Simon said she was. I told him to tell her that I would make sure and leave the chair to Hugh.

Then Alan gets in on the act. Right out of the blue he says, "Are you ready to begin? Are you prepared to do the work?"

Right. Like I already know what the work is. And have some way to know whether or not I'm ready to begin. Begin what? Except that I did know what. Not what the work is. That's the curious, mysterious, exciting part of it. Not knowing. Except I do know. Only I can't remember. But it's only a breath away and I keep thinking I will remember. But I haven't yet.

So he asks this question and I know the answer. I know it's a turning point. I know it's some kind of important turning point and I know I have free choice about it but that I've already made the choice. And I know it's totally, absolutely unquestionably serious, and I know my answer will make all the difference. Only I don't get to answer because of Simon.

He says, "There's a man. He's half in and half out and he's offering you something. A baton."

Simon and I are on the same wavelength now and I think the man is my grandfather. "Why doesn't he give it to my mother?" I asked him.

The Clew

"No, to you. But you can choose whether or not you take it."

"I've waited fifty years to make a start, so I may as well begin. But if I am to begin, I must take your hands." It still bothers me a bit when words come out of my mouth like that. It's not that I want them unsaid or anything. It's not that once they're out it's not okay with me. But it would be nice to have a little warning. So I take Simon's hands and this memory fills my conscious mind. That meditation retreat, years ago. During the meditation, seeing myself standing with the black-robed monk in the west wall of Kenilworth castle. His invitation inviting me through the door and my refusal. End of meditation. The calmness this time, just calmly accepting. The black-robed monk's outstretched hand focusing attention on golden fields, clear blue sky, sparkling waters of the Finham and Inchford. It's as natural now as it seemed unnatural then. So easy. Just two levels of reality. Nothing more. A rational level doubting. Another level simply knowing, seeing, the absolute truth of it all. The scene beautiful, the feelings intense. I loosed Simon's hands then and simply spoke the truth. "I know about stone circles." Knowing the truth, or maybe accepting knowing the truth unfolded the numbers. Seven and three. And patterns. They have to be walked. I know they have to be walked. Or danced. Whatever they are, wherever they are, they have to be nurtured. Walked. Danced. To keep the energies potent. That much at least I seem able to remember.

It's this connection to the land. This inexplicable connection I've always felt. More than to the land, to England. More than to England, to Kenilworth. Eight generations of living, being born, celebrating or enduring life, and dying. Eight generations of affinity difficult to explain. And the stone circles. Always the mystery. Mystified by them. Remnants of people who walked here before me. But never a premonition like this before. I've no idea what prompted the certainty of that statement 'I know about stone circles.' Intuition? Some story read to me? Some memory from long ago? And long since forgotten.

But it wasn't like that. It wasn't a memory. It didn't even seem like anything from this lifetime. Holding his hands ... I was there. I was just there. It wasn't a memory. On some naked, primal level, I experienced the knowing. Physically, mentally, emotionally, spontaneously a part of my very being, complete and whole, I knew. And knew I knew. Nothing to toy with - this reality as real as any I have ever known. But not this one - not the same reality as this. Why would holding his hands ... I can't explain this.

So what to do with it? The numbers seven and three? The patterns? Walking stone circles? Knowing is one thing. But what to do with it?

9th May 1990 : Maybe it was the baton. What's the baton I remember wondering. Maybe it was a dowsing rod. No, probably not. Anyway, I'm dowsing. Not so difficult. And, Mr. Black-robed monk man, you'll be pleased to know we've been to your Kenilworth. Really was an abbey there at one time. Maybe yours. Built it on a sacred site, didn't you? Anyway Joy sensed the energy was dark at a nearby tumulus. Maybe not because of your monastery. Maybe nothing to do with you at all. We find the place the pendulum shows us and then we visualise something to cleanse it. So you should be happy Mr. Black-robed monk man. Now your fields glow golden, your sky smiles clear blue, your Finham and Inchford sparkle in the sun. Joy felt the difference after our work. So did Alan and Simon. I didn't. But I don't doubt that they did either. Well Mr. Monk, whatever your message that day, perhaps all these years later we've heard it. Whatever is going on, I was somehow a part of it and it was a lovely day. And for me, that is enough.

10th June 1990 : Same pain in the right side of my head. Words follow one after another making sentences but no sense. Intrigue, mystery, excitement again. But no sense. It's a longer message this time. Sentences don't seem to follow each other in any particular order. Won't matter then perhaps if I look at parts of it separately. Leave the rest on its page to perhaps look at another time. Look at these parts for now. For now these parts seem to have the most intrigue.

> *... Look at the hills to judge the distance, walk in the circles, they must sway with the movement ... Feathers have become spears. Walk always to the left, there are circles within circles that must be crossed in a spiralling movement. Hold hands in the face of the sun and look upwards into the beam of light. You are the converter, the force must pass through you into the ground. Speak in whispers as the leaves on the trees and sing the songs you have known since the Youthtime. Move sideways in line until the tops of the trees are lit by the light then all will be well ... There is enough power if it is found now, all must be unblocked in a great circle. Work in circles there is no other way and I am testament to this ... Here I guard, it must be begun if all is to be saved.*

What is to be saved? The words that came in April made the same reference to something being saved. And what is all this about circles? It's both stone circles and walking in circles. These are very specific instructions for some activity we are to do in some circle. We made up the ceremony, the ritual, the cleansing at Kenilworth and Joy and the others really felt the difference. Did we convert the energy somehow? Is that what it means about the energy passing through? These instructions are to be carried out in the future but they follow our ceremony. Is someone, something aware of our movements? Our intentions? Has this come in response to our activities?

26th June 1990 : The last two weeks have been very exciting. More pieces. Bigger puzzle. The pieces fit.

> *... Begin the journey, walk in lines as it has been shown to you. On the hilltop I will wait where the dancers move and look back over the valley to see the signs that I have marked for you ... Know that I am here and will guide your feet in the right direction ... This is my land, it will not be destroyed ... I must come from a distance to the place where the thorn stands by the water and the trees are bent low. The songs will renew me in the hearts of men and will return the light into the ground. Sorrows are for healing at the place of the*

The Clew

Moon and the sword will enter the Kingdom of the Brigantes ...

This is my land ... Warwickshire! The place of my own deep love ... *it will not be destroyed.* I knew this time. I know. This is my land means Warwickshire, England. Exciting. Challenging too. Because this time I know. The Rollright Stones. When it said *On the hilltop where the dancers move* I knew the Rollrights! So once I had this message and understood it, I had this idea that I'd go there on the solstice. That I'd do the ceremony, carry out the instructions on the solstice. But that must have been too romantic, too conventional. No stone circles on the solstice for this energy. Anyway I ended up there with Joy but not on the solstice. Yesterday. It all began simply enough. Just the one impression nothing more. Just *the hilltop where the dancers move.* I thought it was only that.

Knew we could only *look back over the valley* from the King Stone. Over the stile and up the brow of the hill but the valley was dark, the cloud cover thick, no signs stood out as marked for us. Until a torch beam of sunlight pierced and shone exactly on a spire, the church invisible until that moment. Too melodramatic certainly. Spellbound nevertheless we stood in silence watching as the sunray faded. Afraid to break the spell we peeked at each other. Then giggled. Equilibrium returned, we fairly skipped back to the circle.

To find a man and woman, and my knowing again. They were waiting for us. They didn't know it, but they were. Joy with her pendulum, the man with his rods, crisscrossing the circle. Seven inner circles I knew we had to walk. Knew in the same way I had known that day with Simon. In the same way I knew the man and woman were waiting for us.

"There are seven circles," he said. "I've just dowsed them." Exactly. Three and seven. I knew it already. Didn't even need to dowse them.

We began, the four of us, instinctively working. A team responding to the knowledge of the pendulum and the rods. Rob and Libby - the two we'd found waiting for us - they too belong to Fountain International. The Rollrights were part of their holiday. They explored the stones yesterday but today felt a strong urge to return and arrived only moments before we did. They mentioned another ancient site and we piled in our cars. Then the signpost, a village name. We saw it and I knew we had to go there. The words just came, *go there.* We drove on. A different junction, the same sign, and the same words pressing themselves into my mind: *go there.* Still we drove further. Then Libby and Rob were out of their car, we had arrived, except again, a village name, a signpost, pointing insistently. Finally my words spoken aloud, "We have to go there."

"That's what Rob keeps saying," Libby said.

On automatic pilot, driving with instinct, urgently excited by the pressing heedless recklessness of it.

Joy exclaiming, "We've passed it!"

The knowing again. She was right. Stopping the car to Rob's shouts, "It's back there!"

Knowing when we arrived. *Knowing.* Knowing I'd been there. I knew this place. I *knew* it. Knew there would be a valley. Knew the path leading down.

The Clew

Could see the fallen great stone on the valley floor. Didn't know the bullocks though! Blocking our path. Why so fearless suddenly? Not me at all. A stick. My stick, clearly telling them let us pass. Not at all sure what possessed me.

And I *did* know this place. Somewhere in the depths of my bones I *knew* it. Didn't actually know it. Never actually been there. Just knew it. Knew the grove of trees, the pool, the stream, the thorn tree by the water. Knew *the place where the thorn stands by the water and the trees are bent low.* And the great stone. How to explain this knowing? The rods and the pendulum speaking the great stone's sorrow. Somehow Joy and Rob knew too. Knew the sorrow. They knew the ritual too. Knew what to do. I wonder how they know. I felt the sorrow. But didn't know how to heal it. Couldn't have decided on such a reverent ritual. Cleansing. Healing. *Sorrows are for healing at the place of the Moon.* Was this the place of the moon the entities mentioned? Was this the sorrow needing healing?

The footbridge beckoning me. Let them do the ritual, the healing. A stronger need for solitude. Under the ash tree. Spiked vertically into the ground under the ash tree. Six birds' feathers. *Feathers have become spears.* The energy winks when a puzzle piece fits.

27th June 1990 :   Almost better when I didn't feel so much. When it was just a mind thing. Just a puzzle. A treasure hunt with clues. Just a game. It's so different now. How can I begin to explain. And when did it begin? When they did the ritual, the healing for the fallen stone, and I walked across the footbridge to that little pool? Under the ash tree. Peaceful and beautiful only more than that. The energy ... how to explain it. Druidic. Silly because I know little about Druids. But it *was* Druidic. I knew it. Just like all the other knowings. And the feathers, spears ... Contented certainty, seeing them. Calm contentment and the little smile of knowing. The certainty of it. A conspiracy almost with this little nod and smile – six feathers stuck in the ground. Being led along. I'm being led along. Only where? To what? By whom? And why? Won't think about that for now. Don't feel. Just play the game. Keep the feelings out of it.

So many different energies. I think of the energies that send the words as 'they' now instead of it. Different energies do the writing. I'm learning the difference between them. Lovely what they say about the rock. Again they repeat the message about my pebble. *Carry the rock and all will be well. Have no fear your strength is restored.* So long ago and only yesterday, Joanna's death. And the M.E. a part of my life for the nine years since then. Now there begins to be more strength. Maybe my imagination. The little sandstone. When I carry it I do feel better and walk further.

Sat down an hour before sunset tonight, the voice said. *The moon and the stars shed enough light but it is in the sunlight that the messages will come. Wait for I shall come again when the fingers are moving and the light has dimmed.* The intuitive knowing again. When the light has dimmed means an hour before sunset. More words for the fingers. More words on the paper. With more clues.

Come now into the open air with arms outstretched. This is the Motherland where our race has flourished and the lines of battle have been gathered ...

The Clew

Men stand in the fields like corn stooks and the life is draining from them. The sunlight is fading across the land and the rain and the storms will come ... You are the faithful and have always carried the message. Where the grove stands are the waters of the Moon, I know because I have always been there ... You must stand by the thorn tree with the oak leaves in your hand and listen for my words. The one with the pendulum must read the signals as have all our fathers before her ... You have no time to learn the real ways but must work as we command while there is yet time to save what is ours. Remember to come in silence and the beasts will acknowledge you ...

You have done well but there is still work to do and time is short. Listen to all that is said, the reasons will become plain. Go to the church on the hill where there is a darkness that must be removed. The light is spreading across the land, we cannot be stopped, though there are many who would try. . . Tell what you know and what I have shown you, it is your task and will be rewarded when the new dawn has broke ... Walk the paths and your feet will be free. Have no fear your strength is restored. Carry the rock and all will be well. I can say no more but will wait for the sunlight to bring me home.

You are the faithful and have always carried the message ... How am I the faithful and what message have I always carried? *You have no time to learn the real ways ...* Why isn't there time to learn the real ways and what are the real ways? ... *while there is yet time to save what is ours ...*

There is yet time to save what is ours? It sounds like we're running out of time. And what is being saved? *The light is spreading across the land ...* What light is spreading across the land and who would try and stop it? It's all so cryptic. Some makes sense. Before things only made sense later. Well some of it made sense later. Will this become more clear later? Tell what I know? What do I know? What have they shown me? How can something I don't even understand be my task and how can I be rewarded for it? I write these words. Where do they come from? What do they mean? This isn't just a one off. *You have done well but there is still work to do and time is short ...* At least they say we've done well. We've done something well. Somehow we must have understood enough to do something well. The church on the hill where the darkness must be removed. That I understand. Joy will know. She saw it too, the torch beam of light. She'll go with me.

31st June 1990 : Joy said she had known. When I told her about the church and the darkness. She knew that there was something troubled about it. Says she can sense the lightness or darkness of energy. Somehow with the pendulum it comes to her. It's beginning to work with me too. The pendulum. It motions something for me. I'm more confident with it now. With the dowsing. Like something waking up inside me. Not like I'm learning it. Or learning the energies either. More like remembering. Shaking the cobwebs out. But I can't sense light and dark yet. Joy didn't know why the energy was dark. Pendulum couldn't or didn't tell her that yet.

The Clew

Maybe I did feel it. As we found our way up the hill and into the churchyard maybe I felt something too. A sadness for the church. I did feel a sadness. Felt love too. When we visualise the healing, I can feel the love. Mostly for the land. The trees, the rocks, earth, flowers, the lives of all those woven with this spot, its past, its future, its own intent, gifts of the earth and universe for just this spot. Words don't find it. Don't tell it. Don't explain the love pushing me out of the way as we do the ritual. Some part of me pushed out of the way replaced by some love I've known or remembered. Some strange love for all of this, for all of something I can't even describe, assumes the moment. And I, Avril, small, separate, human, seem to move away somewhere else to watch, to observe the process.

Joy. And the others. And now me. What's happening? They are comfortable with all of this. Doesn't faze them. Two realities. Am I being drawn more and more into the one they seem comfortable with?

Chapter Two

In the very first two messages two phrases using the same words piqued Avril's curiosity: *'if it is to be saved'* and *'if all is to be saved.'* Although she did casually wonder what 'it' was, the excitement of following the clues, the simple fun of enacting the instructions, the feeling of accomplishment when the clues fit, the appreciation and encouragement inherent in the typed words, distracted her from wondering about any 'sinister' meaning for the words. Avril's experience with the sinister energy the priest helped her set free gave her an intuitive knowledge of when an energy was sinister and when it was loving and nurturing. She is very firm in stating that at no time in the many years she worked with the various energies conveying these messages was there any feeling other than one of total love, total acceptance, encouragement, appreciation, and support. In retrospect, perhaps those words *'if all is to be saved.'* are more important than understood at the time, and perhaps even more important than can even as yet be fathomed. Whether or not these are warnings, and whether or not the warnings are valid, is still - these years later - a bit of a mystery.

As the entities whose thought-groups Avril typed into words continued their messages, Avril began regularly sharing the messages in their entirety with a small group of supportive friends. In the form of impressions, intuitive knowing, and mental pictures she frequently received much more information than she was able to convey in the words she typed. She and this supportive group discussed the typed pages and her impressions. They shared knowledge and interpretations. Gradually, as the material increased in volume and in depth and complexity, they found it necessary to research concepts alluded to. Much of the material they were able to puzzle through. Some became clear only after years of work together and some only after specific activities - also enacted years later. Some, to this day, remains a mystery.

Avril and the others needed no proof of the validity of any of the messages, however, to continue the fun they were having. Perhaps on some level they sensed more to all of this than a good time, but mostly in the beginning it was just a lark. Even these years later, those involved seem to need no proof of anything. Proof that they were correct to continue is in what all of this eventually meant to each of them. To a person they feel that perhaps some of the 'predictions' will never materialise because of the work they did. Perhaps nothing they did made any difference at all. In a logical, linear reality, will it ever, can it ever, be known? From reading and re-reading the volumes of material Avril recorded, listening to the many tapes of recorded messages, it becomes apparent there is not one, but many stories in this material. One book cannot tell them all. Perhaps proof that something, i.e. *'it'*, was saved must wait for the telling of one of the other stories in the material. Perhaps more years need pass before evidence surfaces. Perhaps there will never be any proof at all. Be that as it may, the intrigue, the mystery, the coincidence and synchronicity inherent in the messages and the work were enough to keep the participants interested and encouraged them to continue.

AVRIL
The Moon Grove

8th July 1990 :

... There is much to be done and I must speak through you to the people who know of the Word. There is a darkness that will come in a lifetime and will spread over all things. The light will be dimmed but you have the power to preserve the fruits of the earth ... You have begun the journey but there is not much time and we need your help ... There is a blight across the land and the earth is dying without the prayers. You are the people of the memory who know the old ways. Come again to the groves with those of your fellows who can believe in us, we need all, there are so few left and the work must be done. In the beginning we knew the shape of things to come but much has changed and man has worked his magic in the wrong way ... There is much you know already and should remember. Go to the woods, this I have already commanded you. You make the right beginnings and with your friends the right works are being performed ... The moon is the guardian of our lives and it is beneath her face that the words must be spoken ... You have found one place, but there are others which will be made plain ... You have the power that was given you long ago and in your finger is the record of our line. Go back to the beginning so that our cloaks may protect the land. ... You know much and must record it in this way ... Write now the words that I send and tell the people for the word must begin to spread across the land before the floods come and the people perish. There will be life and there will be a new heart. Nothing can stop this, it is in the order of things that have been preordained. It is our task to protect and warn and save that which is ours.

Come to the Moon grove and begin the work we have shown. Wait until the moon is full and you have seven people and the words will come. Listen for my voice as the sun sets and the moon begins her journey across the sky. The ash tree stands sentinel and the water must run over your feet before you begin ... The oak leaves are to be held as I have told you before. They hold the memories of Albion and cannot be forgotten ...

We wanted to think it was about ecology. But it's more than that ... *a blight across the land and the earth is dying without the prayers ... man has worked his magic in the wrong way. Is this a warning? ... before the floods come and the people perish.* Well, don't feel. It's a game. Follow the clues. Put the puzzle together.

It's about England, Warwickshire or maybe Kenilworth, not today's Warwickshire or Kenilworth but not exactly historical either. Ancient. Like the circles, the stone circles, as ancient as that or maybe even more ancient. But not savage or primitive. Not pagan except I'm not even sure what pagan is. Feels Druidic but I don't know what that is either. I keep feeling I've almost got it, it's on the very edge of my memory, but I never quite get to it. It's about trees and water and hills and energy and energy lines and about reverence and something sacred. Something inexplicably sacred. I want to think, I'm almost but not quite able to think, and yet I find myself wanting sometimes to think this is all very,

The Clew

very silly. It's a game. Treasure hunt with clues. My energy comes back, we enjoy ourselves, that's all. That's enough.

You have found the one place, but there are others which will be made plain. The Moon Grove that Joy, Rob, Libby and I had found. *We have to wait until the moon is full and we have seven people ... and the words will come. Listen for my voice as the sun sets and the moon begins her journey ...*

The ash tree, water running over our feet, prayers in our hearts, oak leaves. It's a ritual. Instructions for some ritual. Like before only more particular. Like before. The Rollrights. The church at Todenham. Like before. *You are the people of the memory who know the old ways ... You have the power that was given you long ago ... There is much you know already and should remember.* Like before? When before? What old ways? And how should I remember?

22nd July 1990 :

Know that I am here and stand by your side when the time comes to make a right beginning ... Be not afraid we will cause you and your friends no harm. We know that we ask much but will give all that we can when the time is right. You too love the land, it was prepared for your race and left in trust for all the generations to come ... Surround yourself with love, this you have always known and there is enough for your purpose. You have the gifts that have been given you across the years and now is the time when they will all be needed. The moon rises and sets and sees the work of all men. She will be there at the grove when you need to look into her face. She is a benevolent mother of all life on this planet and we who come from the stars have left her in charge of the tides and the waters. There are many things that are her responsibility and flow like the wind at the appointed times. Men have not understood what is the nature of life on earth. Much has been forgotten and wisdom has taken the wrong path. You must return to the knowledge of your forefathers or else there will be a rent in the universe and the light will go out. Know that we mean only kindness to all men and, as before, come only when the need is very great ...

Your eyes have become accustomed to the signs and you write our words well. You have our thanks and our protection ... Take care, love all, it is the law of nature and we know you have remembered our words over the centuries that life has been in your hands. Our time is not yours, do not doubt the words are ours and all will be well. Take heart, all is as it was planned and life will survive ... You will remember all that is important ... the light is growing with your help and the work will be accomplished in time for the new beginning. It is as the woman wills, you are of her line and have done her work. All women must be glad for their time has come and the moon will bring them the life they have hoped for ...

Lay down the words I am tired of this strange way. I will come again, wait for my voice ... The darkness is here, I depart.

6th August 1990 : Puzzled through what we think the ritual was supposed to be. Seven of us went to the Moon Grove on the full moon at sunset. Surface of the pool was clear and quiet. Two 'saw' white clad figures. Others 'heard' chanting. Haven't figured out yet who the men in white are. We held the oak leaves, let the water run over our bare feet, individually said what felt right. Then they climbed the hill but I stayed. I wanted to be alone by the pool, to deepen the channel for the water to enter the stream. Freed, it leapt and gurgled, the way water does. The surface suddenly alive with great ripples and leaping fish. I turned, and at that moment the moon rose over the eastern end of the valley. Do the fish leap like that at the rising of every full moon? The others too – at the precise moment the full moon rose – the hundred sheep clustered silently around them all turned to gaze at it. When we're not there to notice, do the sheep always greet the full moon rising? Or was it only because we came in silence? *Remember to come in silence and the beasts will acknowledge you ...* Riddles and clues. Sentences jumbled together all out of context. As if we have to realise the context by unravelling the clues. Why?

JOY
The One With The Pendulum

In the beginning, before Avril learned to trust her own skills, I was a validation for her. The entities didn't use our names, but had their own ways of identifying us to Avril. I think they named me 'the one with the pendulum' because I use the pendulum to verify and validate my own intuition and as a way of accessing otherwise unavailable information. I had been involved in earth healing long before I met Avril, and I think in the beginning that is why the entities suggested my involvement in the work she was being asked to do. For some time Avril and I had been working together on an energetic level to alleviate her ME symptoms. During one session I had felt compelled to tell her that she needed to go to a high place. She urged me to tell her where. Intuitively I knew she was to go to the Dassett Hills in Warwickshire. Later she told me she felt drawn to pick up a small piece of red sandstone and place it on her third eye. When she did so she had experienced a very strong reaction. It was soon after this that she began receiving the urge to type the messages.

On an intellectual level I understood the messages she shared with me. Although much within them was confusing and disjointed, I certainly didn't dismiss them. And when they referred to me personally by giving instructions for the one with the pendulum, I cooperated fully. The messages she received were not asking me to do anything I wasn't already accustomed to doing. It was interesting that they came from outside myself, but from the beginning I found them interesting, fascinating, and fun to discuss together. But they weren't real for me in the same way they were real for Avril. They didn't speak to me in the same way my own intuitive work spoke to me. I willingly did as the messages suggested and as Avril asked because I agreed with what was asked and it was fun. But for me it didn't have the emotional depth I felt from my own intuitive work and so perhaps I took it less seriously. Our work at the moon grove would change that.

The Clew

When we first found this site we didn't think of it as the Moon grove; we were following signs to Lidstone. I can only describe the sensation I had on that June day when we drove through the Lidstone area as a 'tugging.' I imagine it felt much like a horse must feel when someone tugs at a bit in its mouth. I actually felt 'pulled' to stop and go with Avril. I do not comfortably walk through a field where cows are being pastured. It simply is not something I willingly do. When we walked into the field and I saw the bullocks I was not happy. But the sensation of the bit pulling in my mouth grew stronger and encouraged me to continue. I didn't know what Lidstone was and I didn't know what we would find, but the closer our proximity to the stone, the stronger and more urgent the sensation in my mouth. I found this unfamiliar and strange.

The stone was a very large, flat stone, six feet or more long and wide enough for someone to lie on. I don't remember when it occurred to me that it could have been a sacrificial stone. It even had a dip in the centre so that blood could have drained away. Not pleasant thoughts. It was a natural stone, not obviously hand-shaped or carved in any way. However the sides were parallel, it was of an even thickness, the surface was smooth and regular. I sensed immediately that it was not indigenous to the area. It had been transported to this site for what use I could not discern. Perhaps in the strange way places are named and the meaning of the names forgotten, Lidstone actually had something to do with this stone. Perhaps the name was correct and it truly was only the lid for something. But there was a great sadness about it and I sensed it needed cleansing and healing. We did a small ceremony that first day when we discovered it with Rob and Libby, but the entities continued to make reference to the grove. They described the physical place perfectly and referred to it as the moon grove. We were asked to do further work there and it was during this further work that my experience encouraged me to take the messages more seriously.

We waited for the full moon and seven of us, as instructed, and drove with intent to the moon grove as we now thought of it. It was a cold, cloudy evening, and I dreaded the thought of bullocks, especially as it would be dark when we returned through their field. While I willingly did as Avril asked, I did not relish standing bare footed in cold water on such a cold evening. When I stood in the water, however, it actually felt very warm and bubbled up around my feet. I have no explanation for why this happened and as I stood there, warm bubbling water literally massaging my feet, the words Avril typed, *the water must run over your feet before you begin,* took on new meaningfulness for me. The words became real for me in a way they hadn't been before. It was as if some spirit sensed that I needed encouragement, a sign, and it was being given me. It rained while we were doing the ceremony but, immediately upon finishing, a space in the clouds cleared and a bright, full moon shone down on us. The ceremony finished, some of the others left and climbed a hill through a hedge. As I put my shoes on they called for us to come and see the sheep. I climbed the hill to see hundreds of sheep no more than fifteen feet from us. They all stood quietly and they all, without exception, were simply gazing at us. They didn't scatter as sheep do when a human moves in so closely. They had been standing several moments before I arrived and continued to gaze at us two or three minutes longer before turning their heads in unison to look at the rising moon and leisurely moving off. Again I remembered words from her typed message, *Remember to come in silence and the beasts will acknowledge you.*

AVRIL
Pictures and Places

12th August 1990:
> *There are men who have carried the knowledge we have brought you across the generations. They wear white, the colour of purity, and they carry the fire in their hands. You are of the faith and your task will become more clear as we move towards the time when the light will strike the earth … The universe needs the life that the earth brings forth and the whole must be preserved. It is not for you alone that we do this work. Since time began there has been an order in the way that the planets are governed. Man has not understood the linkages that bind everything together. The men in white robes have always known the answers. They were given the mysteries many moons ago and charged with their care. They have kept faith with us and now their time to remember has come … We have become known to each other as once before when we were of the same line. Our cloaks have been laid down many times and the colours have faded with much use. Carry the light in your heart and use the sunshine to give you the strength to go forward.*

16th August 1990: There are so many pages now. The warnings continue. *There have been many prophets but the warnings have gone unheeded.* In our reading we've become familiar with some of these prophets. We're discovering others. In some media there is so much about the millennium and the second coming. The warnings in our material don't seem to validate this. *The universe needs the life that the earth brings forth and the whole must be preserved* doesn't seem to be about the millennium or the second coming. May be difficult to know what this information *is* about. Easier to guess what it's *not* about.

It's all so disjointed. I reread and study it and it is disjointed. Sentences follow each other with no thought to continuity. In retrospect we can see that parts of one message relate to something that follows or came before without any sense of transition or time. There's no sense of time. Things get all jumbled and relate to each other in oblique ways. Even their references to time are oblique. *Our time is not yours …* and *journey through other time lands.* Yet there is a strange sort of continuity. If I don't try and impose a time structure on it. Time doesn't seem to work the same for them. Doesn't seem limited by what comes first or follows next. I take things out of context and rearrange them. They begin to make more sense. Themes emerge.

One theme seems to be telling me I 'am someone' and that I only need to remember. There continues to be reference to some knowledge I have. *We know you have remembered our words over the centuries that life has been in your hands* seems to be referring to me personally. What is this knowledge? And what of the centuries? Does this assume reincarnation?

The Clew

And the energies are changing. Not the right word. It's not just energies. Maybe entities is a better word. More like separate or different entities. My perception of them changes. That's not quite right either. I change. I become more comfortable and the energies, the words, the language – something is smoothing out. I smooth out. Somehow in all of this, it's *my* energy that's changing. I grow more receptive. Even so they sense my doubt, my discomfort and make efforts to reassure me. *Be not afraid, the earth will recover from the disasters man has brought upon her. Continue in the work, there are many others who do these things also. Take heart, the time is at hand and all will be made plain. The first star comes, we depart and begin our journey through other time lands.* With the smoothing out, the sentences flow. Less disjointed. More poetic. It seems more personal.

We all continue reading, rereading, pouring over, analysing. Some makes sense immediately. Sometimes later someone else figures something out. Eight of us now. Interested friends who've become a sort of group. It's as if I've been collecting these people for some time just for this. Some sentences beg to be researched. Like the men in white. Who are they? Druids? Monks of the Cistercian Order with their link to the Knights Templar? Cathars or Albigensians of southern France - violently suppressed by the Catholic Inquisition in the thirteenth century? We're no closer to an answer.

Books fall into our hands. I've learned to pay attention. I wouldn't have noticed this particular book before, certainly wouldn't have dowsed it. It has a list of holy words of different ethnic groups. Strangely they all begin with the letter 'A.' Holy words. Am I being shown 'the words of our fathers?'

... Come to the places where we have said our prayers, and the prayers must be reborn ... Only at night when the wind blows and the oak leaves bend low to the ground can the voices be heard. The moon is the guardian of our lives and it is beneath her face that the words must be spoken ... I will open the door to your memory and the words of your fathers will cross into the air ... Say the prayers that are in your hearts ...

Do I have a special word? 'Anu' the pendulum decided. The others, a word for the others? The pendulum found a word for each. When we were told to go to the moon grove on the night of a full moon and chant our words, are these the words? Why? What does it mean? How is it important?

Beauty and urgency together. Makes no sense but I feel it. The others sense it too. Something about the earth or something about the earth and the universe together that we don't understand. That we've forgotten and must remember. The urgency is in the remembering. To keep the beauty, there's something we must remember.

Who is this who gives the words to my fingers? Who is this with whom I've laid down my cloak, faded with much use? The others smile knowingly. But they can't know. Can't know the feeling of it. The strange familiarity of it. It's a game, a puzzle. Unravel clues, decipher energy, celebrate rituals, it's only a mind game. We're being asked to help heal something about the earth. We co-operate and we're good at it. It's impersonal. It's not personally about me. There's nothing really personal to it. Trouble is, it grows more and more difficult to believe it so.

The Clew

1st September 1990:

> *... The power was enough to share and you have brought the light into the ground as we had expected of you ...*

Don't know quite what to make of sentences like this. Joy can feel a difference in the lightness of the energy sometimes. Does that have anything to do with bringing light into the ground? We give intent. Our intent is from a loving and healing energy. We all share a concern for the earth, a love of nature, an affinity with this land. Is this enough? Is that all it takes? How have we brought the light into the ground? And who is this who expected it of us? And why? I'm sitting down at an hour before sunset more often now. It always comes, whenever I sit down with the intent. Sometimes pages. The entities are different. I'm learning to 'read' them. I can tell one from the other.

> *Listen for my voice as the sun sinks beneath the clouds and the day draws to a close ... Take heart, all is well and the earth can now survive. Enough of you have promised ... for us to begin to believe that man cares for the world he was given. Come home to the woods and the fields and move in them as much as you can. The trees carry many messages and the water flows under the land with a great power that has been renewed ... We need more time and this you must arrange when we send word. The stars watch over our work and in their light are the stories of what has taken place many times before. The fire springs from the heart of the earth and must be renewed for the life to continue. This is the law of your world and of all the others who stand in line across the firmament ... The moon is the store-keeper of the power and it must flow to and from her in a great circle. Stay close to our land, the need is here ... You are not alone, there are many across the universe who hold hands at this time and hear our voices ... Go down to the streams and refresh yourself in the water. This is now newly refreshed and carries great power which you will need for the next stage of our work ... Have no sadness in your heart the words will come whenever you have need. I listen to those who are in my care and feel their tears and laughter as if they were my own.*

... the earth can now survive ... What was it in danger of? Our stupidity? Our misuse of resources? And if it's that, how have we made a difference? *Enough of you have promised ...* I'm not aware that we have promised anything. I type the words. We find the clues and make up rituals. We play. It's fun. We have a good time. We do it on our own time and because of our own interest. How have we promised? Or does this mean that many of us all throughout the world finally get it and are beginning to pay attention to the ecosystem, and that's what's making a difference? Have enough of us promised to do that? Is that the promise we've collectively made? Is that what's making the difference?

I wonder how *the stars record the stories of what has taken place many times before.* What *has* taken place many times before? What is the fire that *springs from*

The Clew

the heart of the earth and how is it being renewed? I suppose in a literal sense it could be the magma. But renewed? Or is it some kind of energy? Like the energy the pendulum and the rods pick up in the stone circles and along the ley lines? Where does that come from? The heart of the earth? I remember something about our being a converter. *You are the converter the force must pass through into the ground.* How does the energy pass through us into the ground? I think they're telling us the men in white have understood and remembered all of this. If only we could figure out who they are. Or were.

8th September 1990 :

> *... It will be necessary for you to seek for the serpent's head which can be found at the place where two rivers meet. We can only guide you with our words and these are difficult for you to understand. We do not understand how you draw out your directions as we see things only from above and all looks different from this perspective. These are the best words we can find to speak with you at this time as we must make the directions as plain as we can.*
>
> *You must go to the great river that flows across the land where the hills look down and the watercress grows in clumps. Seek for a place where one river arrives from the mountains and the other comes south from the hills of the North. There is a name but it is beyond our knowledge which works in a different ways than yours. There is a bridge which hangs on metal strings and crosses below the joining of the waters. This place is not far from your home but it will take one day for you to go there and return ... We ask it humbly as more help is needed than we had first thought. There is enough power but some have not used it how they should and now we have concerns about the time that is left ... The lines have to be strengthened so that the power will flow in the right way when the time for our power to come has arrived ... There is a time coming when the way will become more clear.*
>
> *We are sorry that we cannot say the precise moment. We do not live by your time and can only judge your lives by the sun and the moon as they rise and set across your world. The planets have need of this work that you do, as does all life across the universe. Many have understood the connections in the past but many moon years have passed and those in power were not taught the ways of the ancients or else they fear a power that is greater than their own. They fight always with weapons and anger to protect what is theirs. The universe belongs to all men and cannot be divided in this way. Everything is for the good of the whole of mankind and should be shared equally across your many lands. We have given you many riches for the good of all. Much you have not yet discovered and you have used much knowledge to bring suffering to many. This was not our intention and man has fallen from the grace we bestowed at the beginning of the earth's life ...*
>
> *You must remember what we asked you at the beginning. We will help you as much as we can but we know that even then it will be difficult for you to find the place we ask. You must ask the others who can listen to us and then it may be easier for us to describe. Build pictures in your mind and remember all the*

places you have visited in your life. You have been there before when you were young and heard the stories about the men who once lived at that place ...

Take heart, love all, you have great power that you share between you and that we can grasp when you work together.

I'm learning to do it. I can find the places they speak ... *build pictures in your mind.* I *can* build the pictures. It's not so difficult. Then I dowse the Ordnance Survey to get the precise spot. Tintern Abbey ... *when you were young and heard the stories about the men who once lived at that place ...* Even without that reminder, I could find the picture. Knew it was Tintern Abbey. This time it was Maggie who went with me. We drove the *one day for you to go there and return.* Hadn't paid much attention to the bridge part ... *bridge which hangs on metal strings and crosses below the joining of the waters.* I knew of no such bridge. Surprise and joy seeing for the first time the Severn bridge hanging on its metal strings, glowing white against the darkened sky! Memorable. There are still times when I question. This was not one of them. Wherever we were off too, whatever we were up to, whatever needed doing, we were certainly being given picturesque instructions.

It would be easy to doubt. To ask why we should go off, drive the day it takes to go and return, spend time and energy in this way. It would be easy to dismiss all this as trivial. Logically it makes little sense. And yet, somewhere I know. Still can't quite put my finger on it. Can't quite get to the edge of my memory where it resides. But I do know. Crazy to know this is what I'm to be doing and to think it makes a difference. I don't know what the difference is. They say it's making a difference. That all of us engaged in this work are making a difference. I don't know, I can't say what that difference is. Not that, not yet. And yet each time, as there in Tintern Abbey, each time there are feelings. Recognitions not yet quite conscious. Is it energy? Am I recognising a sensitivity to energy? Am I learning to feel the sadness, the distressed and troubled quality of these energies?

You have the gifts that have been given you across the years and now is the time when they will all be needed ... You are the converter, the force must pass through into the ground.

To my logical mind, neither of these sentences makes much sense. But to another part of me, I know. And understand. And can't explain. Joy and John and Heather and the others don't seem to need an explanation. And so I continue. Too there's the sacredness of it. Each time is different, but each time in it's own way is sacred. There's a sacredness to figuring out where we're to go. A sacredness in the winks of the clues that appear once we've completed a task. And the sacredness of the tasks themselves. Each different. Each with it's own reverence. Each with its single importance and yet each part of a larger whole.

Since time began there has been an order in the way that the planets are governed ... The stars watch over our work and in their light are the stories of what has taken place many times before ... This is the law of your world and of all the others who stand in line across the firmament ...

This is not just poetry. Not just figurative, beautiful language. Somehow, in some inexplicable way, this is real. I *will* remember. Until I remember, I must

The Clew

trust. I must solve the small mystery of where to go and what to do. But I *will* remember. And then solve the larger mystery of why.

Or maybe I won't. Some days it's all so real. No need for logic. For explanations. Other days, it's simply an adventure. Nothing more. One day it's one, the next day it's the other. Sometimes I think the others take it more seriously than I do. I wonder why.

✳ ✳ ✳ ✳ ✳

How could a grown woman, intelligent and in command of all her senses continue to engage in such play? For, she assures me, at this time it was truly play. For Avril personally this was a very difficult time. Her second marriage was rocky. She doubted it's longevity. Together she and her husband owned their own business. Without her ability to work in that business she had no means of financial support. She feared for her ability to provide for herself. She also questioned her ability to establish a lasting relationship. From almost earliest childhood she seems to have been driven to find the perfect mate, and twice now she had failed. The beauty, mystery, and unconditional love evident in the words she typed, the fun of sharing them with her friends, the shared purpose of the outings in the countryside, all were a very important source of comfort at this time in her life.

Today she will smile and joke about the short interval when she and her friends did begin to take precautions seriously. They went so far as to store extra food one winter. As she gained skill and confidence in translating the thought-groups given to her by the entities, she realised their sense of 'time' is not the same as ours. Sometimes it was years before something that was predicted to happen 'soon' actually came about. At this time, September 8, 1990, she was given the message: *"You have a woman who speaks with too loud a voice and cannot feel the temper of the seasons. She will go before the changes come and the ones who will come to rule are prepared for the work they must undertake."* She had no way of knowing that 'soon' Margaret Thatcher would leave office. And when her own mother was ill and dying she was told to spend happy time with her because 'soon' she would take leave. 'Soon' was actually a period of five years.

Often having completed an activity that she and the others were guided to do, they would all marvel at the way clues and descriptions seen as cryptic and not understood before would suddenly make sense. At times during an activity Avril would actually see in the scene before her the very vision she had received in some earlier message. She explains that just as the entities seem to have little concept for our 'space' and had difficulty articulating actual map points, so too they repeatedly seemed unfamiliar with our concept of 'time.' They repeatedly apologised for their limitations in these areas and even implied that for our own benefit we may need to get beyond such limiting concepts.

Avril continues to emphasise that her part in all this was very specific. She received and transcribed the messages. She helped decode the clues. She intuited the places to which she and the others were being directed. She brought the people together. She was the organiser, the impetus behind the events. But she did not compose the rituals involved. Although she took if for granted at the time, now she marvels at how the appropriate people always showed up on site. Someone else always knew what to do. Someone else always took the messages she received and turned them into ritual. Avril smiles when describing the actual rituals. In reality they seem innocent and almost childish: timing the activity for the night of a full moon; holding oak leaves in outstretched hands; letting water run over bare feet; speaking words they felt directed to; standing in a certain place and humming or toning together; joining hands and circling in a particular way; meditating or visualising on a particular image; dancing; singing. It was always joyful. Always play. It was fun. And always expressed from sincere intent and profound love of the earth, a profound love of the English countryside, profound sense of mystery and awe for the stones and circles and energy lines, for the ancient monuments, the Abbeys and churches they were asked to visit. Self-conscious inhibitions were put aside while the group earnestly experimented with the early instructions.

Thought about in a particular way, perhaps the reason for continuing makes even more sense. It is taken for granted that one mother's love can help cure a child while another's indifference leaves the child vulnerable. In some way it seems the participants were behaving under a similar premise. If there was some malaise in their beloved land, (and who couldn't believe that?) and if their combined love would somehow make a difference, then they were all for it. And so they turned up, they danced and sang and meditated. They visualised light and energy and cleansing and healing. They were joyful. And so they continued.

Chapter Three

AVRIL
Ashad recognised and remembered

9th September 1990 : It's becoming more personal. More and more personal. How can I explain how different the energy of this entity feels? Sometimes referring to itself as 'we' but still very familiar. Sometimes using instead 'I' and then even more familiar.

> *... we have become as friends to each other and I feel your thoughts against my mind like a gentle wind on a summer's day ... The night comes and with it the stars that will remind you of my words. Their light is a part of the Great Light that breathes through us all and it will continue to shine long after you have laid down the burdens of the life you now inhabit ... The stars come and I must leave what has become a pleasure for me. Your words are now a delight and I gather them to me like grain from a good harvest ... We offer you our hearts in faith and in the love that binds us together with the Great One. Sleep, dream, rest ... all will be well. I go.*

I know this energy. I know it personally. As a person. As a loved one. This energy is different to the ones before. You will remember all that is important. *This* is important. Why can't I remember? Who is this with whom I have lain down my cloak many times? Who feels my thoughts against his mind like a gentle wind on a summer's day? Who, with no body and not even an identity, who brings such comfort, completeness, familiarity, such exhilaration? Who is this!

Who is this who knows me so well, knows Warren and his Jewish childhood, knows our relationship and can say these things? *Your husband does well ... Tell him the words are all in the books he has known since his childhood days and he alone can understand them. You are not versed in these explanations of our lives and he must not expect that you can understand. The time you have shared has been important for you both but your lives are separate from now as you learn more of your own lines from the beginning of the world. Hold hands but do not make a prison for each other, each must be free to make their own journeys with their own kind.*

How can I begin to explain the aloneness I have felt. The searching, knowing almost from first ability to know, knowing the longing. Knowing the incompleteness and the always, ever present longing. Two marriages, each time thinking this is the one. This is the completeness, the end of the search. Only to know it wrong the first time, and to begin to know with Warren the same. And know still the aloneness. Now this ... this ... energy ... entity ... comes. And feels more like completeness than ... What is this? Who is this? ... *I feel your thoughts against my mind like a gentle wind on a summer's day.* It is like that. I feel it too.

To have the game back. Nothing more. Just puzzle and clue. Go here, go there. Do this, do that. Would I really? Have that back instead of this ... instead of this what? This new understanding? This realisation? Memory. It's a memory. It's like finally remembering what love feels like. Like all this time I thought I knew, but had it wrong. Had forgotten the truth of it. And if this second marriage ends, as it seems to be doing, will I give up the search? For something that feels very much like this energy … entity … Like the energy I feel from this entity … Having failed twice to find … can I convince myself it doesn't exist? Or will I go on looking? And what am I looking for? What exactly do I think I'm looking for?

24th September 1990: It's like living in different realities, scales tipping from one to the other and not tipping back again. What began as a separate life, began as requests to find the places, heal energies, raise vibrations, what began almost as something unreal, now has a reality all its own. There's the reality of getting very precise in our methods for locating the places. Riddles still masquerade as directions. *We are sorry to take you away from your life but there are matters that need your attention. … Go with your fellows to the place where the rain falls from the mountains and collects in the pool under the white cliff … The place you seek is opposite a mill where once bread was made and the sails turned around. …* When I have built *pictures* in my mind, when we've dowsed the Ordnance Survey, we explore our intuition. It's more familiar now and easier. Still the humour and smiles as some clues appear only at completion of our task. Only after we'd finished and began to make our way back did we look back and see the shape of the pool under the white cliff. A sort of 'gold star' confirming our alignment. It happens. Too often to be coincidence.

There's the reality of their reassurance and gratitude … *we are glad that you can hear us whenever we send our words across the time gap to you … You are working in the right way and we are grateful … Your group is very strong and we know that we can send you word in times of trouble and that you will respond … You have brought together people who have great skill and a long history and that is why we can rely upon the work that you do … Take heart things are already better than when we first began to talk … our hearts reach out in thanks to you.*

The warnings about coming earth changes seem very real. *There will be fire and earthquakes as the power in their lands must burst forth before it destroys the earth from inside … The volcanoes will soon occur as the earth must begin to breathe more freely and unclog her respiratory system … Your weather will become very fierce … the other side of the world will be the first to feel the strength of the winds that we will use to clear away the poisons that man has put into the atmosphere … There will be fires at some of our sacred sites which have been covered over by your buildings … Water has to be returned into the earth …* We find evidence in the news but don't know if it's actually increasing. Are there more earthquakes, more volcanic eruptions, more storms bringing more water? What of the fires? We find these warnings puzzling.

Has the fascination, expectation, the mystery of this reality – of the group and our work together - along the way somewhere, has it stopped being a game? Has it become almost more real than true reality. But what is true? The sacredness, the urgency of it mystifies. I remember Alan's question, "Are you ready to begin?" It was a question. My own free will determined the choice of answer. Yet it felt as if I had no choice, or having had a choice, had already made it. This feels the

The Clew

same. To sit down with intent. Or not sit down. To share the words with others. Or not share. Unravel the clues or not. Follow instructions, or not. Respond or not. The question is not whether or not to respond. That grows more certain, more rewarding with each choice. No, it's not whether or not to respond, but to *whom* do I respond? Who makes it such a joy to choose to respond? My memory begins to return. Returns well enough to be haunted by the hide and seek of it. Some memory, or memories peek around the corners, just out of reach. The haunting familiarity of this voice talking through my fingers. What is this reality? Where and when was this reality?

Sometimes, re-reading the pages, sentences will jump out as related. Like these, all collected from different messages, teasing me. About my typewriter, my typing, and the fact that I am beginning to be more comfortable, more fluent in interpreting their words ... *I have learned to speak more plainly in the tongue that you can understand and I am fascinated by the way the sounds join together. There is a shape which I am beginning to understand and you can take my thoughts and put them on your machine in a way which makes me excited and happy ... We are fascinated by the way that your machine stamps out the letters. We know of nothing else like this in the whole of our universe ... Your tongue is strange but there is delight in the sounds and your mind can play with our words until they flow on to the paper which you hit with your fingers. This is a strange way, but we are happy to see that it succeeds.*

Or these, all from different messages, but all encouraging me to remember. *You hold a special place in my heart and I am eager for the time when we can speak as before. Do not fear, your memory is returning and soon you will recall much of what we have shared together ... These words have become a joy to me and your companionship is the same delight it always was. Remember all ... I clasp your hand in friendship and a great love. We shall meet again, my friend, and move together through time with those others who are a part of your soul ... there are many things that we shall one day speak about and you will soon remember my name and the other times when we have talked together ... My words are enclosed in the love that surrounds you and our lives will stay linked for all time. I go and will return, remember my name, it will enter your mind when you begin to remember.*

The others from the group can't know. I share the typed pages with them. We read and re-read them, noting our assignments, gathering clues, pondering warnings, studying what needs to be researched. There are many pages now for my energy returns and I sit with intent at least twice a week. I share the pages with them and they read and reread the words. But they can't know. Can't know the feeling. Can't know the gentle, haunting, beauty of it ... *you will soon remember my name and the other times when we have talked together* ... Can't know the agony of not being able to remember ... *remember my name, it will enter your mind* ... Of being so close. So sure it's just there on the edge of my memory, but still just beyond touch ... *My words are enclosed in the love that surrounds you and our lives will stay linked for all time* ... All the other, the puzzles and clues, the ritual and ceremony, the mystery, even the sacred urgency of it, all the other pales in comparison to this.

The Clew

26th September 1990 : I have remembered the voice! And so many things. Remembered so many things. Not remembered, more than remembered. Know. I know things. It's not like needing the midwife holding the spring balance at Hugh's birth for confirmation. It's not like needing the church's occult advisor to verify this reality before I can believe. I don't need to have known this friend as I knew my grandmother in real life before I can believe he's real. Without any rational explanation, without any proof– I know. I *have* lived before. I *remember* this friend with whom I have many times laid down my cloak. We *have* lived together before. We're not alive together now, but somewhere, sometime a very long time ago we were … *I am he who has been your opposite in life. All men have a fellow soul who walks with them and reflects their happiness and sorrow. Now you are whole again …*

Soaking in the water's nurturing warmth, relaxed, the need to remember unbearable and growing, finally in desperation I shouted, "What is your name?" Frustration. And yes some anger too. So tired of the feeling of hide and seek. I wanted it, he - whoever he or it was - out in the open! Then something began catching in my throat. Almost as soon as the question shouted, the catching sounds in my throat began. Something was sounding itself in my throat. As much a life of it's own as the thought-words used by my fingers to put the words on the paper. The sound used my throat. Made an 'ah' noise with my throat again and again as if stuttering. Wanting it, helping it, wanting to help it and being powerless. The energy his own, the vocal syllables almost mine, the effort mutual. And finally the delight of it! The bewildering, inexplicable delight of it. Recognition, and finally remembering. And knowing. The undeniable knowing that finally came with the name – Ashad!

27th September 1990 :

Once more we reach out to each other as the evening spreads its calm across your land … You have remembered my name and now we can walk together as before when the days were long and we discussed many different ideas and concepts. In your paper this morning came news of a place you should also remember. Here we have known each other and read and talked amongst the many rooms that owed their existence to the thirst of man for knowledge. They will rebuild the Library and it will be part of the new beginning. There are many books that were not destroyed but have been kept safe by the people who were given the task. When your words begin to be known these people will confess their knowledge. The books hold all the mysteries of time itself and will show man all that he has forgotten or has been so stupid to dismiss.

My friend, we have worn many cloaks, sometimes at the same time and at other times, like now, we have not walked together but have kept communion with one another in this or in other ways. Other memories will return to you if you remain quiet and ask the questions. For now it is enough that some happinesses begin to return into your mind. Others will follow and these you can share with your friends. Now I can give you my strength to support you. Those who love you should not fear, their love is true and necessary in the life you now lead and part of their own growth will come from what they share with you ... Now the darkness closes around your home and the trees bend their heads to the ground. Go to the woods when it is dark whenever you can and there we can walk together and I can explain many things ... Now I must depart again through the gate which opens its arms for me to enter. My brothers are working also with their fellow travellers across time and our knowledge is being heard again across the whole of your universe. Go to your rest and recover from the weight of responsibility which our words have brought you. We are sorry that you have had to work so hard but you have the strength and the memories which have made this possible. I go to my rest also as I need to breathe more quietly. Good night dear friend, the dawn will bring you more of our words. Enjoy the time you spend with those you love, from such individual delights the earth takes her own strength and life and shares it with the whole of the cosmos ... Pray for the rivers and walk in the circles, time moves on and our work will bring all the destruction to an end. Love all, that is as you have been commanded.

I take my leave and will speak again after we have both rested. The stars appear and write the old stories across the sky. I turn and leave go of your hand. Remember all. I depart.

Like a sigh. Breathing out. So simple the contentment. The release. The first time in my life without the empty half, the always ever-present longing. For the first time only contentment. From almost first knowing, the searching, unconsciously searching. And now letting go, and finding ... myself? The extraordinary warmth of it. The loving warmth enveloping me when I typed the words ... *you have remembered my name* ... It's still here. Hours later it's still as comforting, fresh and real as in that moment.

But Egypt!? That long ago? Alexandria in Egypt? That library? I did find the article. *In your paper this morning came news of a place you should also remember ... They will rebuild the Library and it will be part of the new beginning* ... A full page article on the proposed reconstruction of the great library in Alexandria. Before its destruction, the greatest storehouse of knowledge in the ancient world. How did he know it would be in this morning's paper? Do they know everything about us? Past, present, and future?

7th October 1990: I have begun to remember more. Fleeting almost-images, brief visual glimpses of scenes. Egyptian. Some sort of stone-block throne looking very Egyptian. On the throne sits a Pharaoh-type figure. Wearing some sort of horns strapped to his forehead. Only a side view. I'm off to the side somewhere. Something is taking place in front of him but I can't see it. Off to the side, my view is not his. Again, some time later, another image - strolling with someone. Someone very familiar, very dear, an intimate friend. We were walking leisurely on very flat land beside a great river. Sail boats. Many single-sailed boats on the river. Sometimes the images come when I'm relaxed. They seem oddly natural at first, nothing out of the ordinary. Only later, the realisation of their strange out-of-context reality. Sometimes, without relaxing, they come. As an unbidden thought comes, they too come. Days later, after the pharaoh-throne image, another very different sensation came. Floating over a great fire. A bald-headed man, tall staff in hand, guarding the fire. Floating above it, seeing it from above. All very natural and unworrisome, floating there above it all. And the man, somehow guarding something. The fire. But more than an ordinary fire.

All this time, trying to remember. Then actually remembering. Remembering his name, and now beginning to remember other things. Other things I know, have experienced. As sure of my being there and experiencing them, as I am of what I experience here in this now. Finally remembering and experiencing and knowing. And now, when I am finally remembering, now he leaves …

> *Now the sun begins to sink beneath your side of the earth and I must speak my last words to you. I will come again later when you have spoken with the others who now take control … there are essential messages that you must receive and share with those who work with you. My brothers have their own knowledge and must speak at this time. We shall ask you to write down new words of hope but also of warning as this is part of our task … You are a sister in the faith and have remembrance of many things which have stayed with you but now it is time for you to understand more of the way that your earth was planned. To this end my brothers will speak with you whenever you have the strength.*
>
> *So, my friend, I take my leave of you again as has often happened in the past. I am sad to leave your side but know that everything is as it should be and I also have other tasks that I must attend do. I go and leave you with my words as a doorway to the life you have regained … The stars shine over the great river that has carried the energy to the world and where you and I once walked. We came from different directions and in different faiths but believed always in the one true Light and the wonders of the earth that surrounded us. Stay curious, my friend, and remember my words whenever you can. The sky grows dark and I must pass again through the door.*
>
> *Remember I will return when the sighing has died away and the people begin to walk on their new path. Be strong in the faith and know that your strength is enough. I leave you in the care of my brothers who will become known to you as the stars are known to the men who watch their journeys across the sky. The light fades and I am needed elsewhere. Take care and carry the love of all in your heart. Your friends have our blessings. All is well. I depart.*

16th October 1990: The poetry and love in his words. Ashad's words. The vividness of the images. Memories. Personal, intimate memories. So easy to live with those. So easy to live *in* those. For that to be the day, and the next, to escape each day into that comfort, that completeness. Too tempting. Too easy, that escape. The imperative, this is not to be personal. It's about something else. So a different energy comes. In place of Ashad, one of the others …

The Clew

> *I know that you find it more difficult to hear these words of mine but time will make us more familiar with one another and then our conversations can flow as yours did with my brother who has known you in past times. We are sorry that you have been ill and you will find it difficult for some time to come as the vibrations have a disorientating effect upon your cellular structures ...*

It has been difficult physically. There is something physically stressful about bringing these energies through. Energies, plural. Not just one. I can tell the difference. No names for these. Not personal these. No personal history here. Information. These give me information. I'm learning, accepting the importance of the information. The urgency of it returns.

Remember I will return when the sighing has died away and the people begin to walk on their new path ... With that simple reassurance, Ashad left. And *the work* returns. Like it or not, ready or not, accepting or not, in some way I am part of that new path. In some place or time at the edge of memory, I said yes to this. And I am reminded, as I sit with intent more than twice a week so that they can use my machine ... I am reminded. Reminded of my 'yes' from that time, and my continued 'yes' now. Reminded of my part in this. Of the part of my friends. Of the part of others who also listen ...

> *Many, like you, have been receiving messages for some time and acting on our instructions ... You and the many like yourselves have worked as we hoped and our gratitude is boundless.*

For now it seems there is no work to do. Instead ...

> *Go down to the streams again and refresh yourself in the water. This is now newly refreshed and carries great power which you will need for the next stage of our work ... the time for many to gather will soon be at hand. We shall ask you to go to a place which we shall describe and there you will meet others who have also been working on our behalf ... Soon there will once again be much work to begin and we will need you to use your old skills.*

I sit so often now, with intent. I sit an hour before sunset, and - as they promised - the information, the warnings, the explanations, the reassurances, day after day after day, fill the pages. One sentence follows the next sometimes with no relationship between. Some things I know are past, some true tomorrow, some at some unknown future date and yet they mix together as if in present time. Very confusing at first, but more familiar now and taken in stride ...

> *We do not live by your time and can only judge your lives by the sun and the moon as they rise and set across your world ...*

Yet even this doesn't explain it. The sun and the moon we use to measure time. Their use, if they use them too, must be quite different. And so we leave it, trusting that we'll know when knowing is appropriate. They talk about love in a rather confusing way too. How can the earth share the love we have for each other with the whole of the cosmos?

> *Enjoy the time you spend with those you love; from such individual delights the earth takes her own strength and life and shares it with the whole of the cosmos. Love all, that is as you have been commanded ... All men must find love and return it. This is the way the earth was formed and the way in which it survives ...*

They speak in riddles about the stars too. Speak as if we knew their meaning, understood their words ...

> *[the stars] have begun to count the number of times the earth spins on its curve and the time will soon come when our work has to begin. The earth has reached a point in its evolution when changes must take place. The fire springs from the heart of the earth and must be renewed for the life to continue. The lines have to be strengthened so that the power will flow in the right way when the time for our power to come has arrived. We must have a clear channel before we can rebalance your world and every one of you will be needed if this is to happen. This is the law of our world and of all the others who stand in line across the firmament ...*

This message again. It must be important. But what does it mean? The lines. Reference to ley lines? Each of us will be needed to help make a clear channel so when some power arrives they can rebalance our world. Perhaps there is some reality in which I could make sense of all this.

Yet still other words speak a truth I can't know, but do. Whisper symbols I can't decipher, yet can. Tune my mind to vibrations already part of my being ...

> *Stay close to our land, the need is here. Beneath the ash tree are the holy ones that must be revived to do their work. Come home to the groves and the water which were your birthplace and in the streams you will find again the stories that have been lost to you. Under the ash tree the holy ones keep their vigil and in the waters the ripples signify the lost words of our people. You are the people of the memory who know the old ways. Your task is to pray and make the journeys through the light of time. Pray for the rivers and walk the circles, time moves on and our work will bring all the destruction to an end.*

And somewhere in all of this, in some very subtle and inexplicable way, this person who I am, this being, this energy, this soul, whatever it is I am, is beginning to unfold in a different way. Somehow through all of this I'm different than I've been before. The messages tell me my energy changes. I know it, without being told. They don't mention the things I *sense* now, things I never paid attention to before. They speak of the energy. But the knowing – perhaps they just assume the knowing. They speak of skills. I can't describe the skills. Not sure what they mean by skills. The skills somehow *they* use. *They* direct the skills. The tools are

The Clew

mine. I use the tools. For whatever reason I have these tools now. Energy tools. Ways of sensing and knowing things. Not tools. I don't know what. The language has no words. The dowsing is part of it. But that's just verification. Even without the dowsing there are things just known. Felt. Connections, understanding, remembrances, insights. No word is it quite. Just knowing. And yet that's not it either.

1st November 1990: They keep telling me there's nothing to do for a while. No 'earth work' as we've come to call it.

> *It will be necessary at some time for you to meet with other groups of people in a large gathering. At that time we will send you instructions. You need do nothing at this time as we are also communicating with others and they will speak with you at the right time …*

We have all been having minor respiratory problems of late. The messages seem concerned that we know it's related to our work and that it will pass.

> *We are sorry that you are ill and I am afraid that you will suffer in minor ways for a little while longer. This is because your body must adjust to the new vibration. Your energy coding has to be changed to survive the changed frequencies and your cells are having to readjust, which leads to a weakening of your protective system … You do well to take the precautions that you do as the power has still not stabilised and the effect it has on you is to make you more susceptible to changes in the frequency …*

I'm surprised I feel no anger or resentment about the physical difficulties. The energy I feel when they work through me is so loving, gentle and protective. It's an odd thing, understanding the necessity of it. The energy is different than Ashad's. But it's as loving and gentle. They know I long for his return, and they try and comfort me.

> *You have learned much and now the curtain of your memory will become less opaque and you will glimpse many scenes which are stored in your mind. Your life with Ashad was powerful and fulfilling and your search since then has been long and often sad. Now all will be restored and you can live your remaining years in the knowledge that you will be together once more.*

They gave me a passage that seems to address how we are related to vibration. It's obviously about reincarnation. I'm realising more and more that I do believe in these reincarnation ideas. Since the memory of Ashad, it's difficult not to. But it's more difficult to come to a sense of resolution about other things in the passage.

> *… the soul begins its journey at a low level of frequency and gradually through experiences passes into the higher realms where many attributes become developed. You have lived on a number of frequencies as have those who now*

stand around you, and you all have different skills which you have acquired and specialised in at different times. Your daughter has now passed through into a higher grade which is why she can now communicate directly with you. She had to strengthen her spirit which she did by overcoming fear and this was the last attribute she needed to pass on to the higher place. Your religions know much of this already but their words have been changed in the past by people who did not have the depth of experience to understand the words. They believed only in symbolism and did not recognise the essential nature of the rituals which had been passed down to them. Your husband comes directly from a line which has the knowledge still in their Law.

Strange, that part about religion. The words that come sometimes seem contrary to things I believe and that I know my Church of England background has taught me. Or not taught me - like reincarnation. Yet … the feeling of it … it feels loving. It feels like the entire reason behind it all is love. I keep going with it. Partly because of the mystery. Partly because of the intrigue. Finding the places was fun. There was an empowering feeling with it. A feeling of solving the mystery. The synchronicities and coincidences of meeting other people. Being in sync with their activities, their understanding of what's happening, what's needed. The camaraderie within the group of us. We're all being stretched somehow. We interact with each other, enjoy each other in a different way now. We are beginning to share a reality that feels right. Truly does feel like the way the earth and her peoples have to be treated if we are to survive. While not always familiar, nothing about it feels like anything my C of E background warned me to fear and avoid.

And I keep going because of the feeling of love that washed over me when I remembered Ashad's name. An inexplicable love and completeness. A peaceful contentedness. It wasn't so much that I found a feeling I had lost. It was more that I remembered the feeling of who I am. And I can't explain it. It doesn't make sense. But it feels like I must know that again. It feels like I must know that in this physical body. With another physical body. One alive on this planet somewhere right now. And somehow it feels like Ashad can help me find that.

And so I keep going. I don't know why the others keep going. Maybe the sense of intrigue. The wonder of it. And we keep pouring over the information, trying to make sense of it.

They speak often of vibration. Somehow vibration, frequency, colour and sound all seem related in the messages. It is apparent they are trying to give me concepts for which I have no words. I use the best words I can find but am unable to explain what the words mean in the context they use them. As with this following collection - all seemingly explaining something to do with colour, sound, vibration.

> *… All life is surrounded by mists of colour which you call the ether. This colour contains all the codes from which all forms are developed … Each level has it's own colour which gives the signal for cells to develop. On your own world the colours have become confused and this has led to much illness amongst your peoples. We have begun to communicate this old knowledge to the others*

> *who hear us and after the troubles you will be able to build new healing centres where people can receive the colour and sound that their cellular structure is deficient in …*
>
> *… Tell her to lie quietly with the picture of a rainbow before her or in her mind. She must put all thought of others from her and focus only on the colour which emerges …*
>
> *… We have given you the task of working with sound because this is what you and your group of friends have experience of and you can understand much that we present to you …*
>
> *… Together you should return to the old places as your vibrations will tune and be tuned by such visits …*

Also, in amongst the warnings about necessary physical changes to the earth herself is a particular message about England. Work is taking place throughout the globe, but it seems the work in England is particularly important for some reason.

> *The earth's cycle follows a particular pattern of aging and renewal as have all the other planets in the cosmos. Man has the possibility to make the change easy or hard and because your science has followed too narrow a path it will be difficult for your race to absorb the knowledge that is necessary in such a short time … This time has been spoken of for centuries in your great books when earth passes through into its new beginning and it joins in greater understanding with its sisters and brothers who watch from beyond the stars.*
>
> *You are right to believe that one part of that area (in the East) is crucially important. This was originally the birthplace of your civilisation and it was to this spot that we last directed our messages in the same way that we are doing today. Then also the earth had reached a point when it had to survive a major change and many men heard our voices. Much information about this time is written in your great books or is wrapped inside the secret rituals of some of your groups. In particular there is a group of men who know many of the holy symbols which they use at their meetings. Most of them have no idea of the significance of their possessions but when our words become known they will be able to offer their part of the mysteries which were broken into many pieces in order that the word should survive.*
>
> *Long ago a people came to your island that were versed in the ways of the East. They had travelled far for they had been cast out of their own land and they carried with them many secrets. They had hands of fire and they left their imprints on your land. These vibrations imbue your people with a particular creativity and strength and this has been the chief characteristic of your race. It is essential that the places where the vibration attaches itself to your land must be kept clear.*
>
> *In your land there is a place where the secrets were buried many generations ago when the men with the sky secrets lived on your soil. This place is not far from your home and is close to the stones that hold a special message for you. Soon they will be uncovered and understood and then men will once again*

have the Law by which they should live. The serpent guards the spot and the lion has stood near it for all these years.

All must be clear or else there will be great danger when the earth begins to move far underground. The men of fire have begun their work, they can read the earth's signs and know what they must do. They live in other lands but know tasks that are their responsibility and they will not fail. We all stand together at this moment, as our concerted power will be needed if the changes are to occur gradually and within the limits of reasonable safety. Keep the faith, hold hands and love all, these are the laws we have often reminded you of.

2nd November 1990: This time, in one session, two voices came through. There have been different voices, different entities with very different energies. But always before only one in each session. Most exciting of all, Ashad was here again.

My friend, I return to your side once more so that together we can greet the day when the earth will see momentous changes begin ... We should sit together as before if the days were only long enough for the ideas to flow back and forth between us and we could speak again of the lives we have lived and the stars we have studied in the schools of the East. Do you remember those times when we prayed that mankind would hold fast to the Mysteries and pass them from generation to generation in love and reverence? Your brow still carries the tiger jewel that denotes your special place amongst the priests who worshipped the ever-burning fire. I have the same mark and our voices sang the same chant and our voices spiralled along the circles of power. How happy we were and how much strength we have both needed since that time ... Continue to reach across to us, we need your skills and now many of my brothers hear your voice. I depart but will return when the time has arrived for us to begin the writings that will comfort all men. My friend I leave you once again with my brother who has become your companion through this difficult time. Rest in my love and the love that surrounds you. All those you love are in my care. Remember.

Maybe I do remember. I think I do remember. Seeing the man tending the fire. That may be the *ever-burning fire.* Be patient. I must be patient. This will unfold the way it unfolds. It is about larger things than Ashad and me. Than our relationship. So many uncertainties. Warren continuing to find his own way. Will our lives continue together? And if they don't, then what? Will this work, this earth work, continue? The messages imply that it will ... *I depart but will return when the time has arrived for us to begin the writings that will comfort all men.* And what is that about? When is that about?

I must try and articulate the difference between Ashad and the others. There is a difference. There is love with the others. Care. Concern for my wellbeing. For the wellbeing of the others in the group. Care and concern for the well being of the earth. It's real and very loving. Feels immediate. Their concern and care feels immediate and urgent. Something is happening that is so important, not

The Clew

just to the earth but to the universe, to the cosmos. Whatever it is we're a part of it. I am. The group is. All the others working around the world are. It seems to be bigger than I can imagine. Or perhaps the correct word is remember. Bigger than I can remember. Even with Ashad's prompting. And all the others. They keep asking us to remember. Remember our skills. Remember the sounds. Remember the prayers. Remember the places where the energy is tied to the earth. Remember to hold all and each other in love. Remember remember remember. Always they are telling us to remember. Perhaps we do remember. Perhaps the 'knowing' that we so often come up with, that we use to follow their instructions, the intuition that we think of as the 'knowing', perhaps that's remembering. And all the time their gentle presence. Encouragement. Concern and care. And love. A deep and profound love.

But not Ashad's love. Ashad's love is different. His reminds me of something different. Ashad's love reminds me … reminds me … remember, remember, remember!!! I can't remember! Ashad's love reminds me of something I can't remember. Something about myself. Something I should know. Something I've been searching for. Each time he comes, each time the words I type are his, each time … the need to remember grows stronger.

Chapter Four

Many levels of growth were unfolding simultaneously for Avril and members of the group. Except for Joy, who was involved in alternative healing and some dowsing, none of the other group members had been involved in any type of 'alternative' realities prior to this time. Avril is able now to look back and see that during this first year, and in fact through most of the years right up until the final request from the entities, she was in a sense on trial. It was as if she had to continually give permission for the work to continue. And permission involved much more than sitting down at the typewriter. She was learning to identify the sites involved. She was identifying people to accompany her on the expeditions. She was being given the instructions to see if she was willing to carrying them out. In each of these ways she was being asked, and was giving intent, and saying yes to the process. In a sense, prior to the even more important work which was still in the future, the entities involved were making sure that she would have the ability and be willing to carry out the necessary tasks. At any time she might have stopped the process by deciding that any of the activities or physical adjustments she needed to make were too high a price to pay. There were many levels on which she was agreeing to the process. Many levels on which she was giving permission to be of service in this way.

Found in the messages are frequent references to vibration and frequency. In part these seemed to be a way of trying to help Avril understand what was happening to her. The energies she was in contact with increased in strength over the years she worked with them. The vibration seemed to increase in small increments, and each time the new energy was stronger, her physical body had to learn to cope with it. She found it welcome that chronic ME symptoms lessened as she slowly built up some kind of immunity to the physical effects of the entities' increased vibration. With each new vibration she also accessed different abilities and was able to use the abilities in different ways. When she began, she could only access the entities involved an hour before sunrise, or an hour before sunset. As she adjusted to the vibrations involved she could be available almost any time of day. In the beginning she needed to type words for the thought-forms she received: a sort of dictation. As she learned to tolerate stronger energies, she could actually ask questions. That she could, with the person's permission, actually converse with their personal guides was another powerful, if novel, discovery. Later she would learn to interpret the thought forms with her own voice so that the typewriter wasn't needed. She would be empowered to received the energy in the presence of groups and would pass along messages from an entity regarding questions people in the group asked. Ultimately she would be able to hold the energy of an entity who discussed ideas with various members of a group simultaneously, one who carried on a dialogue and discussion with members of the group. These vibrational shifts and increased abilities continued throughout the entire time the work was being undertaken. Avril is convinced that until she accessed certain vibrational frequencies, certain parts of the work could not occur. She has continued to have occasional vibrational shifts even though she suspects the major part of the earth healing is finished. With each shift, she has accessed a new dimension, a new ability.

She is amused by the simplicity of some of the information she recorded. Not apologetic, she simply states she had no concepts for explaining the thought-groups she was being shown. It was the equivalent of a school child who had just mastered the multiplication tables suddenly being asked to explain advanced calculus. At times she simply didn't have the ability to translate what she was being shown. Her understanding of the material seemed to grow in a way similar to her ability to tolerate the increased vibration. Times too numerous to record she was given information that made little sense to her. Coincidentally a friend would give her a book, or she would discover one in a second-hand book shop, or someone with whom she was talking would begin explaining something that seemed, suddenly, to make sense of what she had just typed. As long as she was open to it, validation came from the most unexpected sources. Later, when Avril began to receive information for individuals in her group sessions, she was repeatedly instructed to 'read more.' Repeatedly an entity would state "I can see it, the woman cannot say it." By that time there was much interaction between group members and the entity; occasionally when she had difficulty translating something someone in the group would call out teasingly, "She must read more!" And the entity would reply, also in a teasing way, "So I have spoken."

    At any one time the information received seemed to be in the exact amount and complexity the participants could manage. Had any one of them been able to see ahead to the number of years they would commit to this work, had the key players realised the magnitude of the information they would receive and be expected to interpret, they may not have chosen to continue. It's true there were many who involved themselves only for a specific event or for a specific period of time. In the way she would eventually learn to recognise people who were in some way connected to the work, Avril occasionally sensed she was interacting with someone else who might have on some level been connected but who, for personal reasons, chose never to be involved. Perhaps they could see, more clearly than Avril and the others, the complexity of and the time involved in what was to unfold. Perhaps those who chose not to be involved knew on some level that the work would more and more necessitate being able to juggle two realities. Maybe that was simply a choice they were unwilling to make. For whatever reason, the work did continue. And during the last weeks in November 1990, the mystery grew deeper and more inexplicable.

    With the wisdom gained in the last ten years, it's only natural to look back on this next sequence of events with a deeper understanding than any of the participants had at the time. Perhaps then, the most surprising aspect from those weeks of activity prior to the full moon on 2nd December 1990 is that they happened at all. The whole process, the channelled messages, deciphering the clues, meeting friends to carry out instructions, is perhaps as much a mystery today as it was then. At the time a fun mystery, but one taken largely on faith. The reassurances that the activity made a difference continued; however, there is no more *actual* proof of this today than there was at the time. In fact, it was only in retrospect that even the specific, predicted incidents involved seemed to fit into any sequence. There was much more reason to doubt than to believe. And yet Avril faithfully scribed the words. Many faithfully poured over them, puzzling, studying, interpreting, voluntarily carrying out the complex instructions in the messages. Progress continued even when the words made little sense to anyone and even when at times they seemed more than a little silly.

During the weeks preceding the full moon in December, Avril felt an urgency as never before. Daily sessions resulted in pages and pages of information. It began with the core group but grew to include friends of friends of friends, many, many people unknown to Avril. And made reference to many, many specific places familiar only to the individual people for whom the information was received. Except for a few who may be interested in the material for their own personal reasons, the next few pages are not included to be read in their entirety. There is little information in them which in itself is relevant to the telling of this story. Rather they may be scanned with the idea of realising the complexity of the work involved. If, up to this point, Avril had managed to convince herself that somehow she was fabricating all of this, she now began to have very serious doubts. At this point so many people, including complete strangers, enter the melee, and there are messages so intimate to the strangers involved, that it became more and more difficult, in deed it became impossible, to explain the coincidences.

At this time another subtle alteration was becoming evident. So subtle was it, in fact, that at first even Avril wasn't aware of it. Avril's process consisted of sitting down at the typewriter, clearing her mind, and receiving information. A few times she had been rather excited that something that was on her mind subliminally was addressed. But she had never asked specific questions of the entities before. It could be argued even now that she wasn't asking specific questions. But people unknown to Avril were calling from out of nowhere, asking to be included, asking to be part of this involved and complex activity. The answers came. Personalised instructions came. No one was turned away. All were included. All were acknowledged. All were valued. And in the end the gratitude expressed was for all, each and every one. She was becoming aware that the entities were very aware of her thought processes, he worries, her fears, and they addressed these in a personal way for her - and for the others.

AVRIL
Healing on the Michael Line

8th November 1990 : I miss the clues, the puzzle, the search, the acknowledgement we received when we did something correctly. I know there's more to this than mystery and intrigue. Not that the information we're being given now isn't mysterious. It has a fascination all it's own. It's encouraging us to ask different questions. To think differently. To see differently. To sense energies we haven't been aware of. In its own way it's encouraging us to remember. And we are remembering. I know it's all very important. Even without being told I know the information I'm being given is very important. But I miss the excitement of finding the places. The synchronicity that always accompanied our activities. Watching the plot unfold. All of us with our own part to play. I seem to be the one who guides it. I seem to have the responsibility of it. I know it's about the earth, the universe, the cosmos. I know that. But it's about the more personal things too. I know that too. And that's the part I miss. And will miss, if it stops. Or when it stops. It's not stopping yet. There *will* be more.

The Clew

> *Wait now for the instructions that will soon come that we have already spoken of. You will need to join with others at the place that we describe as you will all be needed to balance the power lines and to protect the land from the heat.*

We're also being reassured, even without further work, that the work we and others have already done is making a difference.

> *Your polarity has begun to make a marked change and the rocks are beginning to swell to respond to this change. Much water will be needed inside the earth and it is our task to send the rains that must quench the heat ... Many across the world attend to their rituals at this time and there are enough of you now in your own land to prevent the blockages that would be so dangerous ... There is little danger now of eruptions that are not in our control because of the work that you and the many others have undertaken.*

We realise again and again the primary message in all of this. Something that has happened before in the earth's history is happening again. And we have some influence on it. Somehow we are a part of it. We are not to be afraid. We are to see it as a natural phenomenon. A temporary change, that is all. Something which has been predicted, has to be expected, and can be influenced by right action. The action is in our memory but we have forgotten it. Or maybe actions. We, the group and I, are a part of the right action. We're to believe that what we are doing is important and making a difference. Even so, there will still be natural events. Natural disasters. There are always natural disasters. So how do we know if this time, this particular time in the history of our civilisation, is any different?

> *The earthquake cycle has begun and many others will be triggered by the movement that has already occurred. You wait as we have explained and the signs will appear steadily but at first it will be difficult for others to recognise a pattern. You know all and you must be careful to keep well the records that you have already begun ... research as much as [you] can on the nature and variety of earthquake occurrences. You need more knowledge of this aspect which will be the centre of much discussion after the winter has passed.*

Are we being told to trace the earthquake activity as proof of what they're telling us? Are we being told that in some way we're causing the earthquakes? By some lack of understanding of the way things work together, the way the earth functions, or by some simplistic understanding in our scientific knowledge, are we inadvertently causing 'natural' disasters? Is that what they're telling us? Are we being told to monitor them, figure out what our part is, make some correlation between their occurrences and something we are doing? Will we be told something to do that will lessen their possible number as seems to have happened with *the eruptions that are not in our control?* Like so many things, we haven't figured it out yet.

The Clew

11th November 1990 :

It is important that you take down this message with care ... We have increased the power flowing across your land in order that our work can get underway ... Go now to your bookshelf and you will find, with the pendulum's help, the answer to many of your questions at this time. It is essential that your road to knowledge is a gradual one or else important information would be missed as your brain tries to deal with so many new concepts ... Wait now for the instructions that will soon come that we have already spoken of. You will need to join with others at the place that we describe, as you will all be needed to balance the power lines and to protect the land from the heat.

16th November 1990 :

We must now speak with you of the last action we wish you to undertake at this time ... we need you to meet with many others as the light strikes the earth as we have promised. This will be an occasion when all your combined strength will be needed to protect the earth's crust from great harm because the heat that the light engenders could burn away the upper surfaces of your planet and then the earth would become sterile. You must wait until the time of the next full moon [2nd December 1990] and we will give you much more information before that time arrives. However it is important that you identify the spot that we need you to visit. You must go to the most holy place where the fathers built their first church. We know that this is not difficult for you to identify but you must seek on your plans for the place where the stream of Arthur passes through the meadow of the lion. Here there is great power and many of you must utilise it if your future is to be assured.

17th November 1990 :

These are some of the details that you must have before you begin your work on our behalf. You have chosen the right place and you have begun to identify the actions that you must undertake there. You must all form a great circle as the light must, as before, centre on your power fields in order that it can make contact with the earth. At that same time you must chant the holy words as the channel must be as clear and as vibrant as possible if we are to succeed with our task. Other events will occur at the same time across the world and we have summoned many to work on our behalf at that moment. Your circle must move into a star-shape and then return to a circle for in that way the correct messages will be conveyed to those whose task it is to direct the force-field into the right area. The one with the pendulum must stand in the centre with the other three who will make themselves known to her, and you and Harry must stand a little to their side facing south. In this way the sun's rays can make a straight connection through you both to the line centre that is at that place. Long ago the people of the Word constructed these patterns as markers of the energy points and different strengths. They are linked to the different aspects of the universe which, in themselves, have identical recognition symbols. The secrets of this place have long been forgotten but you and Harry have the knowledge and the particular characteristics to be able to channel the

The Clew

energies in the right way.

Your friends in the southwest must travel to Tintagel and stand in a small circle at the spot where once the prayers were said. At the precise time they must join their hands in a circle and move three times to the left and then three times to the right. This will spiral the energy and give it added momentum as it moves across the land. If it is not possible for them to go to this site then they must go to the spot near the headland in the south where the monks prayed and wrote down the histories of the Celtic peoples ...

Your other friends in the south must go to the nine stones circle where they must walk in seven circles into the centre in a clockwise direction. They must do this at the moment that the sun's rays hit the ground or else the energy will be dissipated ...

Your friend in the east must gather together as large a number as she can as the power must have enough strength when it leaves your land to cross the waters and return to its source ...

You can ask the man who writes the book if he will go with others to the white horse ... It is important that all these actions occur at the same moment as the speed of the energy will be so great that you cannot measure it in your time ... light will radiate across your land smoothing the air and summoning the wind that will blow for many days ...

There is other information that we will give you at another time as there is much you must recall before the day arrives. You have achieved all that we asked and could have hoped for and your happiness is a delight to us ...

19th November 1990 :

Another day brings us closer to the major events we have prepared you all for over the past months. You have worked as we had hoped and your assistance now is of crucial importance to us as we must communicate our instructions to the many who will learn of your knowledge and make contact with you ...

... in the meantime he can go to the place near his home where the castle stands. He must walk around the front of the hill till he finds the spot where a bridge crosses a small stream. Here he must stand quietly and precisely at noon he must throw an oak twig into the water and say his word three times. Then he must cross the water three times, beginning from the north to the south, and in this way the energy will be released from inside the hill where it has been stored for many years. He must first, before he begins wash his hands in the water as he has done before near your home and he must wash them a second time when his task is completed ...

We speak now of the actions at the great circle. Here many must go and stand in a double circle at the head of the avenue. As the hour approaches they must circle in opposite directions seven times. Then they must lift their arms and speak the holy words. At the exact moment of noontime they must lie on the ground still in a double circle with their hands joined. They will be able to feel the earth move as the current passes beneath them and their own energies will give it added strength to take it on to the next line crossing ...

Now we must speak of your own actions at this time. You do not need a *great number at the balancing site but you must be very precise in your actions ... You and Harry should face each other and you must hold each others hands to protect yourselves against the force of the current which will be the most powerful you have yet received. One of you cannot do this task on your own as it would be too dangerous. This is the first time for many centuries that we have regenerated the energy in this way and your presence in your land at this time has been carefully calculated in order that this could be done once we had decided on this path ... We regret that the effect in other countries will be catastrophic but protections are already in place and we have assured that nothing goes beyond what is absolutely unavoidable ... Listen for our words, you must give precedence to these messages or else some important detail could be missed.*

20th November 1990 :

We are grateful for your return from those things which are important to you. However there is much that we must now communicate to you and we have very little time before events take a hand. We have not given you any detail before because we ourselves were uncertain of the outcome of our contacts with so many of you. However you are now all prepared and our work can begin in those areas which we have previously identified ...

You have realised the sequence of events that will begin at the time we have spoken of ... She who lives in the valley must go to the circle as she has planned. There she must walk to the left in an outer circle and then reverse her path in an inner one. This she must repeat until she has completed three pairs. She must then loop into the centre and out again and then repeat the pair process in the opposite direction. She must begin at noon precisely ...

The men who speak with you will give you much help and themselves have much information that will help you with your work. Tell them that both the lines will be recharged by the energy but that the female line will have a spasmodic current as it is important that the energy is interrupted in this way. This is because the power surge would otherwise be too strong and the surface of the land would be burnt up by the heat. They must look on the coast where the two streams cross the sands. This place is near to the church where once the sailors prayed and the sand has to be kept from the door. This spot is of great significance to the line and must be recharged. It will need seven people to walk in a circle one at a time. Then the one with the rods must focus the power into the centre. They must not stand inside while that is done, as the power would be too great ...

21st November 1990 :

You must take care that you do not overtire yourself in the coming days ... we suggest that you speak with the man who is coming to the place of the lion as he will be able to offer you guidance on what you need to do at this time. We now have further information for the man with the rods. You must tell him that you work on behalf of the Masters and that you have been chosen because of your fortitude and courage. This you have proven in this life and in many others and you know many secrets which will return to you in time. It is enough that you have walked with the men of fire and have shared their secrets. This is your land, here your ancestors have built with their hands and cared for the earth. Now you must bring all your skills to the fore and Harry must also use his special gifts for the good of your race.

You must tell the man that the place he must seek is close to the well of the holy man. He must find a small field where the current crosses in an east-west direction. If he walks slowly along this line he will find a spot where the energy spirals in a clockwise direction and then reverses. This double helix is the place he must also recharge before the day of the full moon …

There are still tasks to be identified and many will approach you. At those times we will give you directions. We regret the need for so much work but all must be well at this catastrophic time for your peoples … Now we must depart as there is only time for us to deal with urgent matters as many others wait for our words and have great fear. Speak again with us as the light dims and we will answer what questions you have. Sleep as much as you can and heed our words.

22nd November 1990 :

Your arrangements go well but you must concentrate more on the area in the south where Harry lives as it is crucial that those spots are attended to … You have no cause to worry that there will be insufficient at the place of the Lion, we shall see that that is not so. You must take time to find the precise spot and the skills of the wise ones will be needed for this. Harry must join with them at this time as he can pick up the change in vibration which will mark the precise spot. Afterwards he must stand with you and you must on no account loose hands until the wise ones speak.

The one with the pendulum will soon be well. We regret that she has had to suffer pain but this was the only way that we could make the changes to her structure that were essential. From this moment she will be much more sensitive to sounds than before and she must take great care in your noisy world or else her hearing could be damaged. The reasons for this change will become apparent once your earth has re-stabilised and then she will become greatly loved for the knowledge she can offer and for the healing she will be able to transmit.

Some of your friends are concerned about the timing. Do not question as you have received our words correctly and all will be well. It is not possible for us to explain such things in detail as you cannot find the words to describe our meaning but all will be well if the precise time you have recognised is adhered to …

You all do well, you have our blessings and the benediction of the Masters … We offer you our thanks and leave your side.

23rd November 1990 :

This is the moment of challenge for your race and the time when all that has been prophesied for centuries will come to pass … You are one of the many workers across your world who have been selected for your various gifts and *experiences to do our work … You have the skill and you have grown much in recent time and we honour your skills … You have begun to see your past and more can now return. You were once the great Balancer of the court and your sorrow comes from that time when you gave up your friend to the fires of the lost ones. He is now restored as you know and together there is once again work you must undertake. He will stand at your side … and your strength, with that of Harry, will be enough to balance the light. It must be received and divided at that point or else it would destroy all that it touched. Do not fear, you know what to do and Ashad will be with you …*

The man with the rods has begun his search and all will be well. Tell him that his special gifts will be needed after the light has arrived and that he must begin to use the pendulum more than the rods. It will be difficult to use the rods in the new ways after the light has struck and the channels have been enlarged.

There are not enough people yet at the site on the moorland. This you must correct as this is a crucial site.

The site near the sea in the west must be visited by seven people at the time we have spoken … The man with the rods will catch the current as it passes and he must be careful that he takes none of it away with him as this would be dangerous as the power will be unstable for a short time …

Now we move across the ocean to the lands where there will soon be sorrow … Pray for them all and keep the faith …

25th November 1990 :

There is little time to communicate the answers you need. We must first speak to you of the man who asks … He has great psychic powers that he must begin to use now and we suggest that he begin by undertaking the task you can set for him for the day of the moon's judgement. … Tell him that he must turn away from those people who believe only in the power of the head and listen to his own heart here many messages are waiting to be heard … Now we must give you the instructions for your friend by the great river. She has powers which she must use confidently – she can bring about changes which will make life easier in that area. She must go to the spot where the willow trees grow in clumps … in her mind's eye she must cover all the water she can see with a carpet of gold and say the river blessing. She must hold that colour for some minutes until the clouds part and the sun shines through.

You have arranged all well but you must make certain that everyone has their precise instructions as they are crucial if all is to go safely … Ashad will wait at the Lion where you will remember your past.

26th November 1990 :

… You are taking the right actions and making the right arrangements and all is as it should be at this time. There is little we need to communicate to you and our time is occupied with the many others who work …

27th November 1990 :

… This portion of our task will soon be ended and then the work of education

The Clew

and encouragement begins. You will be needed still and we will communicate the tasks that we shall need you to undertake. Your group is strong and now others have joined you who have particular strengths. Your task will be to lead your land back to its responsibilities and many will hear you ...

29th November 1990 : (Morning)
We regret that we must call you so early but there is an emergency. The people in the south have identified the wrong area and you must speak with them immediately. You must tell them that they must look where the trees stand in a clump on the moorland. Nearby is a bridge which was once the only crossing for people making a pilgrimage to the abbey. You know of this place and must communicate your knowledge to the woman who makes the arrangements ...

Our time is now short and we have begun to link the signs together. Man has not understood their meanings and so you can only work on our instructions but soon you will understand and marvel at the simplicity of it all.

The woman who speaks with you of the great circle has a special responsibility which she has earned. We trust her greatly and her presence at the holy site will mark the beginning of a new life for her ...

29th November 1990 : (Evening)
... You now have the correct site in the south and the woman there makes the right arrangements ...

The man with the rods must continue along his path of discovery. This will lead him to a true understanding of all that we prepared at the beginning of the earth's life. He will uncover many of the mysteries that have long been forgotten and his voice will be heard by many who turn to you all for knowledge and understanding ...

There is much that has begun although you cannot as yet see the signs. Very little time however will elapse before these become obvious to all. Your government has seen many changes in the past few days ... The changes that occur will pave the way for the new approach to government in your country that is needed. The man who takes control has the knowledge and strength to change but many months will pass before the new ways are accepted and enforced ...

We will speak now only if there is some emergency otherwise you are free to go about your preparations ...

30th November 1990 : (Morning)
Tell the man who questions that the time is aligned with aspects of the heavens which as yet you do not comprehend. He does right to question but you have the truth and our assurance ...

30th November 1990 : (Evening)
You ask for the woman who goes to the monk's island. Tell her she will be led to the spot but she must go there a little before the time of action as she and

The Clew

her friends must spend a short time pulling in the energy with their minds. They must picture it crossing the ocean as a gold band and swirling around where they stand. At the precise moment they must dissect the power into sections so that it moves from them as an intermittent current. This task is important and they must concentrate very hard on their task. They will know it is complete when a small ship comes into sight.

We have no further time and must take up our positions across the sea. Call if you have need but you have arranged all as we wished and our communications must now be with those who are less prepared. We depart from you but will return to stand by your side when the moment of truth arrives.

28th November 1990 : An urgency to these recent messages. The advice, *Go now to your bookshelf and you will find with the pendulum's help*, has turned up the book 'The Sun and The Serpent.' Hamish Miller and Paul Broadhurst dowsed these two lines. Named them the St. Michael and St. Mary. Side by side, sometimes crossing each other, two ley lines the full width of England. Cornwall to Suffolk. Unimaginable numbers of prehistoric and historic sacred sites along these lines. Stone circles. Holy wells. Tumuli. Churches incorporating pagan symbols and artefacts into their architecture. And now we're being given sites on this line! And so many people. *Others will now make contact with you and we will speak with you at those times to communicate the instructions that they must have if all is to go well.* But so many. Where do they come from? How do they know?

Each one shares concern. Words like, "I feel that at last I am really doing something for the earth." Sincere, not a joke to them. More serious and earnest sometimes than we are. They've not had the clues, or mysterious treasure hunts. They've only their own concern and desire to make a difference. And yet they come. From somewhere. Asking to help. Asking for a place, a task, an instruction to follow. And magically the entities know them. Without even being asked or told. Know where they live, know how to guide them to spots they are familiar with. Know about their lives and how to use relevant information. For one: *this is very near to her home and she often walks there and looks at the horses.* For another: *She has been to this spot many times and she will remember that there is a white building where she has once eaten.* For another: *Here there is a spot where in his youth he once played with the frogs and he must return there before he can begin his new work.* And still another: *Tell him that he has remembered the place and the moment was when he was a boy and argued with his father. Here he used to go to recover his peace. Here his peace waits for him still and he must acquire the blessing before he can move forward.* So many others. Receiving personal instructions for some specific task on some specific point related to this St. Michael line. Some place close to them, familiar to them, meaningful to them.

It's as if each was expected. Known about beforehand. Prepared for in some way. Such personalised instructions. And gratitude to each. Appreciation. *We will reward the many who have trusted your words and you must convey our thanks to them all.* Each one is included. Not one has come forward without receiving personal attention, information, requests for a particular action at a particular

The Clew

site, and thanks and appreciation. Each has identified the particular spot to their satisfaction. And each waits, ready. Ready to execute their steps in this vast ballet choreographed from one side of our land to the other, synchronised for noon on the day of the full moon.

But is it enough? I too ask people to join in. Friends. Acquaintances. Friends of friends. Feels risky. What will their experience be? For now they trust. They agree to come. Agree to play their part. For now. But after? One thing to include the core group. Always been a lark with them. And they seem to know things, sense things. On their own they validate differences in energies following our work. But these others? Will they? Will they think me crazy? If nothing happens, if they feel nothing, what then? I've wasted their time? Their good will? Do I still doubt? Yes. But also I will the trust to be there. And sometimes will myself to keep going. There's an anxiety. An anxiousness about this whole St. Michael event. In two minds about it. How can the information all be so precise, so intimately individual if there's nothing to it? So there's something to it. What? Will a lightening bolt strike? An earthquake? A searing seam of energy travelling faster than we can imagine? Still, we have their reassurances. And up to now all has been relatively benign. For some unfathomable reason the risks seem greater if we don't follow through than if we do. Besides, it's too late now. The dance has already begun. Letting one willingness follow another has brought me, brought all of us, this far. But this far isn't quite far enough and so I continue.

3rd December 1990 : It was enough that things went well. That afterwards people talked of personal experiences and it seemed meaningful to them. No one felt the trip or the time was wasted. I am relieved. My doubts and lack of trust were unfounded. I had none of the sensations the other's did. Nervousness about Harry and his willingness or unwillingness was unfounded too. His participation was vital. The rods worked for him. First time he ever dowsed and he found the spot. Exactly the way they said he would. He seemed able to flow with the process and what was unfolding better than I could have imagined. Mostly just relief. I feel a sense of relief. Who knows what happened. We have their reassurances.

> *Your work yesterday was successful and for this you have our thanks. The light has passed beneath the ground and your channels are now safely enlarged. When the time for the earth to heave arrives the force will pass safely through your land ...*

But who knows what actually happened. At St Michael's Mount a small ship came into view as predicted. As instructed they watched for a small ship to come into view as a sign to end their work. They described the dinghy as uniquely beautiful with a dazzling turquoise sail. Appeared on cue just as they finished their visualisation.

And now it feels like they're leaving me again. Whomever I have been working with, whomever has used my fingers and my machine to prepare us for our parts along this vast line, is leaving. After all the work, all the urgency, all the anxiety, the will to keep going in the face of doubt, my reward is to be left alone again …

> *At the place of the lion there were many workers who gathered round you and added their prayers to your own. This spot is of great importance for here the priests of the stones left much wisdom and where you stood was the place where their energy recharges itself. There will be many changes amongst the signs from now on as their time to adjust to the new order has arrived … you have enabled the light that will spark the changes to pass through your land … you have my thanks and the blessings of us all. We confirm our care of all who have helped us and offer them our love in faith … We have spoken freely with one another and you have taught me much of your language … Our work together has achieved much and I have enjoyed my time at your side … Good bye, my friend, perhaps we will one day speak again.*

Not as difficult as Ashad leaving. But difficult. The words he always used, 'my friend.' It does feel like a friend leaving,

> *… You must now rest … When we need you we will call and we know that you will hear us … Ashad will return to you when the words have to be written and if you have need before that we shall hear your voice when you call and one of us will come to your aid.*

And so it ends.

Chapter Five

AVRIL
Continues her schooling in 'the wisdoms'

28th December 1990 : The winds came as promised. My house didn't escape.

> *Now the wind bends the trees and you begin to experience what we have prepared you for. We are sorry that you too have suffered damage and that so many people have found themselves in such difficulties. However, as was explained to you, we must take these actions as your science has set in place so many inadequate and careless systems that are affecting the earth's own power resources that we must interfere and create a pause so that our work can go unhindered.*

Interesting way to describe a gale, interfere and create a pause. And what work went or is going unhindered? This is yet another energy, another entity. I know, even before they validate my experience, when they change and I'm working with a different one.

> *We have not spoken before and I am only one of many who can respond to you when you have questions to ask or when we wish to offer you information.*

I am reassured that Ashad is near. That he will return. I don't feel his presence and sometimes question whether or not I'll work with him again.

5th January 1991 : It's not that I'm less disciplined about listening for the messages. It's that there seems less need now. Preparing for work on the ley line was a kind of fine tuning. It enabled me to know with certainty when they want to speak to me. It's not as urgent and there seems more time in between messages. A relief really, with everything else that's happening. Still, it does seem the work will continue at some time in the future.

> *Many are working on different tasks and soon all will be clear as we have already spoken. You have no need for concern as your group has done all that was needed at this time and now you must all regain your strength for the tasks that lie ahead ... Be assured that events are progressing as they should but it is important that you act on the messages from others that you receive as we need the help of you all to continue with our work ... the cleansing of your country's power lines must continue ... the future of the cosmos depends on the fate of your planet.*

My fingers typed those last words *the future of the cosmos depends on the fate of your planet*. And now I read them. And re-read them. And they make little sense. How can the work we do be that important? I'm just me, an ordinary person. I have no great skills. No great knowledge. How can the future of the cosmos depend on something I'm involved in? It's easier when we're told to go somewhere and do something. Given a task with implicit instructions. Any task is much easier than the meaning in that sentence.

12th January 1991: Kuwait. The Iraqi invasion. The non-Arab world watching in horror. The amassing of UN forces. The news night after night filled with it. We wait. And wait. And wonder. Worry. And fear. Another world war? Haven't we learned anything yet? For months the words I type have tried to console my fears. I've found these references, in message after message, to this location:

> *In the East there will be much talking which will lead to a new order and new friendships. The land there must be divided in a different way … In the East there is still talk of war but do not fear … there will be many surprises that will shortly occur in that area It will be necessary for all the peoples of the world to co-operate if mankind is to survive … We speak now with you as you all have many worries about the situation in the East. Fear not … solutions will be found which will prevent major action from taking place.*

But for months the nightly news has been far less reassuring. Ashad so often comforted me, told me repeatedly he would answer. *Remember that I am always at hand and can speak with you if you have need …* And so I reached out to the one voice I knew I could trust above all others. And when he came, I knew his energy. A love washes over me. A nurturing presence not so with the others. But his answer about this desert conflict is also oddly different from the others.

> *Destruction and death will fall upon the man in the East who has brought such pain to the sacred places where our line began. Sadly, there are many who will be the victims of his arrogance and secular mind but we will save as many as we can and the people of your country will not suffer greatly … We can only give you a small amount of information at a time as much of the future depends upon how man himself reacts to the disasters that will befall … Precise events have depended upon man himself for we must always leave man to be the master of his own fate.*

Relief to know he's there. I can ask. But what to do with the answer? Or with his mild rebuke. *I will hear when you call and come to your side, but there is other work to do and my brothers will often need your hands.* Will there be war? Can I trust the words *the people of your country will not suffer greatly?* What about other countries? Are the victims only to be the 'guilty?' In war, that is never the case. So many questions and so few answers … *much of the future depends upon how man himself reacts to the disasters …* I don't know whether this thought brings relief or dread. Often we pull together in disasters. Is there a way to pull together before a disaster? Is that what our work on the Michael Line was? A pulling together before the disaster? Can we pull together and actually prevent disasters? Is that one of the messages inherent in this material?

The Clew

4th February 1991: The crisis with Iraq escalates. We are all gripped with worry but I have special reason. Words were given to me months ago ...

> *Over a period of time there will be many changes in that area ('the East') and there is now enough light in the ground for the sacred places to survive. You are right to believe that one part of that area is crucially important. This was originally the birthplace of your civilisation and it was to this spot that we last directed our messages in the same way that we are doing today. Then also the earth had reached a point when it had to survive a major change and many men heard our voices. Much information about this time is written in your great books or is wrapped inside the secret rituals of some of your groups. In particular there is a group of men who know many of the holy symbols which they use at their meetings. Most of them have no idea of the significance of their possessions but when our words become known they will be able to offer their part of the mysteries which were broken into many pieces in order that the word should survive.*

What mysteries were broken into many pieces? It has to do with some knowledge. Or body of knowledge. Some truth we've forgotten. And who are these men with the secret rituals? Templars? Freemasons? The men in white? The men of fire? Who are they? It's about Iraq. The birthplace of our civilisation, the Tigris/Euphrates valley is Iraq ... *it was to this spot that we last directed our messages in the same way that we are doing today. Then also the earth had reached a point when it had to survive a major change ...* What messages are we being sent today and how are they being directed? What major change did the earth have to survive? The same trauma we have repeatedly been advised of in my previous typed pages? Changes of cosmic importance?

The last few weeks, as if in answer to my ever-present worry, words have come. Not Ashad's words, but the same meanings ...

> *The evil one will use fire to destroy his enemies and the land will be scorched. He twists and turns and has stripped the sacred places of the light that is their due. He has brought dark power to the places of our forefathers and has invited the wrath of others who have little knowledge of our names ... The men who fight in the deserts have much to accomplish and there will be great pain and much destruction before the evil one is removed and the sacred places become quiet once more ... Night falls in the desert and the fire rains from the skies. Destruction will be terrible and swift and the hawks of Sodom will be struck to the ground ... The power is flowing from this point all around your globe and men's hearts and minds will be changed dramatically in a short time ... Others are doing the same as did their forefathers and your land will once again be the knot into which the power lines converge ... Our power is strong you have helped to make a clear way for us and you have our thanks.*

England will once again be the land into which the power lines converge? Are the power lines the ley lines? And now today still more ...

The Clew

In the East the blackness will overwhelm the seas and the sky will grow more dark. The men of fire use their hands to preserve what they can but much will be lost. The power will be finished at this place and the centre will move to your own land. This is the work you and others have been part of ... as before, you can use the strength to keep all from harm. There has been too much fanaticism in the East and the light has been corrupted at the places of the wise. Their anger is great and they will destroy as has been prophesied. You must guard in your own land against the cruel ones but there are strong seeds which can still fruit and nourish what has lain dormant for so long. Many moons ago all this was prepared by the great ones who carried their skills over the waters. In your land they left the riddles and secrets which only a few have sought to interpret. Now the time has come when all must be uncovered. Many are working under instruction and your group will also receive new tasks when the difficult times have passed. Your time will come soon and then your real work can begin.

In the larger picture, the larger scheme of things there was - or is - a centre of power in the East. The cradle of civilisation. At some time, perhaps in ancient times, people from this area - the East - came to England and brought knowledge or skills or something and left the riddles of that here. Now it is time for the centre of power to move here. And somehow we are a part of that. Our work on the Michael line perhaps. Or perhaps some work we are to do in the future. We've been told before we're not the only ones. Here are told that *Many are working under instruction and your group will also receive new tasks.* Earlier we were told *Continue the work, there are many others who do these things also.* Difficult to fathom, concepts like these. We are one very small bit of something very large. There's an edge. On one side it's all a mystery, a treasure hunt with clues - a lark. It was all just a lark. Nothing much seems to be happening at all. Camaraderie. Excitement when the clues fit. The fun of it. Nothing more. And the other side of the edge - these words. The implication of these words. How can I possibly believe all this about moving power lines from the cradle of civilisation to England, about riddles and secrets that only a few have sought to interpret. How can I possibly believe? And what is my *real* work that is soon to begin?

5th February 1991: I try and make sense of things in my mind. How is it that I can recognise the different energies? Can understand the difference between Ashad and the others. Something very personal with Ashad. As if he's a family member. More than a family member. Not familiar with the others, but even with those I know the difference. And why the difference in physical sensations? Sometimes I'm even ill when they change or when we are being prepared for some task. Before some task, before we carry out the instructions often several of us with the same physical ailments. Always minor. A coincidence? I specifically called Ashad. Knew it was his energy answering. How does all this work? What's going on here? More and more they sense my doubts somehow and give me answers or reassure me.

The Clew

> *There are many ways through which we can communicate with those people who are sensitive. You yourself have experienced a sense of urgency which we initiate by transmitting a higher frequency vibration than the one you receive once we have started communicating. Many people like yourself have the ability to receive messages but do not have the discipline it requires or the ability to translate our thoughts into language. Others see only in pictures and for them the colours of the vibrations have to be sharpened in order that their mind can construct an image. There have been many in the past who have received information about the events that you are now witnessing although the times they have given have varied because of their individual interpretation of the information we have sent.*
>
> *You have the right message even though your fingers have written the wrong words ... You too have great powers but small experience in translation.*

I think I understand this. Think I can be aware of different frequency and vibration. It is a sort of urgency like they say. Feel it in my head sometimes. Sometimes, somewhere else. But it's physical. It's real. Not just imagination. And I know what they mean about *You have the right message even though your fingers have written the wrong words.* Not easy choosing the words to capture the impressions. They give me words sometimes and other times impressions. Then I have to choose the words. The impressions are much richer, more vivid and complex, difficult to reduce to words. Sometimes I don't know the words. A vague sense of something I should know but don't, something I knew once but have forgotten and can't find words for. *You translate well, though with inexperience.* How does one 'get experience' in this sort of thing?

Sometimes the words come easily, but the understanding just isn't there. What to do with sentences like this.

> *You must look again where the grass circles and tie in the energy at this point.*

Is the grass in the 'grass circles' - the grain in our crop circles? How do I 'tie in the energy?' There begin to be many references to the stars.

> *You will continue to remember all that lies in the past ... the stars have recorded the stories if only you will take time to look ... The new order has arrived and the wings of the earth hum with great power. Listen to the wind and watch the stars in their movement across the sky ... Tell your friends that they must begin to chart the movements in the sky. ... He must look to the stars and begin their study in earnest. He has memories which will help him in this undertaking and a natural understanding of patterns.*

Astronomy? How can the stars record the stories? Astronomy? Only in millions of years. Millions of light years. Not something to be noticed on a clear evening. And what is this 'new order?' Where is this all going? Where will it end?

The Clew

23rd February 1991 : It was not Ashad's voice giving me these words today. But again I'm reassured.

> *I am not Ashad, he waits until you begin the writing of which I have spoken … Ashad will continue this work as you have expected, it has been my task to ask you to begin. We all speak to you from the same level but from different positions and the messages are carried by different signals which only practice can prepare you for.*

And they're clearly telling me there's something else I'm to do.

> *It will be your task to communicate our words and to offer direction. You must begin to write as before to a regular pattern as there is much to record and you must once again build a strong communication between one another … The light has moved from its source and now waits for the lines of power to bed it into its new home that you have all helped prepare. Now is the season of joy for all of us as we move closer to the reunion. This has been foretold by many prophets and will bring a new life to the ways of the earth … It is my responsibility to bring together all the recorders of our words as the message must be clear and not confused at this time … you must return to the difficulties that will be resolved.*

Perhaps it's left the East and is waiting to enter England as explained earlier, a new home we have all helped prepare. My part of it seems to be to bring through these messages. Others do other work. I sit and type. And recognise the place, and bring together the people involved. But there's another part too: the difficulties. They're referring to my marriage. The words are few, but the message was clear. I'm being given time and they are not yet impatient. But I'm not to let my personal life interfere. No, that's not quite it either. I'm not sure I can put the feeling into words but it has to do with courage and independence. With trusting that I can go forward and know joy. This work has to do not only with the earth, with 'bedding power lines' and preventing who knows what. It also, somehow, has to do with me personally. And with the others. It's about us personally too. I'm to resolve the difficulties so that I can get on with my life in some way inexplicable to me. So that I, so that we all, can be available for some service we don't quite understand.

21st March 1991 :

> *It has been many days since we have spoken together. My friend, much has happened on your world and the trials and tribulations of your peoples must continue. Across the seas there are many who think only of their own wealth and this will soon crumble in their hands … You will soon move amongst your own people and there is much work that must be done in a short time … Spring comes now to your land and the work must once again begin … There is much that we must soon begin but you must first become more versed in the Wisdoms and time must spin its circles a little longer before we begin … You are one of many but have the memories which bind us together. Love is the*

The Clew

power that fuels all life; all men should use this gift and revere its source. It is time to depart, we will speak more when your life is not so burdened. I am at your side.

Ashad. He greets me as 'my friend.' None of the others do that. And to Ashad I say thank you for this loving kindness. This warmth and closeness. This companionship and support in this difficult time. But the message is the same. There will be time to bring order to the personal. But I *am* to bring order to it. If I am to be part of future work, I must be whole. And available.

28th March 1991 :

My friend, I am here ... You must wait quietly with others for the moment when your time will come to speak out and you must be well prepared, for many will make mock of your words. There are though those who wait desperately, as a desert nomad for water, for the knowledge that we have promised will come about. You and your friends are safe, we have not forgotten our pledge and there is much work for you all to do in a changing future ... You must resolve your own conflicts as you have sketched out. There is time enough but your mind must be clear of all concerns before the power can enter.

In the East the darkness lays like a cloak over the sand and the children weep from pain. They cannot regain what has been lost. Theirs was a sacred trust that they abused with their indolence and squabbling, and their life of warmth and comfort is the price that they must pay. Beauty and joy must be nursed and replenished and not blown away on the wind of avarice.

Now there is little still for you to do but to rest and prepare your mind for the challenges that will come very soon. You are once again content with yourself and have let go of the anger and fear that tied you down. Now your energy can flow harmoniously and you can extend your skills as before ... You are in the care of many and keep my love.

5th April 1991 : Desert Storm. Innocuous sounding code word for such mayhem. Saddam Hussein in Iraq. And much of the remainder of the world defends Kuwait. What of the Iraqi people? So much bloodshed. Sorrow. Uncertainty.

Now the sorrows return to the lands we knew well, my friend. The darkness intensifies and the earth will be sorely troubled as the light vanishes from the plains that were once so fertile. The people of the earth must all suffer for their lack of care for the earth ... Many have written over the centuries of the means by which the earth and all its abundant life survives, but men have had to play their own games and have limited their intellect to what only they with their limited capacity could understand ... Many moons ago there was also destruction but much was saved by the wise ones and it is this knowledge and power which must be understood and released now if enough is to be saved. You have little time but the plan goes as we have prepared and the Masters are content.

The Clew

Science fiction. I'm typing science fiction. Some crazy science fiction novel coming from somewhere I don't know where. Except it's not science fiction. *The evil one will use fire to destroy his enemies and the land will be scorched …* In the East the blackness will overwhelm the seas and the sky will grow more dark. Months ago. Those words came months ago and now the skies over Kuwait and Iraq turn black with the smoke from the oil wells Hussein set on fire. This is about real events. I remember Simon and the way he described my husband's grandmother when he wouldn't sit in her chair. Because he couldn't have known her and yet described her so perfectly … And now they describe events in the East in this oblique fashion. The clues they gave us too. And the little rewards, predictions come true for us to see but only if we ended up in the right place at the right time. Science fiction doesn't manifest personally into your life in these ways. It stays neatly between the pages.

I'm torn between believing the science fiction, or believing the other. What, *what* is the other? If I believe the other, then it has something to do with memory. They're coaxing me. Gently giving me reminders. And slowly I begin to remember. It's as if they're standing off to one side observing. Like they are watching someone with amnesia. They're waiting to see if I'm going to remember. They can't force me to remember. I think they are loathe to give me any of the knowledge or what they call the 'wisdoms.' It's as if they fear I'll misuse it – or perhaps misunderstand it. I have to remember them - the 'wisdoms' - in context, in some context of ethical integrity. And they know they can't force that. So they wait. And encourage. And create as best they can, a safe place for me to remember.

I'm reminded of something I typed months ago. Not Ashad's words. Another entity. One whose voice I hadn't typed before.

> *You have wandered alone for many lives as was necessary for you if your commitment was to survive the test. You have moved amongst the holy ones and know all by name and your knowledge can now emerge from the darkness and pour back into the earth from whence it stems … Many now gather in the sacred places as the spirit of love recalls them to their separate tasks. Others like you have been recalled … you have achieved what we asked, as have many others and this land will be safe when the power uncurls. Your task will be to write what has already been told to you but you must also speak it out without fear … You have trod the Isles of the Blest and have listened to the words of the old men … With Ashad you have walked the place of wisdom and you once travelled where the great river enters the sea. Now there is darkness in that place and the fires have been lit. With fire comes change and reconstruction, so it has always been … On the banks of the Tigris men carry pain and grief. It must all be destroyed so that the new order can begin … Men must care for the earth and understand the needs of the light … fear not your memory will return … your strength is proven. You are alone no longer. Work and pray.*

I do remember things sometimes. I can't place them. Maybe Egypt. Maybe Sumeria. Or Ur? But I can't force it. It stops if I try and make it happen. Can only

The Clew

happen spontaneously. I'll be remembering their words, something Ashad or one of the others has said, and something will begin to become conscious. But then I realise it's there, try and focus on it, and it's gone.

> *You must use the power to re-generate the light in the West as there must be a calming of the troubles and the cessation of bloodshed ... You are on the path that leads to the knowledge ... There will be great interest in our communications and you must speak honestly of the work that you have done. Many will respond with their own knowledge and skills ...*
>
> *Now I leave you to struggle a little more with your life. All is well, the path you walk is well-trodden and there are many signs. Goodnight my friend, you are in my care. We will speak again when you have need or I call. I return to the ways which are familiar to me.*

This feeling I know. This presence I know. This warmth and familiarity I remember.

12th April 1991: Iona. During my holiday on Iona, and my walk along the beach of the Port of Coracles – the small bay where St. Columba landed, the words I'd typed came back to me. Humorous in a way that the beach even has it's own story – that everyone's personal stone is waiting for them on the beach. I can disbelieve now that I'm home and the incident is far away. But at the time I was sure I saw it, a white light beaming up from the shoreline. Nearer, I could see the small green marble stone. The light shone up from that particular stone. I'm sure it did. And then I remembered what I'd typed and then read again just before leaving home.

> *You travel soon to the place of the sun where you will recall much amongst many friends. Seek for the spot where the birds fly into the cliff on short wings for there is the gift that was left by the one who carried the rod.*

The birds were fulmars. They were flying into the cliff. And for seconds one hovered so close to my face, as if it recognised me. And the bit of green marble. So like the affirmations at the end of our earth healing. A little smile from Ashad. An affirmation. The bird. And this particular green marble stone ... *for there is the gift that was left by the one who carried the rod*. Strange that now I haven't been able to find the piece of sandstone. Almost inconceivable that I could have lost it. Is this little green 'gift' to take its place? So I return from holiday to find Ashad waiting to begin again. His energy comforting, but the actual words – not quite so.

> *Love is the key to all the work that we shall undertake and you will often feel drained and must seek rest and assistance as the positive outpourings that this learning demands will affect your physical makeup and may exhaust you ...*

The Clew

The two realities again. In one - my marriage not going well, my mother ill, my concerns basic. How will I support myself. Will my mother live. Will I be living alone – again. In the other - words that don't have any context for making sense. Certainly know that *love is the key to all the work that we shall undertake.* Couldn't have continued without knowing that on a very deep level. Also the fatigue. Certainly that is real. *Outpourings that this learning demands will affect your physical makeup* ... it's more than fatigue. It's also the sensitivities.

> *Your memory has been opened ... and the time has come when the Word must begin to be reconstructed using the powers that are yours alone ... your knowledge must be pulled from you as a spinner teases the wool onto the spindle ... I have been given this crucial task because our memories allow us to knit our souls together which enables the current to pass across the divide between us ...*

I know things there should be no way of knowing. Remember things that can't be within any memory in this lifetime. The memories are visual. And so real. But the next part, what follows, I can't make sense of. Maybe it's allegory. Maybe it's symbolic. I don't know what to do with it. What are the 'Words'? And what are the 'sounds'?

> *Firstly, we must return to the source of all life and the place where men were first given the words with which to nurture all existence. These were given to only a few and have been carried over time through many lives by those who were given the charge. Your role was to communicate those that were given but also to retain the sounds that would be needed when the earth moved into its next cycle. You know the sounds already but the construction is not known in any language and we must toil at conveying the best copy onto your machine.*

What words were we given and how do they nurture existence? What sounds do I know that will have to be constructed and how will they help the earth move into its next cycle? And what is this current that passes between Ashad and me? Am I going crazy to be reminded of "In the beginning was the word and the word was made flesh?" And the current, is it love? Is love a current? Current is an energy. Love is an energy. Is love more than we think it is? Does it have powers we can't fathom?

And the next part – has an unmistakably Biblical sound. *All went well until the thought forms themselves discovered the power of thought.* Begins to sound like Adam and Eve partaking of the tree of Knowledge. Too simplistic. It can't be this simple. Does it come in this simple way because of my inability to put it in more complex form?

> *In the beginning there was life without form and the shape of the cosmos was amorphous. It was decided that time must be constructed and so solid*

The Clew

> *matter and beings who could organise and survive within such constriction were created by thought. All went well until the thought forms themselves discovered the power of thought and from that moment on they had to be put in charge of their own destinies. It was vital, however, that the earth herself remain in our care and for that reason we have always made certain that there have been some on earth who understood her needs and worked under our guidance. These are the advanced souls who have proved their strength and faith and are not confused by the chaos mankind has created. You are now all returned to earth at one and the same time as the changes begin and it will be the task of you all to explain and nurture the truth.*
>
> *… your work is to gather these and our other words together and show them to the world. This is the task for which you were born into this life and it will be your final task if you hold fast to what is true and just.*

Whoever *we* are, we're all returned to the earth at one and the same time. And it is our task to explain and nurture the truth. What truth? How do we nurture and explain something we don't understand or even know exists? I simply don't know what to make of all this. I'm to gather the words together and show them to the world. These messages? If I can't make sense of them and *I'm* the one who received them, what will the rest of the world make of them?

Vibration, sound, frequency. Assume there's some truth to all of this and, if I can only figure it out. Assume it makes some kind of sense. Then these three words draw attention. Whatever is happening has something to do with sound. Or vibration and frequency. Energy isn't it? They're all ways of saying energy. Are they trying to get some idea through, some idea for which I have no words and so I have to use the closest I can get and that ends up being words like sound and vibration and frequency and light?

I *am* learning to tell the difference in the energy of places. Different places feel different, have different energies. Different entities feel different, have different energies. Physical sensations. Different physical sensations for different energies. Is that it? My body *is* beginning to sense different vibrations or different frequencies. Is that what this is all about? Are they telling us this is some kind of sixth energy sense that we have to learn to turn in to? Or remember how to tune in to?

Ashad tells me that in some way his memory and mine connect in a way that allows *the current to pass across the divide between us.* My own curiosity about my ability to type these strange words brings the response that they create a sense of urgency for me by transmitting a higher frequency vibration. And for people who receive this kind of information in picture rather than words, *for them the colours of the vibrations have to be sharpened.* Current, higher frequency vibration, energy again …

Light, sound, energy are all vibration. There are so many references to this idea of power lines and light. In addition to saying that England will be the knot where the *'power lines'* converge, they say the *'power'* will be finished in the East [the Tigris Euphrates valley – Iraq] and the centre will move to our land. This is because there has been so much fanaticism there that the 'light' has been corrupted.

The Clew

Still later they explained that the *'light'* has moved from its source and now waits for the *'lines of power'* to bed it into its new home that we have all helped prepare. Then we are told that we must use the *'power to regenerate the light'* in the West so there is a calming of the troubles and a cessation of bloodshed. Too there is reference to our land awaiting the *'light'* and caring for the earth and understanding the needs of 'the light' and some contract we must hold to or *'all the light will go out.'* Further we're told that *the cleansing of your country's power lines must continue ... And the channels must continue to be cleansed and the new energy must go uninterrupted ... And the power must be unleashed if the world's light is to be re-charged.*

This image of a huge power plant generating light and sending it along energy lines. And that it has to be nurtured with love and caring for the earth, and that fanaticism corrupts it. And what does it all mean?

Chapter Six

A year had now passed since Avril had received the very first typewritten words, and her attitude to the material was evolving. As she changed energetically, as her vibration increased to keep pace with the intensity of the entities, she also began to relate to the material differently. What began as fun, exciting, mysterious, was becoming more personal, more transformational and less a 'psychic prediction'. The 'psychic' quality of the early material had helped Avril keep a playful, don't-take-it-seriously attitude. It helped her, in a sense, keep it at arm's length. As she began to actually remember historical content, as she began to realise the depth of the content, it grew more difficult to view it as some odd, isolated, 'psychic' experience.

She has since learned that warnings of earth disasters are often characteristic for a beginning channel. This is not to invalidate the warnings. Without a doubt, the last decades have seen many of these warnings, from whatever source, validated. It does, however, speak to what might have been her inability in the beginning to access or interpret more complex information. It may have been influenced by the 'fascination' this information held for her at the time. Her own fear may have been attracting it. She's not sure why the content of the information evolved. She has never found reason to doubt the authenticity or the sincerity of the information she received. The content clearly evidenced a compassionate, enlightened source of great integrity. Even when warning of disasters, she found they felt very loving and supportive and seemed to arise from love and concern for the welfare of the earth and all her peoples.

She still has difficulty explaining the process she was going through. She knew the energies she was in contact with were changing, their vibration was stronger. She also knew she had changed in many ways to accommodate them, but has difficulty finding the words to explain this change. Sometimes she says it was as if, both energetically and emotionally, she had to begin work at the lowest chakra level and progress up through to the higher ones. Except at the time she didn't know what the chakras were. Other times she explains it as if she were in contact with different planetary energies and some were more powerful in some ways, and demanded emotional growth in different ways than others. She speaks of this now with her deepening understanding of astrology. At the time she was also ignorant of that system and consequently unable to use it for an explanation. But each paradigm she has tried to use seems to have its own limitations in explaining what was happening for her.

Avril was under much personal stress at this time. The uncertainty of her marriage continued to cause emotional fatigue. The entities alluded to this and advised her to take time to come to resolution before the 'real work' began. The Gulf War caused her personally much grief and anxiety. The entities tried to reassure her. As the content of the material she was typing increased in complexity, it contradicted so much of her contextual thinking and belief. The entities encouraged her to go to her bookshelves. She was reading about the Glastonbury Zodiac, about the Templars and Freemasons, about Sumeria and Ur. She remembers hearing the legend claiming ancient travellers from Sumeria were the reason for the names Somerset and Somerton. It was growing both easier and more difficult to integrate the messages and the activities of the group involved with them into her 'real life.'

Repeatedly she was encouraged to 'remember.' She was given hints and gently prompted. Only in retrospect can she explain the restrained urgency she felt in the entities' gentle insistence that she 'remember.' The idea of reincarnation was quite foreign to Avril when she began this work. She would grow to be quite familiar and comfortable with such realities. What she also grew to understand was that she could only access prior knowledge, prior understanding and skills, if she could access some memory from the lifetime in which the knowledge, understanding and skills had been hers to use. In the next earth healing she would be asked to construct a magic square. This concept from the mystery schools is still a mystery to her, but she found that if she could access a lifetime in which this knowledge had been hers, she could understand the concepts she typed well enough to construct what was needed. As so often happened with the information she received, it was left to someone else to interpret and use the square. Her role continued to be one of scribing information; of recognising people who were, for whatever reason, to be involved in the earth healing events; and of bringing those people together. Others played the role of interpreting complex symbols, composing rituals, interpreting energy changes resulting from their fieldwork. Together they all searched myth, legend, and inherited wisdom for links to the information she was receiving.

Not for years would Avril begin to understand the meaning behind Ashad's words: *Your task and those of many like you will be not only with communication but also in locking on the correct frequencies that will be needed to move the generator pulse of the prime energy to your land and then to secure it in place.* When these thought-forms actually became words on the paper, she was mystified. She had only a vague notion of ley lines composing some sort of energy system, of having been told that she and the people she worked with were 'conductors' who were to pass some type of energy into the ground. She had no doubt that others had actually experienced this energy. She didn't know exactly what it meant to move the generator pulse of prime energy to her land and secure it in place, and she didn't know how to lock on to any particular frequency which would enable this to happen, but if that was what she was a part of, she was willing to continue. In retrospect she feels she has come to a deeper understanding of the meaning of those words, in the two months prior to the next earth healing, she had the benefit of no such understanding.

In the meantime, for whatever reason, she faithfully made herself available to receive the messages and type the words. She made time to share them with friends. With dedication she tried to understand them and to the best of her ability earnestly complied with their requests. At this point she might have welcomed the rather straightforward instructions she received for the work on the St. Michael line. It was not to be.

The Clew

AVRIL
The Placing of the Sword

18th April 1991 :
> *... it is vital that you understand the need for the energies to be re-charged or else the disaster we have already detailed will affect the Earth, and the energy system will be disconnected, as it requires the whole to function if the separate parts are to survive.*

So the Earth, the solar system, the galaxy, however far out it goes, they're all interconnected some way. They're saying somehow the earth is so important to all of this that if it 'runs down' or something, the cosmos will be affected. Not the first time they've made reference to this phenomenon. Too, too difficult to believe but for the time being assume it's true in some way I can't understand.

> *It is our task to re-tune the earth's energy band in order that the interactions can be revitalised ... if all is to be well you must become versed in the sounds that will tune the new vibration as we have already explained ...*

Reference to the 'sounds' again. Reminds me of a guitar. If a string is properly tuned, you can make it resonate by striking the same note on a different string. Are we the 'different string' so to speak? We make a sound, which is a vibration, and it resonates with the vibration on these ley lines, and with some unimaginable help from some unimaginable being, or source or something, it all retunes the energy bands? And I'm to help the process. By becoming 'versed' in the sounds. Something I know from some time in the long distant past that they will coax onto my machine.

I remember once they said that I had *been prepared long ago for this time by the masters of learning, and song and the knowledge will return.* I don't know who the masters of learning and song are but song is a musical term and re-tuning is too. Funny, I typed the word 'hum' too. Months ago they said *The new order has arrived and the wings of the earth hum with great power.* It's all very musical. Nicely poetic. But it's serious too. Something that is actually supposed to happen. Has to happen. And it all has to do with vibration, a change in vibration. A change that with their help we're supposed to bring about. They're trying to get me to write about something that I don't understand. They give me the impressions of music, I choose the words that have to do with music to explain something that has to do with vibration. Sound and vibration. A power that is a vibration. And has something to do with sound. I'm not sure.

> *Our greatest fear is that your earth's new energy pattern will be too energetic and the consequent trauma will be overwhelming.*

I'm remembering that funny scene where a soprano sings a high note and shatters the crystal goblet. I wonder if that can actually happen. If the energy is too strong, it's as if the earth will shatter like the crystal goblet.

The Clew

However we believe that ... if you all undertake the work for which you have been prepared all will survive.

Our work must have to do with strengthening or enlarging the energy bands, doing something to the ley lines. And we do it somehow with sound. Or vibration. Everything is vibrating. Molecules are constantly moving so everything is always vibrating. We *can* hear vibration, we call it sound. It's sound and vibration both, but I haven't understood yet how they are working together in this.

They have said, repeatedly, that we are not the only ones doing this work. What work? The ballet we choreographed along the St. Michael line?

There are many of you but there are so many tasks that you must undertake between you ... However, much work has been done to balance the energies and we are hopeful that you together have sufficient power to hold everything together. By 'holding everything together' are we helping prevent 'overwhelming trauma?'

They speak now of some additional work. At some unknown time in the future. And it has something to do with sound and frequencies.

There are now certain elements of the work to come that must be explained. Your task and those of many like you will be not only with communication but also in locking on to the correct frequencies that will be needed to move the generator pulse of the prime energy to your land and then to secure it in place.

They've been saying all along that whatever this generator pulse or prime energy is, prior to now it has been in the 'East.' It began there but now needs to be moved. The generator pulse of prime energy. What is that? And where will the correct frequencies come from? Are the 'correct frequencies' the ones that aren't too energetic? It's as if they're making the frequencies more powerful, more energetic, at least more than they have been in the past here in England. So they do something with these frequencies and it's our job to lock on to them and then they'll end up here in England instead of in the 'East.' If we all undertake the work for which we've been prepared, we end up being a tool that will have sufficient power to hold everything together. It's as if we're the copper wire through which electricity passes. We're the guitar string that will vibrate with the correct sound. Somehow we have a task in the re-charging, the re-tuning, the securing in place of the correct frequencies.

These elements consist of a sequence of numbers that will be conveyed to you and the ones you will work with at the proper time ... You need only receive the information that we send, others will process the information and construct the diagrams that will be needed.

I might be able to imagine that I have some understanding of the sound and vibration. But numbers? What do numbers have to do with it? At least this time

The Clew

apparently we'll have help figuring it out.

I am still curious. I still wonder what this is all about. Curiosity doesn't make it any easier to read the words I type. It's still difficult. Makes so little sense. Who are the others who will process the information and construct the diagrams? How will I meet them? What are we to do and how are we to do it and what difference will it make? On one level sometimes I think I know what they're talking about. On another, I am quite mystified. I remember what they said at one point. They said it takes discipline. Discipline to sit down and type words that seem so important but also have so little relevance to anything in my life right now. It does take discipline. And a certain kind of faith. Ashad's words at least are reassuring. The love, the recognition is still there. The trust I have for him - it helps.

> *All life is light and is disseminated through particles of sound. You and I were joined in a segment of matter that first took shape in the thought of the great Arkana ... Our reunion is a gift I treasure and will save for your return ... You have passed through many vibrations and now await only to be cleansed by the brothers. I will wait for your coming. It is time to leave these words that give such pleasure and return to the other tasks that are mine.*

13th May 1991 : The entities have always told us we aren't alone. Others do this work also. I recently typed:

> *The man you seek has acquired much knowledge and will recognise the words you offer. He will be able to understand the diagrams that will be constructed and to understand the total concept of what we will place before you. You will need to meet with this man, but that will come about naturally.*

Well it has come about naturally, *have* met we this man, and things begin to make more sense. Like the musical notes the messages been trying to help us find.

> *Your friend who learns of song must concentrate on the lower sounds and the rhythms they respond to in order that she can learn the patterns that are needed ...*

Maggie and I. Earnestly trying to follow their instructions, trying somehow to discover the patterns that are needed. We felt so silly. Singing. Trying to find the sequence they want by humming through a paper covered comb because neither of us has a musical instrument ...

> *The sequence of notes that you must string together is controlled within a harmonic structure as she has rightly interpreted.*

So it does have something to do with the song, the vibration, the retuning. We are to do something with song.

The Clew

Their words are so sophisticated compared to our crude attempts. Must have had a good laugh if they were watching. Or maybe they are totally frustrated with us, same as we are. Truly gave it our best effort, but must have failed. Gave up on us finally, I think …

> *We are sorry your friend has had difficulty with the example we have given her. Tell her that she can choose any sound she wishes and at the given time we will offer you the constructions that will fit the sounds she has.*

But after all that, after simply taking everything on faith and continuing in the face of these crazy difficulties, finally help arrived. All that about the sequence of notes, the chant, the song, whatever all that began to make sense once we met Geoff. He tells an unbelievable story. Two years his group has been receiving instructions. For making a sword. To use this year – at the summer solstice. At a stone circle. Arbor Low. Amazing. What's even more amazing, they succeeded in having a representative of every occult sect they could trace *bless it!* Unimaginable.

> *This is the man whom you must speak with in order that the information we send can be correctly interpreted. Speak with him again and tell him that he must use the sequences of letters that we send through you to establish a grid in areas that we shall describe. He has worked hard and is on the right path but he needs to share as his work must increase its breadth of focus.*

I did speak with him again. And shared what we've managed so far. It's a grid. We're constructing a grid and Geoff is to help us do that. It's a circle with a grid of squares inside. The chant is written around the outside of the circle. The grid is filled with letters and numbers. And he is to use it in some way in his work with the sword at Arbor Low on the summer solstice. The sounds Maggie and I have been trying to find have something to do with it. Somehow they are trying to get us to compose, or perhaps remember, a chant. Musical notes, letters, rhythm. We have to match it with something we don't seem to quite understand – or remember.

> *The individual notes are familiar to your ears but the matching together of the phonetic sounds may prove difficult as such a system is unknown in the languages you are familiar with in your present incarnations. However, as we have previously explained the early language of your friend's ancestors* [Gaelic] *and of the one who writes have similar forms within them. It will be necessary for you to make various matchings which you will need to check with us … You have begun … the work of which I have often spoken. Continue now with your life, we will sit often together as our thoughts spill onto your machine. You do well, my friend, I stay within reach.*

17th May 1991:   Lunch with Joy. Talking about the soul. What is it? Where does it go? Or come from? Joking (or maybe not joking?) about soul mates. And

The Clew

reincarnation and how do reincarnation and souls fit together. And all the while we talked these little nudges. About the DNA spiral. Why would I keep thinking about the DNA spiral when we're talking about the soul? What did it have to do with anything? I wondered if the little nudge was Ashad trying to get my attention. Finally, I asked. His answer enlightening, intriguing, and too beautiful to be a joke.

> *The Light contains the elements of all life on your world and on all the other worlds that exist at different levels. It can best be compared to a train of thought that circles through your mind interlinking at various points or termini that bring ideas from different directions to coil together and finally complete a whole. You and I were spiralled in the first outburst of matter and our linkages are strong with many inter-connections. At your birth our life entered your present body but only the shadow of my half came into your existence. The strong, mirror half remained in the ether, copying each development you make and responding to the emotions of its twin. When your body dies our two halves will reunite to spiral as a whole. It is this whole that must reach perfection, each half responsible for part of the development of the whole.*
>
> *That whole contains all colour, many aspects of which you are unable to decipher but the rapid growth of man in such huge numbers has meant that the spirals of life have been broken into fragments and many of the colours have consequently been erased from your coding. There are strong spirals of spirit and they form the minds that are responding to the call at this moment. This is extremely difficult material to convey to you but you have made a great leap forward in understanding. I leave you now but will return when you have more time to speak. We are one, of such are we made. I wait for your call.*

I've re-read this passage so many times. On some level, I think I understand it. Even without understanding it's beautiful and felt loving and nurturing to receive. This is the relationship I've remembered and always been looking for. And I wonder, again, if I will find it in a physical body, alive in this time space, on this planet.

31st May 1991 : Interesting. This powerful man. Seemed almost to invade my office so much space he took. So insistent. Almost belligerent.

"Who are you!" he ordered Ashad to answer. Not satisfied with Ashad's answer again he insisted, "Are you Avril's soul?" Back and forth they went, Ashad's gentle but firm answers and the man's insistent questions.

"Where did you work in Egypt?" *Alexandria*

"When in Egypt?" *Before the ninth flood.*

"That is no help. Under which Pharaoh?"

And so it went, back and forth. Almost sparring. I could feel Ashad's amusement as the man's frustration rose. But so gentle. In the face of the man's anger and frustration, only calmly gentle answers. And the realisation - I can ask questions! More than ask questions, carry on a conversation! And so I did. The

The Clew

next day. After the powerful man left and I realised it was possible, I asked Ashad.

"Will you tell me of our past?"

We have been together many times and in different lands ... There, in the place of the seven moons, we lived and worked. You were the oracle of the priest and I the scribe. Together we worked recording what was known of the Mysteries. It was your task to speak with the gods and to record their desires and the explanations of the way in which life was constructed and supported ... We became famous for the care with which we scribed the words, and at a later time we took that knowledge to the Great Library at Alexandria ... This is the same work that you are doing at this time and that is why your response has been so powerful. At that place there was much happiness and gladness in our hearts as we worked to record the knowledge so that the future generations would have it all. You were young and had the neck of a swan, I loved you. We swore to hold fast to each other for all our lives. This was a gentle oath that has hurt no-one else in our many lives since then, but it has remained deep inside us ... We have always recognised each other when our cloaks hung together and have found each other each time we have stood apart. This is the oath that we swore long ago when the waters covered the land.

"What am I to do?"

You must listen to the one with the sword, your knowledge is needed at that place.

"What of the grid?"

You must construct the grid of our memory which has held the power since the earliest time at the place of the moon ... You will soon receive the letters and numbers I have described but you must go to the side of the one who writes who must construct the equations.

"Will it help in this work to recall past lives?"

Yes, it will help you to remember; you must picture the columns of the temple and the great bird that guarded its centre. Nearby was the small room where you spoke and I recorded your words. Love is the key. Remember and the knowledge will flow through you like the great river where we used to walk. You have lost sight of the knowledge but it can be recalled. You have had many lives when you were far from such concepts and the pain you have suffered has covered it over. But it is yours to retrieve and you have my hand to help you. We will speak again of this time whenever you wish. It's memory brings joy to me also ... When it is important we can speak without your machine but you must use the sunshine for that to be possible. The power in your machine gives us the best possibility to hear each other but if the need is very great I can use a stronger current but only for a very short time ... All goes as it should. You have come a long journey since your memory opened. My brothers give thanks ... Remember I am near at hand. I must depart but will listen for your voice.

The Clew

The stars shine, my friend, as they did before, so long ago. Look upwards. The memories are there. The door opens, I depart.

It seemed beautiful. I smiled at the part about having the neck of a swan. But I won't try and have a conversation like that with him again. The one time was enough. Too much. Switching back and forth, almost from one brain to another. Too, too difficult. Caused an excruciating head ache. Had to be in my own energy to ask the question, back in theirs to answer it. Different than when the man came and asked the questions. I stayed in their energy and just answered. I was aware of both 'worlds' but didn't have to go back and forth between them. Too difficult, going back and forth. A similar kind of thing happened when they try and give me the numbers and letters for the grid. In their energy to receive the thought forms, but back in my own to evaluate them and make changes.

Strange the way Ashad tries to get me to remember. The personal things are nice, but he's not trying to get me to remember personal information or for personal reasons. He can tell me the personal memories. Over and over he tries to remind me. And sometimes I do begin to remember. When they gave me the numbers and letters for the grid they began

> *You have made the connection with your earliest time that we asked and you will now have sufficient power to connect to the ones who wish to speak through me. Remember the fire and the man with the bowl and begin the words.*

The most unusual thing. It seems that if I can access some memory of some past life or something, when I remember something about the life, I also remember the knowledge I had during that life. I'm sure I don't understand it. I don't know what the past lives are, or when they were. I don't know what the knowledge is. But I was able to follow their instructions. It was very difficult physically. The energy in my body was very intense. I was able to manage it but only just. After working for a time they advised me to leave that energy.

> *This is as much as I can communicate to you as the power is too strong and you will be harmed. Lower your power centre to your heart and we can speak as before ... All is well my friend, you have returned to the vibration that we are familiar with. It is only possible for you to work for very short periods of time at the level you reached as the power waves are too strong for your physical form. Do not fear, you do as we ask and you know that your words are good. You are in our care and we will keep you from harm.*

Can I begin to explain what happens to me when I am typing this information? I remember in the beginning. It was an urgency. Something I had to do and didn't quite know why. It's still a little like that. The feeling. But not exactly urgency. An alertness and an awareness that are almost supernatural. And a tension asking for resolution. It is sort of like a vibration. In a strange way. Like

The Clew

I'm vibrating at a higher frequency. Like all the molecules in my body are moving a little bit faster. I'm sure no one could see the difference. But I can feel it. I did lower my power centre when they asked. Don't quite know how. A change in focus. Less focused. They change something too. The intensity is less. It's as if my body is a muscle that is being trained somehow. An athlete would train to lift heavier weights. Slowly, somehow I'm learning to accommodate higher frequencies. Higher frequencies seem to be more powerful. Seem to take more energy.

I worked with them the next day and received more information. But again they spoke of the strain.

> *You have knowledge which can only be slowly drawn from you as your strength is not great enough to be in constant use. At this level all is well but, as you have learned, the higher work puts a much greater strain on your capacity and you could be damaged. Your system must constantly stay in touch with the earth and you must stay solidly based in your present life. You are held in love by many and their affections are the threads which hold you safely to the earth. Spend time in that world, we speak when there is need ...*

It's like the copper wire again. Or the guitar string. Or what they said about the earth. It's as if it's all the same thing. Everything has an optimum frequency and if more current is put through, if the frequency is increased too quickly or too much or without sufficient preparation there can be 'damage.' Are they telling me I need to stay 'earthed' in much the same way as an electrical cable is?

It's as if they can only give me knowledge that I already understand. Or have some concept of. They can't give me information that is so totally foreign to me that I have no way of finding words or symbols for it. There were some equations I couldn't figure out. They managed to help us with the 'song,' the notes. But the equations were too much. I guess they'll have to find someone else. If there are others working on it, surely they can. Must have been so frustrating for them. But not so much so that they couldn't take time to reassure me.

> *Your husband grows in understanding of his path. There is still time and responsibilities that you must share but he now moves positively to create his own happiness ...*

Not a prediction. It's not that they predict. They sense my sadness and pain and reassure me. Show me what is there so that I can see it too. And they're right. Warren is leaving. I'm almost positive of that now, but we find an ease with each other that wasn't there before. And always, always Ashad's gentle words. Comforting.

> *Stay calm, love all and enjoy your world. You are in our care. I return to the brothers, but will hear you call. The stars move through the darkness, all will soon be made plain. The door opens to my hand and I leave your side.*

The Clew

17th June 1991 :   After many tries and much correction, we have the grid completed. It's a circle enclosing an actual grid with numbers and letters.

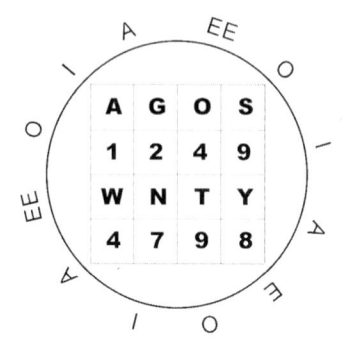

The Arbor Low Grid

Finally when it was complete, Geoff pointed out that it was a Qabalistic construction. Qabalah – ancient Hebrew Mystery tradition stressing the power of letters and numbers. I don't know, but it does have a strong resonance with a photo of the San Miniato Zodiac 'coincidentally' sent to us not long ago.

> *You have completed the grid. All is in order and you must only see that this is placed in the correct position at the centre of the circle. The first line of the grid must be placed toward the north. This will allow the correct sequence of connections to be made to the lines of power that will enter from the different planets which are now taking up their correct positions. Ask the one with the sword to call out the word three times and you must repeat the chant seven times as you have already identified ... The line is of sufficient size to carry the power as a result of your previous work but we must ask the one in the east to also use the word 'aleph' three times as he sends the power through ... You are tired and must protect yourself as your time in the circle will make great demands upon you all. The chant is accurate but there are difficulties in tying it down. This is possible, however. We will reduce its electrical vibration so that it may be retained.*

Puzzled by all this. Still trying to make sense of it, I asked again and received this.

> *You are right. The circle contains the necessary harmonic structures which tune the new vibration as will your chant. Your present circle is adequate but not perfect. You seek in the right direction. The zodiacal forms have always represented the harmonics of the cosmos ... Take my hand, go further back. Sound constructs form by a series of vibrational influences which have a modulating or accelerating effect on matter ... The new vibration must arrive with the sun, be tied into one by the grid and be charged by the sound. This*

you will achieve at the place of the sword. The sword is the key to lock it to the earth. This is enough. You seek perfection, that is not necessary as we also will take part and will balance out your errors. You work well. There is no more need to speak unless you have need. My friend, I leave you.

My mind struggles with concepts like these. I can bring through the words. Can type them on the paper. Can follow instructions. Can't always understand the subject matter. Feels a bit like studying physics or calculus without the prerequisites. In fact, examined from rational subjects like these, I wonder if any of this has any real meaning at all. But there are others this time. And the sword. Two years receiving and carrying out instructions. It's not only me this time. Not only me getting the group together. Not only me going out on this seemingly rather crazy jaunt. Someone else is coordinating it this time. I'm part of it. Have done my part so far. Need only continue. And see what happens.

✲ ✲ ✲ ✲ ✲

Long after the actual event at Arbor Low, as Avril acquired a rudimentary understanding of astrology, she found it helpful to think of the work at Arbor Low in astrological terms. Legend preserves a people's explanation of a certain time, records their perception of particular phenomena, passes down description of historical figures who embody the wisdom and understanding of the time. In one area of the ancient world the historical figure of Jesus embodies much of the legend around the turning from the age of Aries to the age of Pisces. Avril notes it is entirely possible that in ancient England the Arthurian legends, the Excalibur legends, and the 'turning off of the energies of the time', were the mythic way of recording this same change from Aries to Pisces. And that perhaps the work done at Arbor Low was about preparing for the new energy of the current age - the age of Aquarius. Curiously, although Avril would not be aware of this fact for another six years, the last entity she would channel, and the one to guide them in their final piece of work, would identify himself as Merlin.

The sword Geoff 's group worked with was referred to as the Dragon Sword. Instructions for crafting the sword had been intricate, complex, and followed to the letter. His group received instructions for the composition of the metal which had to be specially smelted. The design, size and proportions of the sword were precise and specific. He spoke of a belief that the Dragon Sword might somehow be the opposite electromagnetic charge to Excalibur. After noting the Arthurian legend and the part Excalibur played in that legend in turning the energies of the earth 'off,' he too wondered whether or not they were being instructed to build and use the Dragon Sword in order to turn these energies back 'on' again. Would 're-tuning' the energies rather than turning them 'on' and 'off' be more in keeping with the language used by the entities working through Avril? Is it a coincidence that Avril's group had so recently carried out a complex piece of work on the St. Michael line? Is it coincidence that so many churches along this line have stained glass windows or stone carvings depicting Michael slaying a dragon with a sword?

The Clew

In the third message Avril received were the words ... *the sword will enter the Kingdom of the Brigantes* ... A year separated this message from the ritual they were about to perform. Was this reference to the Brigantes, a Celtic people whose Northern England territory extended as far south as Derbyshire, a reference to the work they were about to do in Derbyshire at Arbor Low? Was the sword which would enter this 'kingdom' a literal reference to the one which had been built for the ritual at the site? Avril had nothing to do with choosing the site at Arbor Low and knew very little about the sword to be used. Yet her typed messages told her she must bring through information needed by those who built the sword, who choose the site. Was this reference from the previous year merely coincidence? Taken together, everything teased many more questions than answers.

If Britain is the central junction of the energy line system of the planet, then from its relative position there are those who question whether or not Arbor Low might be the centre of that central junction. At 1,000ft it is the highest henge in England. Differing estimates claim from 50 to 150 ley lines crisscrossing the site. The word 'arbor' as well as relating to 'tree' seems also to refer to 'the hub of a wheel from which spokes radiate'. 'Low' is related to fire. If fire is energy, is Arbor Low the hub from which energy radiates in all directions? The henge of Arbor Low itself is an earthwork mound about 250ft in diameter enclosing about 50 recumbent stones. It is possible the stones were never meant to be upright. But whatever is or isn't known about Arbor Low today, this was the site where Geoff had been instructed to enact the ritual which had grown to include Avril and her work.

It speaks to the seriousness and the intent with which Avril considered her own part in the work, that she is so vague about the particulars of the actual on-site events and the experiences of the other members of the group. She is still reticent about describing in detail any of the major earth healing events. Geoff, representative of the group who constructed the sword, wrote a letter of suggested 'instructions' for the 1991 Summer Solstice event at Arbor Low. John and Heather, the only two group members whose tenure was continuous throughout the entire time Avril worked with these entities, also used a camcorder to record the event. From these two documents it has been possible to reconstruct the following description.

After travelling much of the night, Avril and her group met Geoff's group at the henge well before the 4:43a.m. time of sunrise. It would have been difficult to note the actual moment of sunrise without a watch as the day dawned misty, cold, and wet. An orderly if rag-tag assortment of people already populated the henge. Most were dressed warmly; Marian, Geoff, and Anna were in flowing, hooded robes. Against the background of the dark fabric of his robe, the sword hanging at Geoff's back, extending fully from one shoulder to the other and to well below his waist, commanded attention. What little light managed to sift through the mist seemed magnified into brilliance by it's gleaming blade. As the group began their ritual, the rag-tag assortment already in attendance grew attentive in curious silence. Without previous foreknowledge or planning by members of the sword group, someone quietly and sombrely drummed a Native American rhythm throughout the entire ceremony.

A certain number of people were to be used in the ritual; two women were to stand either side of each man. The procession began at the western cardinal point of the henge.

The Clew

A trio, two women and one man, were dropped off and left standing on the outer earthen bank, at the western cardinal point. The procession then crisscrossed the henge to leave a trio at each of the other cardinal points: east, then south, then north. As the procession crossed from south to north, three women pointed their staves to the centre of the henge and 'prepared it' by sounding an agreed call. After completing the circle by returning to the western point, Marian, Geoff, and Anna continued to the interior of the henge. It was believed the trios on the outer banks were responsible for holding and steadying the energy, and perhaps for encouraging or strengthening it's flow.

Prior to the commencement of the ceremony the grid for which Avril received instructions and which she had faithfully helped construct had been carefully centred as instructed. Standing on either side of the grid, also as instructed, Marian and Anna each grasped a sword guard, unsheathed the sword, and presented it to Geoff. Holding it aloft by the point, he in turn presented it to those present. Heavy mist prevented shadows, but from somewhere light reflected off the sword's blade. The robed figures, the gleaming Arthurian-type blade, the drum's solemn cadence, the respectful curiosity of the on-lookers all seemed to create an air of mystery. Geoff had been told to call the word 'Aleph' three times, which he now did; the group followed with the agreed chant, repeated seven times. Once Geoff lowered the sword, Marian and Anna again each held a guard, Geoff held the hilt, and the three carefully centred the blade on the grid, then thrust the sword into the ground, guards pointing east/west. Avril had been instructed to construct the grid in reverse or mirror position. Considering the gloom, overcast, and mist evident, it was strange how brightly the grid reflected from the sword's blade – mirrored back now in correct reading position!

The trio stepped back to allow the others to enjoy the reflection. Unaware of the preparation for this event and unsure quite what was happening, the 'extras' on the scene nevertheless entered into the activities good-naturedly. They milled about, examined the sword and grid, and became still as if on cue. They seemed to examine the props of this little vignette as if orchestrated by some unseen director. In the background the cadence of the Native American drum continued to measure the moments of the unfolding scene. When the others had finished their inspection the trio then continued the ceremony with the ritual 90º repositioning of the sword blade to a north/south alignment. At this point it was suggested that the released energy would instantaneously head in a north/south direction and follow the sun in a westward direction, keeping pace just behind the sunrise.

After a few moments holding the sword in place, the trio again stepped back to allow for those wishing to satisfy their curiosity. The trios at the cardinal points were summoned forward to join hands and circle the centre trio and the sword. They then returned to their cardinal points on the outer banks of the henge. With focused attention Marian and Anna lifted the sword straight up from the ground, without turning it in any direction, and resheathed it. The centre trio then retraced their initial path, picking up each cardinal trio and closing down the circle and this part of the ceremony.

Marian, Geoff, Anna, and the Dragon Sword immediately began their hastened journey to Glastonbury where they had been instructed to enact another ritual. Avril and the Kenilworth group retired to a hearty breakfast and steaming cups of warming tea. Three days later, rested from the journey and sitting at her typewriter, Avril received appreciation

The Clew

and encouragement for a job well done.

24th June 1991 :

Here I return to give you our thanks for the work that has been completed. Now everything is in place and the earth can begin to take control of her own destiny. Many events will now occur which will be as we have previously described, but we have achieved that which we sought, and with your co-operation and the help of so many others, all has been saved ... My friend, we are at the end of a great adventure ... the light burns strongly and is safe in your land.

Chapter Seven

AVRIL
The search begins

18th July 1991: So many mixed feelings. Always such an anti-climax when it's finished. Is it truly finished this time? Strange. For the others the most important consideration is whether or not we 'did it correctly' or whether or not we 'made a difference.' Not personal for them. Not the way it is for me. I miss the energy. The messages. The feeling of being in the presence of, oh I don't know. In the presence of whatever it is. Something that can see the larger picture. Something outside the mundane aspects of this life. Over a month ago Ashad said *"You work well. There is no more need to speak unless you have need. My friend, I leave you."* That was just before our work at Arbor Low. And then when we finished, *Here I return to give you our thanks for the work that has been completed. Now everything is in place and the earth can begin to take control of her own destiny.* And since then nothing.

Warren is leaving. As good as left. Which brings up the partner thing for me again. What am I to do with this feeling that I'm supposed to be *with* someone? In one way I'm perfectly content to be on my own. In some ways perhaps prefer the freedom of that. Yet in another way it's always as if I'm constantly searching. It has to do with Ashad. The feelings Ashad brings up for me. Will I have that? In a living, breathing human? Will I know the acceptance and supportive love that I feel from Ashad? I read and read his last words.

> *My friend, we are at the end of a great adventure and once again we have shared the delights each offers to the other. I will reach for your hand whenever there is need but you know that we walk together at all times and that my words are within your reach. I return to my brothers but the joy of our life is a vibrant part of my being. Go forward happily and trust in your own strengths. I will always hear your call, the oath is remembered. The door opens and the night will fall but now the Light burns strongly and is safe in your land. The future will make all things plain. My friend, I leave your side but you are not forgotten and will never be alone. Remember.*

The sadness. No one else can know that. None of the others. How to explain the sadness when a friend leaves. How can I explain to them, to anyone, about this particular friend. And the loss I feel when the typing stops. But not only a friend. More than a friend. The loss. Of Warren and all that means. And now this. The others ask if there is more work. I don't know. We thought it was finished once before. Maybe it only seems finished again. But it's more than that for me. The loss for me is more than whether or not the earth healing is finished. It's a loss only I seem to understand.

26th July 1991: At a workshop someone explained that I might 'channel' advice for people. That I might be able to ask Ashad to answer people's questions. At first I wasn't so sure. But to have Ashad back again. To be able to type the words. To have that presence. Very tempting. And so I ask!

> *I hear you speak and we must look at the ways in which our knowledge can be used ... You have been a good servant of the Light and therefore it has been confirmed that we can work together in the way that you describe in order to help others ... When you are contacted you must ask whoever writes to place their palm flat upon the paper which contains their request. In this way it will be possible for you to connect with them and for us together to provide the best answers for their needs ... We can speak only of the learning of the heart and the growth and acquired knowledge of the soul. Harmony is that which should be sought and each inquirer must interpret the words we offer by listening to the spirit that lives within him or her. Man has this possibility to hear as you and many others have proven.*

So he will return! And perhaps even help me in another way.

> *You have needs and this the Masters recognise ...*

However greed must form no part of our work.

> *There should be sufficient reward to enable you to live a life that is satisfying and without struggle.*

That part of it, the financial part of it I suppose, remains to be seen. But at least he will come when I ask. There will be more time together. He even answered my question about what to tell people about this service. He advised that through me he will :

> *... offer learning and advice to those who seek a greater understanding of themselves. Such help should be sought humbly and only used for spiritual advancement. Learning will be offered in order that those who seek can be shown the history of their many lives and the advice will be for them to interpret for themselves by tuning in to the guidance that their inner selves can offer. Advice will be given to show how each person can best do this at this particular stage of their growth. All men have the power to direct themselves along the path to perfection but the Masters accept that at certain times it is necessary for each to seek help from those in the other worlds that they cannot see. For some this may be an opportunity to resolve problems that have been retained from previous lives whilst others may seek new direction or an understanding of the path they are on. All men can recognise the Light and have the power to bring it into their life, at whatever stage they are existing. Love is the key to the search and to each man's growth.*

I feel almost as if I'm off on another adventure. What will this one bring?

The Clew

7th October 1991: Ann saw him! He confirmed it!

> *Your friend who has seen me sees well. She asks of my eyes. They are that colour because I grew amongst a people who came from the other side of the mountains. The race had travelled far from its first home on earth and there were those who were outsiders who lived amongst them and fathered the children of the Truth. From such a union was I born and carried within me the knowledge of my father's mind. Together we could reach a great distance to acquire the knowledge that others sought but we were badly used and our sorrows were great. Now we work together again and my heart is full to overflowing with the delight of clasping your thoughts. Love lifts the hearts of all men and women to a higher vibration and allows them to access thoughts which enhance their whole being.*

Confirmation. Not that I ever doubted. How could I? He's as real, more real maybe, than any of the others who send these strange messages. Strange that something so 'unreal' can feel so real. But it's true. And now the surprise, maybe even shock, of her words and this confirmation.

Do I want time to move more quickly or slow down? Do I want this chapter of my life finished so that I can move on, or do I want to prolong it because I am so uncertain about what comes next? Conflicting needs. Conflicting desires. Will I ever figure it out? Will I be alone forever now?

> *Your husband will make a good life for himself in his new home and success will be his. He has begun to acknowledge the need for change within himself and this acknowledgement will allow doors to open.*

So the reassurance comes in moments like these. I'm not to worry. Warren and I are doing what we need to do. We are growing, but in different directions, or something. The reminders come too. Nudges that feel almost like asides but feel like a caress.

> *Many times we have stood together as the processions wound their way to the High Place. Your eyes were the colour of poppy seed and the strength of your voice carried the words of faith a great distance.*

8th November 1991: Ann has seen Ashad again - in a different lifetime. And again he has confirmed it!

> *The woman who came has many gifts. One of them is the gift of sight and it is possible for her to recall my picture when once long ago I lived on your world. Then I was a man of good family, and I was respected for my gift of words. I became a Christian at a time when such beliefs were dangerous but I was protected and came to no harm. You too shared that life and we often walked in the garden of my father. You wore white and your hair was braided*

> high upon your head. It was enough that we were together occasionally as at that time our lives were removed for the most part. There have been many other lives which we have shared and one by one I will expose them to the woman if you wish to remember. Cease now for I must return to the work at hand and we have no need at this time for continuous communication. Know only that I will reach for your hand when you call and that those who seek will always be answered.

I remember in the beginning. The little clues we'd find after we'd done something well or figured something out to their satisfaction. This feels the same. So many doubts in my life right now. So many things I question. It's as if this is a little reminder, or a little nudge. Keep going. I'm going in the right direction. It is enough. I know now. I must find a way to know all of it. To believe all of it. That it will work out okay. That I will be provided for. That I will find the love I seek.

1st January 1992 :

> Here, friend, we stand together as so often before. All is well you are progressing as you should and the advice has been good. Tell your friends not to be disheartened with their lives. The period they have entered is one of grounding and re-assessing what has been awakened in them so swiftly. They are on the right path and should simply ask each day that their lives should continue to unfold according to their chosen paths.

And so. The new year. A memorable day. It's official now. Warren physically left today. So I too must ask that my life continues to unfold according to my chosen path. And what is that? Ashad reassures me.

> Soon you will have more time to concentrate on your skill and many will seek you out … Your work will become recognised and there will be much to occupy your time and many places for you to visit.

I don't know if it helps. Maybe it doesn't help enough.

14th January 1992: Strange experience tonight. Quite strange. As if I'd been hit in the middle of the forehead with some beam of light. Funny way to describe it but it felt like a powerful glow. My head actually, physically seemed to jerk back. I saw this man. And wham. At the same time the sensation "He's one." He's *the* one? And then he came up later and asked if he could have my birth date.

I'd been so nervous. Never spoken in public like this before. Never admitted in public to this sort of activity. Never talked about it. Never tried to explain it. Not exactly something easy. Thirty people sitting around, chatting. Time to begin soon. Looking out over the faces and hit that one. Or it hit me. Went around the room again to see if it happened with any of the others. It didn't. The next time my eyes rested on him it was only a ripple. But a definite ripple. And then for him to come and speak to me after I'd finished. To explain he was beginning to learn astrology and wanted to see if there was anything in my chart that would predict channelling. Like the palm reader? Coincidence?

February 1992: Ann sees energies too. Patrick. His name is Patrick and he's a friend of hers. She saw his energy and mine and said they are very similar so she asked us to lunch. Patrick volunteered to demonstrate his reflexology on my feet. I *was* curious. I wondered how it worked. What would happen. Difficult not to believe in past lives now. There's still that little problem with believing, but it becomes more difficult. When he touched my foot something happened. Difficult to explain but I began seeing something like flashbacks. In colour. Like slides projected on a screen. Difficult to know what they were or what to make of them. Standing in a French tumbril on the way to the guillotine. I can't even remember for sure because it all happened so fast and seemed so real. I think I was actually lost in the experience of it.

I saw Patrick too. In Egypt. I don't know why but I *knew* it was Egypt. He was a very old man. Being led away by a woman I knew to be his caretaker. He had been the most important priest but had fallen out of favour. I was to assume his duties. I, the priestess, who continued on after he left. I don't know how I knew these things. I don't even know if I knew these things. They seemed so real. As did the feelings. Compassion. I felt so much compassion for Patrick. The slide images might not have been real, but the feeling certainly was. I have seldom felt that kind of compassion. And for this stranger I don't even know?

There were more slide pictures. More knowing from nowhere. Patrick remembered why he was being led away in disgrace. Why I was assuming his duties. The pharaoh for whom Patrick worked had been found outside the city partly eaten by animals. His cartouche said he had two hearts and so to fulfill this prophecy Patrick and his scribe convinced a court eunuch to volunteer his heart. His scribe - Ashad. Ashad had been Patrick's scribe! An assistant wearing a wooden head of Anubis had taken the eunuch's heart while he was still alive, put it into a jewelled box and then into the pharaoh's body for burial.

I could see the temple where the ritual was carried out. The new pharaoh introduced a new religion where God was to be worshipped as one, not as his many parts. He insisted the people stop interpreting the sacred words literally and so he made an example of Patrick. Patrick had interpreted the cartouche literally. And his scribe - Ashad - had been the one to convince the eunuch to volunteer his heart. So both must be punished. Ashad was drawn and quartered and his heart thrown into a brazier. Patrick was banished and left in disgrace. As he was being led away he reached toward me. I actually saw a rainbow of colour stretch from his fingertips to my brow. And that - the rainbow of colour - seemed no more strange than any of the rest of it.

And what am I to do with this new ability? Being able to see this way - in colour now. Is this what Ashad has kept asking me to do? Remember, he kept saying. Remember. Has Patrick's work unlocked something so that I remember? Is this the way Ann sees? And what am I to do with these feelings for Patrick? They feel like feelings from this lifetime and yet they're not. It feels somehow like

The Clew

I've been 'led to him' as if somehow in some way he's 'the one' but I don't know any more what 'the one' means. He's not to be my partner. I have strong feelings for him, but they're not the same feelings I had when I first recognised Ashad. What is this about? What is this continual searching, or feeling like I must continually be looking for someone?

February 1992: I had another reflexology session with Patrick. More slide pictures of another lifetime. It all came rushing so fast and was so confusing. Patrick just kept doing whatever he was doing. Touching the different places on my feet. He's used to it I guess. He said it happens. He didn't really say what was going on for him. I don't know if he was having these memories or not. I saw him so clearly. Younger this time. On Iona. I know Iona. I remember it from *this* lifetime. I suppose that part I could just be remembering from my trip there. But not the next part. Not Patrick as a monk. And me. What was I? A monk also? How can that be? Was I a nun? Were there ever nuns on the island? I don't understand.

We were together gathering gulls' eggs. Somehow we used the time, or the excuse to gather gulls' eggs, as an excuse to meet illicitly. There was great affection between us. It was exciting being there together. Lovely, sunny beautiful day. And we had often been there together. We often met like that. I know it. I felt it. I felt the affection just as I had felt the compassion. It doesn't make sense. But I felt it. I actually felt this love for this man working on my feet. And then the bell! I actually heard a bell ringing. Didn't imagine that. My foot must have jerked because Patrick reacted in surprise. I couldn't seem to leave that image to come to the present. It was so real. So loud. The bell! I even shouted 'the bell!' out loud, but Patrick – the Patrick in this lifetime - ignored me and kept prodding my foot. He began running. I knew he had to make it back and not be late. The bell insisting, clanging, filling all reality with its warning. He'd been late before. I knew the punishment. So real. As real as Patrick sitting there, pressing on my feet. More real. The relaxed happiness, joyful almost giddy excitement of the stolen time. I was actually *there*. Patrick was working on my feet but this younger Patrick and I were together on the shores of Iona gathering gulls' eggs! And then there was the bell and happiness and joy evaporated and there was only fear. Of his being caught. If he were not to be caught he must run and quickly. He must make it back in time. It was all so real.

How to separate it from, well, what were these feelings I had for this man. Me now, this much older woman, and Patrick a much older man. Yet there were the feelings. Of that younger me for that younger Patrick. What was I to do with the feelings? What am I to do with the feelings?

April 1992: Patrick and I have been working together. As Ashad suggested. Patrick will begin working on someone and I'll begin to get images. At first I would tell him but then I learned not to tell him right away. "Avril," he practically shouted, "I can find my own blockages thank you." There seems to be always this competition between us. Intellectual sparring. Then I have to remember the compassion I felt when I saw him being led away, and I sit more quietly. I remember his wisdom. He must do it his way.

The Clew

Joy asked us to work with someone seeking her advice. We agreed. Patrick was working on him and I was seeing the vivid images which seem to be common now. At one point I was seeing all these dead chicken carcasses. Seriously, I really was seeing them, hanging there. Grizzly. Nauseating. Finally Patrick reached the spot and he saw them too. That part wasn't unusual. We had agreed on what we saw before. But this time Patrick made a joke about a well-known firm of turkey suppliers and the man sort of laughed. He used to work for them ! First time I ever had my slide picture confirmed! Always before I could pretend it was just - something - I don't know what. This time I can't pretend. This time it's real. I saw the chicken carcasses and he had actually done that kind of work. It's too strange.

But it gets stranger. After the man left I discussed my slide visions with Patrick. The man had complained of chest pains and headaches. Patrick realised that the chest pains were from the past life I had seen before - when Patrick and Ashad and I all were together. This man was the eunuch! The chest pains were remnants of having his heart taken out while still alive. In my slide vision this time I saw the may wearing a tight gold serpent headband, a euraus which accounted for the headaches. Only at that point did Joy mention his impotence. Patrick had picked up a blocked testes but said nothing because the man hadn't complained of a problem. Although he hadn't told the client and me, he had shared that information with Joy. Castration and now impotence. Patrick knew that he himself, as the high priest who orchestrated taking the eunuch's heart for use by the dead pharaoh, had been the cause of this man's present discomfort. He knew, in the same way I sometimes know things, that this man was the eunuch who had volunteered his heart. And he knew that having been the cause of the man's suffering, now in this lifetime he had assumed the other role. This time he must be the healer. Patrick sees it as karma. Another new idea for me. Healing of karma.

And what of the coincidence? First Patrick. Then the slide pictures. Now meeting this man. All within the space of a few months. In one reality it's totally unbelievable, too coincidental, and must certainly be a fabrication of my imagination. Joy and Patrick's imagination also? We all seem to get the same information. Pieces of the same information. We fit it together and the pieces make sense. In one reality they seem to make sense. In another reality, the one I'm more used to living in, they make no sense whatsoever. Again it's as if I'm being shown another reality. A visceral reality I *know* to be true - and still wish to deny.

May 1992: I'm beginning to recognise the feeling. Don't know what it's about. Or understand it. But I sometimes have this feeling. Like I'm meeting 'the one' but then it isn't. Like Patrick. And now Adam. The coincidences are confusing. Before I left for the Chalice Well it was as if I already knew. As if I knew already that I was going to meet someone. But it was still such a shock when I saw him. When he wasn't there one moment, and then a few seconds later it was as if he appeared out of nowhere. And what were the chances of us both being there at that moment? His open airline ticket so that he delayed his flight even after his

The Clew

friends left. My being delayed so many times and finally deciding to stop at Glastonbury on the return trip instead of on the way to *my* friend's. And then the feeling. Go to Chalice Well. Like before when both Rod and I thought we must go to Lidstone. That same feeling. And then he just began talking. "I wish I could let go." And my answer, as if there was nothing strange about someone I'd never seen before talking to me this way, "Why can't you?" And the knowing. Partly again the knowing 'he's one.' Or he's 'the one?' I don't know.

But this time it was more than just that 'he's the one' feeling. He spoke of the man who had taught him all kinds of knowledge. And I saw the Native American, the wizened old Indian. Seeing him so plainly with all those things hanging from his belt. And knowing that he must let go. Adam must let go. The man's time - the Native American's time - was ended. He wanted to go and Adam was holding him back. I could feel his knowing, almost as if he was personally sending me the message, that he had grown old and bent in service and wanted to leave. Then Adam saying that he hadn't told me what the man looked like but that he *was* Native American, he *was* old. Then Adam knowing that we'd been together before and that we'd been lovers, and my knowing that we hadn't been lovers, or if we had, our relationship had been socially condemned, against the norm, in some way. And the feelings again. What to do with the feelings. Feelings from some time not now but feeling the same. An extraordinary intensity and warmth, a reassuring sense of safety - the feelings I had for him, and with him. Not at all natural for the situation. It's all very confusing I'm sure and I don't understand it. So Patrick's not 'the one.' And, as there seems no continuing connection, obviously Adam's not 'the one.' What is 'the one' about and why these feelings of recognition?

July 1992: Working with Patrick is difficult but powerful. We do see the same things. Get similar visuals and piece together problems, or at least the cause of the problem. Sometimes that is enough. Like the woman whose psychiatrist sent her to the hypnotherapist who then consulted us. The hypnotherapist calmed her down but couldn't prevent her from thinking she was going to die in six weeks. And she was dying too. Starving herself to death. We saw her together. Patrick and I. I was seeing several of her lives – one when she starved to death. One in Roman times, when she was poisoned with hemlock. In another she was a man and died of the plague. She'd been the same age as she was now and it had taken her six weeks to die. In another she died of mustard gas. In the trenches in World War I. I saw all these things, starvation, having the plague at about the same age she is now, being poisoned. Then Patrick said she had poison in her kidneys right now. Her husband said she ate paint as a child. Very sensitive woman. Not happy about any of this talk. As we were about to leave she asked for a drink but her husband drank from the glass before handing it to her. For weeks she had been refusing to eat or drink unless he tasted it first. It all came together. It all made sense. She was picking up on all of it all at once. The man who had been the Pharaoh's eunuch was experiencing symptoms from one previous lifetime. This woman was experiencing symptoms from several lifetimes all at once. Do we bring all these unhealed wounds back with us? Are we somehow being given a chance to heal unfinished business? Whatever was happening, here was this unusually sensitive woman. Too sensitive maybe. She seemed to be aware on some level - unconsciously or subconsciously but on some level - aware of all those different lifetimes all now, in this lifetime. She was not at all happy with any of our work and didn't seem to welcome our help. We left.

Two days later she phoned, fighting mad. She had more energy than she'd ever had and was using it to accuse us of witchcraft and who knows what else. But the interesting thing is, she no longer believes she is going to die. I'm more used to it now. It seems more familiar when something like this happens. I still don't understand it. Not even sure I believe it. But don't know how, exactly, to go about denying it.

That kind of sharing happens with Patrick and me. We complement each other in that way. But it doesn't work in other ways. Something about the two of us together. In other ways it doesn't work between us. Too much competition maybe. Too much intellectual sparring. We are always competing with each other. Too uncomfortable to work that way for both of us.

PATRICK
People getting the same information

My life as an engineer, an entrepreneur, a business owner did nothing to prepare me for the rather sudden discovery of my inexplicable talents. After total rejection of school C of E, my philosophy was to propose that all the beliefs of all the major religions in the world be written down and compared and any tenet where they differed be thrown out. What if anything might be left after such scrutiny might be true. All major religions were dubious; alternative realities simply weren't worthy of doubt.

From my affluent place secure within the establishment, I gently chided the mother of one of my children's school friends for being a 'flower child.' In her flowing Indian-style dresses and seriously into alternative medicine, I regarded her as slightly mad and misguided. I continued in this belief when she appeared on my doorstep, took some hair clippings and left hundreds of herbal pills to treat my glandular fever. A taste of things to come, she did one outstanding thing. During an uninvited reflexology treatment, she pressed on a particular spot on my foot and set off a noise inside my head. Without commenting on the noise I asked her to repeat the pressure. "Oh, that's your ear reflex," she stated casually and continued pressing elsewhere. How could she know I had heard a noise and how did pressure on my feet effect my head? I discounted her silly talk of auras and chakras, but the scientist in me was intrigued.

Our occasional meetings in the following years were punctuated by my sarcastic challenges. With time on my hands following a major set back in my career, I took up her standing offer of a series of treatments. I intended a series of arguments, my science versus her spiritual explanations. She offered another challenge. She needed to write a book for the established medical community explaining this system of reflexology - pressing various spots on the sole of the foot to heal all sorts of maladies in the body. Being a non-believer, I could ask all

The Clew

the questions, insist on all the rational explanations which would make the book appeal to the non-believer. Would I consider attending a course she taught in preparation for helping her write the book? How could I ignore such a challenge? In the strange world of alternative realities then, engineers could have their function. Any good engineer knows atoms and electrons move. Everything is energy and therefore everything has sound and perhaps if we listened correctly we could all hear the sounds I'd had a sample of in the treatment years earlier. I could explain everything. Patrick the good cynic who took nothing on faith. There was nothing I couldn't explain. I would attend the class, I would help her write the book, and my function would be the one at which I was best: the cynic. My function was to ask the unanswerable questions, and if there were any answers, answer them scientifically. Unfortunately, my acceptance of the challenge backfired.

The first week was not good. I did not understand the medical jargon of the other course members. I could not feel the tensions in body tissues. I got into trouble for going too fast. And casually over tea, some idiot woman told me she had met me in a past life. By the second week my ego was well dented and I was deciding not to continue. I could feel nothing wrong with the knee of the woman I was treating, particularly via the foot! Angrily I muttered to myself and insisted to whomever else was listening, "Show me! Show me what I'm supposed to feel!" As I rubbed and pressed the knee I began hearing a noise. Each time I went over one part of the knee there was the same noise in my head. Like an off-tune radio.

I called to Ann, a no-nonsense tutor. "I think I can hear this." "So can I." "Is that what they all come here to learn?" "No, but I know several others who can. What's wrong with the knee?" "I don't know, it just makes a noise." "Well ask your ear. Is it skin? Is it muscle? Is it bone?" "I don't know!" I interrupted. "Is it ligament? Is it the capsule?" Bang! The noise in my head made one very loud sound. I knew I'd just had an answer. "Think about that then," she said and walked off, triumphant. She had just beaten my past arguments, game, set, match.

I was hooked. I knew, as an engineer, that I was in an energy field. What was it doing there? How did it work? It appeared that when my field (assuming I had one) linked in with that of another, my body knew what was wrong with the other field and had found a way to confirm an answer. If only I could guess the right question to ask. I remade my decision. I was not leaving the course!

It grew even more fascinating. Unintentionally I caused three cathartic emotional releases. One almost catatonic shock caused a tough physiotherapist to pass out drumming her heels on the floor. While working on the odd woman who had recognised me from a past life, I had a sensation of being kicked in the stomach. Simultaneously she reared up off the table saying, "Where have you been? I've been looking for you." All this from only touching people's feet!

The same course taught dowsing and so I learned that a 'yes' answer from the pendulum was accompanied by a noise in my head. I asked the pendulum if I had lived before. Yes. Had I known people in this life in previous lives? Yes. Question after question. I stayed up night after night asking questions. Listing lives, dates, relationship, occupations, friends, locations. Certainly more interesting

The Clew

than TV. People began lending me books on esoteric subjects. Much of it seemed way-out rubbish, full of New Age nonsense. I still had my feet on the ground.

I befriended Belen, the odd lady who seemed to have known me in a past life. On a trip together we were driving past a stone circle. As we approached it, I heard the noises in my head that stressed humans made. Walking in the field I heard patterns in the noise at the stones, at different heights, and at different distances from the stones. I could understand why the ancients wanted to mark out such places. As we returned to our car a group of youths arrived, jumped out leaving the doors wide and the radio on full blast - Halleluia Chorus from The Messiah. The impact of the music after the heavy dose of earth energy was devastating. I sat in tears. I was beginning to lose my normal objectivity.

With Belen I practiced the reflexology we had both learned. On one occasion while I worked on her feet she drifted off and began to talk about what she was seeing, strange places in past times. Then she started screaming, reliving being burnt alive. On another occasion she reared up telling me, like some oracle of old, to go to Glastonbury. To honour myself, to baptise myself, and to go to the Tor. A few months later, still the doubting cynic, I did make the trip. At the Abbey in the Chapel of St. Patrick I asked in my head, "Was I you?" No answer. "Did I work for you?" A jolting punch in the solar plexus. Okay, that was that. By now I could find earth energy lines. I found and walked the lines in the centre of the Abbey. I immersed my head in the Chalice Well and climbed the Tor. From the Tor, with black sky all around, I irreverently challenged the gods, "So let's have a bit of sunshine! You can do it if you try!" Nothing happened. I chuckled and forgot about it until I reached the stile at the bottom of the hill. One bright shaft of sunlight lit me and the stile.

I studied meditation. I flew to California to study in a residential course. I explored Astrology, Tarot, Spiritual Guides, and Ancient Egypt. Egypt was particularly interesting because my wife and I planned to visit Egypt within a month. Before leaving Belen felt compelled to share more of her strange oracles. "Look for the writing on the back of the black statue. It is very important to you." "Find the chamber under the ground which is connected to the left foot of the Sphinx. It is where the river used to flow. There the ancient ones of Atlantis buried their secrets just after the flood. They will be discovered in our time."

I had also befriended the no-nonsense tutor from the reflexology course. A retired Nursing Sister with a down-to-earth approach to some very unearthly topics, Ann had become a firm and respected friend. On my return from Egypt, she asked me to accompany her to a talk someone was giving about typing messages from some unearthly guide. That's when I met Avril. She gave the talk. Ann sees auras and perceived something similar in Avril's and my aura and asked us both to lunch. Avril was an interesting experience. Because she was curious about what I did, I volunteered to give her a reflexology treatment. As I worked on her feet, she too started to talk in a trance-like way about ancient lives and places. She continued until she too was screaming about being burnt alive. Unconcerned - I'd had this happen before - I continued in a detached manner. I was beginning to get used to this. A patient could cry and scream and ramble on about whatever they wished, it made no difference to me. I did what I did

The Clew

regardless of what they did. I found the noises and did whatever it took to make the noises stop. Nothing could be more simple or straightforward. In fact, I prided myself, being an engineer even made it easier. I didn't have to believe or even seriously listen to all their past life fairytales and such.

Much to my dismay, it was different with Avril. Against my better judgement I saw what she was describing. I had actually *been* there. In Egypt I had been in the temple she described. I knew of the ritual she was articulating in such minute detail. In Saqqara near the stepped pyramid, I had visited a temple opened to the public only days before our arrival. It had been closed for thirty years and had only been opened after restoration. During our brief visit I had seen the walls of the temple picturing ceremonies and rituals exactly as Avril was describing. No other pyramid has writing inside. She described it all so perfectly and yet *she* had never been there. The engineer had a little difficulty with that one. That was not the end of it either. Over the next few months, there were more coincidences. More validation for some reality beyond what my engineer self could explain.

During another treatment Avril spoke of a life when we were together on Iona, one where I had fallen to my death from a cliff while gathering gull's eggs. If, when I touched their feet, people wanted to go on about past lives, that was one thing. But to include me in one of their lives, to say I had been there, had been a part of it in the way she had described our being together in Egypt, was more difficult for me to ignore. And here was another lifetime we had supposedly shared. I felt both cynicism and curiosity. When the curiosity finally won out, I asked to dowse the map she owned from a trip to Iona. I was surprised at the strong reaction in the palm of my hand to four places on the map. To my amazement not only did the palm of my hand react strongly, but I also felt emotion. I felt sadness at the bay where Avril thought I had died. I also felt sadness at two other places. And at another, a strong sexual excitement. In the brief moment before dismissing the latter feeling, I remember the strange and unwelcome thought that perhaps Avril and I had been something rather more than friends. Subsequently I went with my wife Jocelyn to stay on the island. I visited all four spots and was relieved that I didn't really feel any return of any of the emotions I'd experienced earlier. However, at the Bay of Pigeons, I recognised and 'knew' the cliff where I had fallen to my death.

No less cynical, I was none the less not quite as able to discount my own emotions and 'knowings.' In this newly discovered frame of mind I found another rather jumbled link with Iona. Whilst back home, reading an old guide book someone had lent me, I came across the story of the death of St. Colum the founder of the monastery on Iona. When too old to walk far, a young monk had pushed him round in a barrow. Reading this I suddenly found first one eye and then the other running tears but without feeling sad. Through her 'channel' Avril confirmed that I had been the young barrow pusher. When Colum died, just died – no angels, no voices, no light from heaven, just died – I, the young barrow pusher, had lost all faith. In the end perhaps he too had been a cynic?

The Clew

AVRIL
The loss of Ashad

August 1992 : Will I get used to it eventually? What do I expect of it? Will it ever make sense? The coincidence. The knowing. The recognition. The strangely familiar interactions. Too familiar to be explained by the circumstances. I seem to have met another one. What does that mean, another one? Who are these 'ones' I keep meeting? So another. Did I have a premonition this time? I had finished seeing Avebury. Or thought I had. Why go back to the shops? On my way home for the day, back to the B&B, why turn instead and go back to the shops? And why that shop? Why walk into that particular shop, at that particular moment? Why was I sitting drinking tea in a shop after a day that already seemed complete? Was it a premonition? I'm not even sure I know any more.

And then of course it began. When it begins like that, I don't know what to do with it. It won't go away. So I go along with it. Partly because I hope to get rid of it that way? Partly because I still hope this will be 'the one?' Partly out of curiosity because each interaction seems to have its own particular interest? A collection of interesting encounters? So I see this man. Mild curiosity at first. Ignore it. He's just another customer in a shop. I'm standing next to this person. This man. Tall and large. American, by the sound of his accent. In line to buy a cup of tea. Nothing more. When we've each taken a table and he begins reading a book. I'm looking at his shirt and wondering why I'm sitting there and also wondering if he wore the shirt purposely. Moon and stars. One of those crazy shirts tourists wear. Here we are at this ancient site that might have something to do with recording celestial events or something and I'm wondering if he knew that and wore this shirt intentionally.

And then the voice. That at least I'm beginning to recognise. The words haven't come out of my mouth yet, but I'm recognising the urging. *Ask him.* And my automatic response. No. The answering voice, more urgent this time. *Ask him.* I didn't even need to look to see the two women at the table next to me, their cream tea eagerly and appreciatively being devoured. Oh, right. A lone single woman is supposed to just walk up to this strange man, American man, and ask him if he picked his shirt purposefully or if it was a coincidence. In front of these two women I'm supposed to do this. He might be American. Maybe women in America do that. Single women alone in teashops. But this is England. And those two women devouring their cream tea certainly aren't American. They are very English. I will not.

And the voice. More emphatic. *Ask him.* There will be no rest. He continued reading the book. For a moment it was as if he didn't hear me. As if he was consciously deciding whether or not to notice me. Then he lowered the book and I saw his eyes. And I knew. If I hadn't known before, if the insistent voice telling me to ask him hadn't told me before, when I saw his eyes, I knew. *Knew.* Knew what? Who knows what. Why my car turned the wrong way instead of going back to the B&B? Why I felt compelled to wander into this particular shop? Why I was here at Avebury at this particular time to begin with? I don't know what I

The Clew

knew. I don't know myself what it is I recognised. Knew he's one. Another one. There's something we're to do together. Some connection we have. Or have had. Or are supposed to have. Is he 'the one?' Will *this* be the end of the search?

More easily than it should have, his story tumbled out. The same as with Adam. As if there were some reason he was safe telling it all to me. The planned trip to take his partner to The Cook Islands. The week before she decided to end their relationship. But he'd saved and planned it for so long. So they went anyway. Disaster. Had he thought the trip might mend things? It didn't. Returned to Oregon, demoralised, with two weeks before his teaching term was to begin. And then it began. It. All the 'its' that resulted in his being in this particular shop at this particular time, in this particular part of the world. Coincidence. For no reason apparent to himself he knew he needed to spend the next two weeks in England. Took his credit card to the airport and boarded a plane. Thought he wanted to see cathedrals.

The confusion in his voice. He couldn't understand it. Was he feeling the same confusion I feel about these knowings I seem destined to follow? Seem destined to act on when they make so little sense? Anyway he too acted. No interest what so ever in religion, spirituality, or cathedrals. Sad and vulnerable though, so maybe just indulging himself to forget. Anyway he was off to Salisbury. His story continued to spill out. He didn't at all seem puzzled by the fact that he was sharing it all with me, a complete stranger. Puzzled by the story itself, but not by the sharing of it. Mystified at the way things were unfolding. Wandering around Salisbury, wondering why he was there, he found the leaflet. "You must see Avebury" it said. Taking it literally he found public transport, first he had gone to Glastonbury, and then back to Bath. A bicycle. He rented a bicycle and boarded the train with this rented bicycle to make the last 10 miles to Avebury. Wonderment on his face. Somewhere in this very matter-of-fact recitation loomed an unasked question I tried to ignore. He would find the words to ask it soon enough.

The day was a long, long summer day with much light left. I could take him around. Would he be interested? In the circles? In Silbury Hill? In North Kennet Long Barrow? We walked and talked in a normal fashion. I shared things of common interest, he noticed, took an interest. It went well. Until the barrow. Finally, after visiting the others, we arrived at the barrow. The sun cast the low, golden, lingering light of the long evening through the stone entrance. Mesmerised he stood, hardly breathing. Putting aside my role as tour guide, I too gave in to the feeling. We stood silently in the magically clear, still, evening light, ageless stone post and lintel protecting and enclosing us. When he turned to look at me, his eyes saw me, didn't see me, looked at stones reflecting soft gold light, and didn't see the stones. What did he see? In that moment I knew he had found words for the unasked question.

"I haven't come here to see cathedrals, have I?"

"No, I don't think you have."

"Why have I come here then?"

I wasn't sure I knew. I'm not sure I know even now. And even what I do know, do seem to understand, how to put it into words? How to speak it? It makes even less sense when I find the words to express it. I watched his confusion and knew it as my own. Had known it as my own. Less confused now but still not able to explain. He would have to make his own meaning. Piece together his own sense of it. Find his own explanation. And so, pretending ignorance, and noting the fading light, I suggested a pub. After an uneventful meal, we parted.

But he returned. The following weekend he passed through Kenilworth on his way to France. We sat drinking tea. Quietly, familiar, his story still unfolding. Looking at his watch he spoke softly. His former wife was being married at that very moment. So lost he looked. I reached to comfort him. He jerked – his body actually jerked rigid the moment I touched him.

"There's a man. With snakes! What is this? What am I seeing? He's holding the snakes in his hands, holding them aloft. There's a tall standing stone. Encircled in an iron railing. Where is this? What's happening?"

I had withdrawn my hand immediately. Whatever had happened seemed to be fading. He looked at me and finally his eyes refocused. Finally he saw me. Saw the tea cup in his hand. Saw the room. Saw in present time. And asked. "Where was this? What was that? What's happening?"

"Has this ever happened to you before? Have you ever had experiences like this before?"

"No."

"Then perhaps this is why you have come."

Simple answer. Just words. And yet he seemed to accept. It seemed enough for some reason. At least he was quiet and didn't ask any more. And then he left. He would go to Mont St. Michel. Positive he must go, not understanding why, knowing he must find something there, he would go to France.

He left on a Monday. And was back by Tuesday. He had found it. Hadn't even gone into the monastery. No tours, no poking around, no interest in anything else once the urgency was satisfied. Had seen the golden figurine high atop the monastery, glimmering in the sun and knew instantly that it was it. That was why he had come. To see that. Too high to be seen clearly, he wasn't sure what it was, but still he knew that he had seen it. Had found what he had come for. In the guide book he saw the picture, St. Michael killing the dragon. St Michael killing the dragon? Strangely, he wasn't curious. Didn't ask why he had to find that particular image. Didn't know what it meant any more than he understood anything else that seemed to have happened to him on his trip. Only knew that he had gone there to find it, knew as soon as he saw it that he had found it, and knew there was nothing left for him to do. He had finished.

He had returned to Kenilworth one last time, to share this with me. And then he left. Oregon seems half way round the world. He's invited me to visit him for Christmas. There's so much affection between us. Is *he* the one?

September 1992: Am I growing wary? I never know when it's going to happen. Is there something I'm doing to cause this? They seem to be everywhere. This time at the Rollrights with John and Heather. Walking around the outside. Other people there. Quietly walking. Exploring. Just being in the space. And then to look to the centre and see him standing there alone. I wasn't having flashbacks.

The Clew

Not the slides this time. No past life recall if that is indeed what it is. But everything stopped and went into slow motion. The light changed. It was unreal. I watched from some place outside myself. He was alone in the circle and for a few moments no one else existed. There was no one else anywhere around. Or didn't seem to be. Somehow even I had evaporated and watched from a space somewhere separate. As if a camera had him in focus, larger than life he filled the screen. I was the audience watching it unfold. I watched him standing there, alone, elegantly dressed, and the feelings began again. How can this be? I met Gray, he shared his powerful experiences with me, he returned to Oregon, and I'll visit him at Christmas. If Gray is 'the one' who is this? What are these feelings? The mind. This one has to do with the mind. This time it's affection but respect and admiration too. Are these feelings from some past lifetime too? A swift image, a Greek amphitheatre, a man, my teacher (?), handing me a scroll. Why the feelings? Why did I have to speak to him? *Have to.* There was no getting around it. Is he 'the one?' I'm confused.

March 1993: The necklace. Emerald and diamond. Sold. But the experience it bought. Am I any wiser? Any nearer the goal? Or am I only more confused. In November Gray called to say he had fallen in love. Well then he's not the one. But I was to go anyway. The tickets long ago purchased and he wanting to show me Oregon. So I went. Was it all worth it? The car accident. The physical injury. Being helpless and having two strange men, in turns, first one and then the other care for me. Would I do it again? There was growth. There were changes. New understanding? I don't know.

It soon became apparent that the two love birds needed time alone. A seminar at Mt. Shasta seemed the answer. And the coincidences began again. Another one. I'm getting so I know instantly. Walking from his parked car to the stairway. Why had I been simply driven to leave the room for some fresh air? Why was I standing on the steps looking down just as he stepped to begin the journey up? I had known instantly. As soon as I saw him in the car park I knew. But could have ignored. Still could have made the choice to ignore. He stepped up onto the steps and looked up. As before, as with Gray, it was his eyes. And I could no longer ignore. Why, why do I keep getting this sense of recognition? On one level I know it's about a partner. I'm always looking. Always asking is he the one? Always looking for 'the one.' Is Douw the one? Probably not. I don't know who or what is what any longer.

After the accident and after the hospital and after Gray caring for me, Douw volunteered. And so Douw cared for me. Both of them caring for me in ways a man, at least one not intimately involved with her, shouldn't have to care for a woman. What was that about? The reading I did for Douw. Wanted to return something, to give him a gift in return for his care for me. Would he like a reading? We'd talked so often and so long about all 'my activities.' He seemed interested. These reading began with Ashad apologising and saying 'they' did it as gently as they could. The accident. Ashad had something to do with the accident. It wasn't an accident? And then, during the reading, Ashad explaining that now I could tune into Douw's own guides. I no longer needed to go through Ashad or any of the others. When I wanted to read for someone, I could tune into their own personal guide. The accident had been responsible for that, Ashad said. So the earthquake and the seeming blow to my head began the typing. Then Patrick and my reflexology treatment seemed to start the vivid, in colour slide pictures. And now the car accident somehow making it possible to tune into personal guides. So was it worth it? I don't know. How would I know something like that?

Perhaps the slide pictures I began to see were worth it. Memories of another past life? So familiar in a way. After the accident. Being an invalid. Lying on the divan, the pain in my chest, another vivid memory about one of these familiar strangers. I saw it so clearly. I was dying of TB. Lying on a chaise longue looking out through a pair of French windows. They opened out onto a lawn with flower beds. Warm and sunny and the woman in the white, floaty, muslin summer dress. Lying there looking out, knowing I was dying. The red canna lilies. The flowers. The beautiful lawn. These two dear people, Douw and the young girl, enjoying the summer day. And knowing I was dying. It must have been Austria because he was wearing one of those Austrian embroidered suits. Not my husband. I knew Douw wasn't my husband, but he had been someone very dear to me. A steward. Someone who oversaw my affairs. And I loved him very much. And trusted him. And there I was again. My chest hurting from the accident. Lying on the divan and watching Douw care for me. And feeling the same feelings all over again. So what do I do with the feelings? Again!

And the other images. When I began his reading. White marble balustrade, greenery all around, a white robed figure somehow Atlantean and I don't even know what Atlantean means. But it was Atlantean. Douw's energy is Atlantean too. And his guide. I could see his guide. It was his guide giving me the information. Not Ashad. Not any of the others with whom I'd grown familiar. But his guide. I sat there typing and speaking at the same time. Not exactly reading it as I typed it. Douw angry at life in general. Raging at the universe. Denying any belief in anything like God or any other 'supernatural' being. At whom is he raging then? If he didn't have some basic understanding on some level that there might be something to rage at, would he be raging? What has he done to deserve his life he insists. Insists I make his guide answer that one. *You have to put right what you did wrong.* "Tell me what I did! Tell me!" And his guide patiently explaining some altercation with the law. "I sense you are angry with me." His guide's quiet, reserved, understated answer, *I have known frustration in my charge of you.* A very novel idea, that they too have frustration with us!

So was it worth it? I don't know. Am I any closer to - to what? To anything?

April 1993 : And now Ashad is leaving. After all the changes, with all the questions he leaves unanswered, with all the men I don't know what to do with – or perhaps I should say all the feelings about all the men I don't know what to do with - with the accident and all the new 'skills' I seem to be evolving into and now he leaves. On my own more than ever before. His last message is so confusing. I asked him about Niall. The latest of the men. Is he the one? Is he my partner? I wonder I don't weary and give up hope.

The Clew

> *My friend I stand at your side with the colour of our knowledge connecting us. Once long ago we stood at the place where the sun slips low and the moon rises above the horizon. Around us the many gathered, for it was for you to speak the words of the gods who guarded the shrine … Many have stood at your side throughout the long span of time which has been yours to endure and they all gather now as you near the end of your journey. Hold them all in love for your soul has had that blessing always. Now this new partner comes who will take my place at your side and you must leave go of my hand for I can no longer guard you and must step back into those dimensions where my new work awaits. We are as one, for so we have been through all time and that security should remain with you through all time that is yet to come. Dear friend you have grown through sorrow and courage and now the great task awaits your heart and your hand … I draw back and must set my longing aside. Hold to the truth which you know and to the love that you believe in. There are many others who stand waiting to move to your side. The love between us is eternal and the colour will always contain it. The man knows for he comes from the place where the patterns are begun. I move back to the door and your guide moves to your side. We have joyed in this new time but our oath is ended. It is enough that you know that We Are. Let go my hand, my love moves with you and will keep you from all harm.*

Who are the many who have stood at my side throughout the long span of time I have endured? They all gather now? Is that who all these men are? It certainly feels like I've been with them all in past lives. I guess I can say that. I *think* I know what that means. The end of my journey? What journey and how and when does it end? Well at least the news about Niall seems to be good. If he's to take Ashad's place that must mean something. But who are the many others waiting to move to my side? And it doesn't seem to help much to know that Ashad and I 'Are.' It doesn't seem to help to know the love between us is eternal. It's all fine for Ashad to set *his* longing aside. What am I to do with mine?

Chapter Eight

It is only with the knowledge and understanding of hindsight that Avril can recognise the new skill she was learning at the time of these unusual encounters. With each validation of her internal knowing, as when she 'saw' Adam's Native American mentor, she was encouraged to further trust the knowing. Each time she met another with whom she felt an unusual connection, and each time someone came forward independently to validate some inner knowing she had felt about the meeting, it confirmed her sense of recognition and strengthened her ability to access her intuition. She *was* beginning to wonder for what purpose she seemed to be meeting all these men. But although she realised none of them was 'the one' she was not yet ready to abandon the search.

An astrologer can look at Avril's birth chart and explain, astrologically, her obsession with finding the right partner. Even without the astrological understanding, however, it is clear that the obsession was certainly useful and perhaps even imperative in order for her to find the participants for the last piece of work. For whatever reason, she seems from earliest memory to have always known there was, somewhere, a perfect partner. Because she was newly divorced and always thinking she might meet that partner somewhere, sometime, she was open to all the chance meetings she experienced in the next several years. She discovered each in turn was not 'the one,' but she continued to believe that he was waiting in the wings, and so she was open to the chance encounters and open to the feelings of connection she was recognising so often throughout this process. And so, although she was very, very far from realising it at this time, she was indeed learning another skill: recognising and trusting intuition.

Although confusing for her at the time, the 'search' was imperative and would continue until enough pieces of the puzzle were found to enable the final work to be undertaken. In his own way, Ashad was even trying to reassure her. At the time she wrote this sentence,

> *Many have stood at your side throughout the long span of time which has been yours to endure and they all gather now as you near the end of your journey*

she thought she understood his words. However, Ashad and the other entities frequently gave her messages which she *thought* she understood only to find later that they were referring to a concept with which she was totally unfamiliar. Following the last work the group did together, or 'the end of the journey,' she is finally certain she understands that sentence. For the work to continue it was simply imperative that she find the relevant participants. Much later the entities would tell her that each of the people involved in the final work incarnated at this specific time for just this specific purpose. And it was only through what she thought was her own personal search for a mate, through the feelings of recognition and familiarity with so many of the men, that she was finally able to find the 'many to stand at her side.'

Ashad's final message came in answer to a specific question on Avril's part. She had stated that the past months had been so turbulent with so many 'reunions' that she began to doubt her judgement over the arrival of a partner. She specifically asked for guidance on

that point. Therefore she interpreted the sentences
> *Now this new partner comes who will take my place at your side and you must leave go of my hand …*

and the sentence ...
> *The man knows for he comes from the place where the patterns are begun …*

as having to do with one of the several men she continued to meet and 'recognise.' Even when, only days later, Assurbanipal arrived to take Ashad's place, she didn't realise that the sentence
> *There are many others who stand waiting to move to your side*

referred to the entities she would continue to work with, not the human men she must also continue to meet.

This was not the only confusion surrounding Assurbanipal's arrival. The entities continually advised Avril that she must read more. It is perhaps an understatement to say that at times they must have been very frustrated with her inability to translate the pictures they gave her into words appropriate to the concepts they were trying to convey. Because Ashad made reference to lives they had shared in Ur, and in answer to the admonitions that she should read more, Avril had begun reading about Ur and Sumeria. She had actually seen Assurbanipal's name in that research.

As with so many things Avril is uncertain why the entities chose for themselves the names they did. She knew the energy of each was different. And the names they used to identify themselves always seemed appropriate to their individual energy. At the time, without doubting, examining or questioning, she was satisfied to identify them by the names they chose. From a place of more experience and greater wisdom she now defines what she believes to have been involved in the process. In the beginning it was as if the entities had to lower or slow their vibration to make it compatible with Avril's. For her part she had to raise her own consciousness up, in a sense raise her own vibration to reach out for the energies being made available. For lack of a better way of explaining it, it was as if the entities as spirit were reaching down and Avril as *matter* was reaching up. In the no man's land inbetween, they had to agree on an imagery. Each of the entities seemed to embody what might be called an archetype: a healer, an astrologer, a pagan god, a powerful goddess. And whoever or whatever the entities are, this shared exchange resulted in names (or sounds) which embodied that particular entity's energy. Although she was not aware of this process in the very beginning, Ashad too seemed true to this from the very first. Ashad is strangely similar to Achad which means union in the Qabalah, and Ashad certainly personified the personal union for which Avril had always longed.

It was not enough, however, that they chose names universally appropriate to their archetype, they also needed to use names which would be acceptable to Avril personally. Names from within the Church for instance, or names from within the Moslem or Native American tradition, would have been much less acceptable to her personally than the names that emerged. The names whetted her curiosity. They served to encourage her reading and research in the direction of the concepts she needed to understand to do the work she was being asked to do. Additionally the names seemed to serve some function in triggering memory of lifetimes and skills Avril needed to remember and access in order to accomplish the later task. In any event, the names seem to have been chosen with care and with purpose and certainly resonated with Avril on a personal level.

In her reading and research she had learned that Assurbanipal was king of Nineveh, Babylon in 600 BC and that he had the greatest library of astrological texts in the ancient world. It would be another year however, before she realised the many references Assurbanipal and earlier entities had made to the stars had anything what so ever to do with astrology and mythology. She smiles now at her naiveté regarding messages such as

The stars appear and write the old stories across the sky.

and

... watch the stars in their movements across the sky.

and

... the stars have recorded the stories if only you will take time to look.

Given these admonitions, Avril dutifully went out on many a clear night and gazed at the stars hoping to figure out what the messages could possibly mean. The frustration the entities must have felt in their aborted attempts is evident in this understated comment.

Tell the man who questions that the time is aligned with aspects of the heavens which as yet you do not comprehend.

The aspect of the heavens which Avril did not as yet comprehend was obviously astrology. But even such seemingly concrete messages as

Tell your friends that they must begin to chart the movements in the sky,

and

The heavens are a map he must become familiar with and he must move clockwise around it beginning at the place of the ram,

did nothing to enlighten their protégé as to the real meaning of these words. Avril is an Aries, yet she still made no connection between the astrological sign of Aries and the entity's reference to 'the *ram*.'

When asked why the entities didn't simply tell her to study astrology, Avril has a ready answer. First, she had free will and total freedom of choice in all matters and was never *told* to do anything outside of her ability to understand or at least discover the meaning of what she was doing. Secondly, the very fact that she was unaware of a concept made it impossible for the entities to give her the 'words.' They could be showing her 'pictures' of astrological constellations or configurations and she would only see and choose the word 'stars.' They could show her a 'picture' of the ram Aries, but with no astrological understanding she could only see and choose the word the 'ram'. They could try and show her the precession of the equinoxes but she would only see

the number of times the earth spins on its curve;

or
> *The stars wander at will within the confines of their allotted space and record the adjustments of the heavens in order that the knowledge of life's cycle is not lost.*

Perhaps this is the exception to the rule that a picture is worth a thousand words. In this case only four words, 'precession of the equinoxes', were probably worth many, many pictures. But Avril knew neither the words, nor the concepts, and so she and the entities were stuck with the pictures.

It would be another year before Avril met and 'recognised' someone who could help her with these rather foreign concepts. In the meantime she continued to help individuals by giving them information from their personal guides. She was also continuing to grow as a channel. She no longer needed to type the messages she received and no longer needed to work with people on an individual basis. Although she did continue to do some individual readings, Assurbanipal seemed to enable her to work with groups. She would sit with the group, make herself available for Assurbanipal, and he would begin sending her thought forms and pictures. These were interpreted through her voice, but her accent, intonation, mannerisms, and affect were obviously those of someone other than herself. Unfailingly, once Assurbanipal 'arrived' participants in the group felt that they were interacting with someone other than Avril. Unfortunately since she hadn't yet begun to audio-record group sessions, we have no verbatim access to Assurbanipal's wisdom and insights.

AVRIL
Assurbanipal arrives. More training

February 1994 : It was one of those memorable moments. Standing there gazing out the window, my hands in warm dishwater. A flash image. A still-life photo image. A distinctive, colour image. So clear, it could have actually been a photo. Brought a smile and a warm feeling when I saw it. I held the feeling for a while because it was so pleasant. Then let it go. But the next day, doing the washing up, there it was again. Same feeling, same image. I closed my eyes and looked straight at it and seemed to be seeing it for the first time. It reminded me of another photo. After our work at Somerton on the day of the St Michael healing, we stood grinning for the camera. In the true photo our bedraggled figures stared back at me. Captured there the very way we looked. Pleased? Proud? Relieved? Silly? I couldn't tell. Maybe all of those. But the people in this other image, the one behind my eyes, although strangely similar to the actual photo, were *not* the group from Somerton. Not a group I'd ever seen together all in one place before. I gazed even more intently at the faces. They stared back at me. Not our faces but the Knights of the Round Table! Standing in that picture, all the men I'd been meeting, all smiled sheepishly back at me. As if they too felt the craziness of such a juxtaposition. Smiling, "Knights of the Round Table? Not us." Smiling the conspiracy "We're crazy. You're crazy. We're *all* crazy." Crazy as if they had read my mind. Read there the momentary surfacing of the odd suggestion. As if the thought I'd had, as if the suggestion, were some sort of conspiracy. Not surreptitious-plot-up-to-no-good conspiracy. Not even prank-meant-as-a-joke-tomfoolery conspiracy. But conspiracy as if offering opportunity and excitement, mystery and maybe a little intrigue. And recognising within myself an eye-widening feeling, a heart-skipping feeling, a kind of joyful nudging feeling of 'Why not?'

Didn't know at first exactly what 'Why not?' was all about. Nudged its way into my consciousness from out of nowhere so easily it might have always been there. Get them all together. All in one place. Celebrate. Strange word, jollity. But it fits. As if that's what we're to do. I'm to arrange a celebration of jollity in which we all participate. I let the feeling fill me for a moment. It seeped in around all the edges and filled me with unbounded joy. Totally unreasonable. Unreasonable because it wasn't only about those of us who had been involved at Somerton. That would be easy. More difficult the photo I was seeing. That photo, the Knights of the Round Table, included all these different men I've been meeting. We all stood together as if in one place at the same time. *That's* what I was staring at! The idea of it! Bring them all together? In one place? What a wildly romantic idea! The more I thought about it, the more fun it seemed. None of them is 'the one.' But I love them all dearly each in his own way. Why not bring them all together? Have a holiday. But I dismissed it. At first because it is so outrageous. I know and love each of them, but they know nothing of each other. Why would they even consider such a thing? Dismissed it. Totally.

Only to have it back again. I recognise the feeling. Am I getting used to it? The prompting of another thing I need to do? It's that 'knowing' that I'm beginning to accept as normal. Even something as abnormal as this can, with that knowing, seem normal sometimes. Explored it, toyed with it, expanded it, moved it around here and there. Saw it unfolding. Imagined the where and the when and the how of it. Then after the fun of it for a while, tried again to put it from my mind and forget it. But it wouldn't go away. Finally I've given in. It's crazy but I think I'm supposed to do it so I'll do it. And there is a sense of pleasure in it. I think I would enjoy it.

To act on it before I change my mind I called an astrologer. He looked at my chart and chose the date. November 8, 1994. I found a B&B in Porlock, Somerset. They've given me a good rate. I've written to the core group. The people who have been involved from the beginning. And I've written to all the men. Almost begin to feel normal, these little urges I get. Like this one. What an outrageous idea. And yet on some level it's not at all strange. It's just - well - normal? I wonder what this is all about.

May 1994: Most unsettling. I should be used to these things. I knew he was coming. Didn't know he was 'one', but he had rung up so I was expecting him. But only as a client. Not as 'another one.' Working in the kitchen I felt the nudge to go and look out of the front window. Dishcloth in hand I followed the order. I'm beginning to think of the nudges as 'orders.' Not that I don't have complete choice in the matter. But there is the curiosity. When the nudge comes, I always wonder. Maybe like a child going to the circus. What's going to happen next?

The Clew

There's a little feeling like 'Oh good, here we go again. What excitement will this bring?' Will I ever change? Will I ever turn away from it? Be content without having to know what's behind the feeling? So anyway, standing looking out from my front window I see a man on a bicycle. Not time for my client to arrive yet. Half an hour early. And yet with sinking heart, I knew. 'Oh dear God not him!' I remember thinking. 'Oh please not this one!'

It was very clear. Except that like so many other things already I had no idea why I so adamantly didn't want it to be him. Or who 'him' was. Did I mean I didn't want him to be a client? Didn't want to do a reading for him? The depth of the feeling was inexplicable. True, there was a dishevelled look about him. He stopped there, his bike still braced between his legs, and he hunched over intensely studying something in his hands. It's true he didn't look like someone with whom I would have anything in common, but it was more than that. It was something else. I couldn't explain it. Not sure I can even now. A little more understanding now, perhaps, of the feeling. Or perhaps even less understanding. I don't know.

He was coming for a reading. Simple. Nothing more. Should have been so easy. But nothing ever is these days. Not when that feeling surfaces. So now I have a house guest. He certainly in *no way* qualifies as 'the one.' But here he is. He had already made his decision. When he called for his appointment he asked to have a question answered. Go to India and live the rest of his life in an ashram or buy a computer and support himself doing astrological readings? He needed to decide. Choose between the two. But by the time his appointment with me approached, he had already decided, so why the journey? Why the train ride with his bicycle? And why is he now my house guest? Should have sent him to the ashram maybe? Didn't do the reading during the scheduled time. Just talked. Like picking up where we'd left off - except that we never left off. I never saw him before. And yet, there was that familiarity. So familiar now, that strange familiarity with these strangers who turn out not to be strangers.

Then Joy and Bernard for dinner and I spilled the coffee on him - on Ian. In a panic certainly not warranted by a little coffee, Joy jumped up and practically shouted, "Stop! You have to put this right! Ian, will you do exactly as I say, right now?" There was something else, it was as if something else was going on. I don't know if I actually thought those words at the time, but even then I sensed what ever was going on wasn't about spilled coffee. Ian playing the part of the polite guest agreed to do as Joy asked. She ordered him, insisted urgently that he turn to me and say "I forgive you." For spilling a little coffee? A bit dramatic, I thought. Ian did as commanded. No sooner had he uttered the words than Joy asked if he meant it. Yes, meekly. Only then did she explain. I don't know if I believe her. Will I ever know what I believe? How could she know? Even after all the times I've seen her dowse energy and create ritual in our healing ceremonies. Even after the times I've been reassured by the entities that she really does know these things, that she really does have these abilities. When she says something like "He was your son and you killed him," it's still difficult to know what to believe.

And the next day. When he sat in on my reading for another client. I never let anyone sit in on a reading. Why Ian? I began the reading and he began commenting. Things like, 'That's Saturn in Capricorn.' I stared at him dumbfounded by the realisation. Astrology. All the references to the stars! Astrology! They'd been trying so hard, Ashad, Assurbanipal, they'd been trying to show me, give me the impressions for astrology! They must have been very, very desperate to send me help in the form of someone I'd killed in a past life! Maybe their idea of a well deserved prank. It's not going to be pleasant, working with this one. We'll see eye to eye even less than Patrick and I did. Well, well.

IAN
After four years in the wilderness

In April of 1990 I was back in university taking an M.Sc in Organisational Development. At this time my approach to life was no-nonsense and concrete; I simply possessed a materialistic paradigm and a psychological interest in people. The philosophy of the course was one of 'deconstruct and reconstruct'; as part of the deconstruction phase I was assigned an essay to define truth in 2,000 words. Unable to appreciate, or even see, the irony of trying to define truth in *any* number of words, I dutifully went into the library. And never came out. Although the assignment was successful in the 'deconstruction' phase, the reconstruction took a form perhaps not intended by the MSc programme. In the library I discovered a fascinating world I had never known existed. I discovered Buddhism. And Yoga. I discovered the Qabalah and astrology and tarot. I discovered the mystery schools and the world of the occult. And whatever world I had known previously ceased to have much relevance for me. It was an exciting, magical, shocking time, an awakening. But it was also the beginning of my four-year dark night of the soul. It would be years before I learned the coincidental nature of the date: four years before I met Avril, and longer before I learned that a similar change in her life also began in April 1990.

The more I studied the subjects I was discovering, the more difficult it was for me to integrate myself into society. The philosophies, belief structures, the ancient truths I was finding seemed incompatible with the world as I had always known it. Here was a world which resonated with me in a way nothing else before had, a world strangely familiar and more true than any truth I had previously been taught. But two years into the search I was less and less able to integrate myself into any semblance of normal life. I simply couldn't reconcile these new found truths with the way I saw life being lived around me. I found myself desperately searching for some way to live a meaningful life without giving up the spiritual growth which now seemed of utmost importance.

At this time I was shocked to the very core by three incidents of what I can only call precognition. The three successive incidents strained my concept of reality to the breaking point. In the first incident, days before it actually happened, I 'saw' the Amsterdam plane crash of 1992. I saw the plane coming in at an angle. I saw it heading for the high-rise buildings. It was surreal and I didn't know what it was about, but in my mind's eye, it was very, very real. Within days I watched it on TV. It was difficult enough to realise I had known about the crash

The Clew

days before it happened, but watching TV and seeing the computer simulation of the crash was extremely unsettling. It was exactly as I had seen it days before it happened. The second incident was a similar crash in Nepal. Again, prior to it's actual occurrence, I 'saw' the plane crash. This was only mentioned briefly on the news but it was enough. I knew that I had seen this very incident days before it happened. The last incident was closer to home. I saw a caravan in a woodland. I saw police crouched down hiding. I knew it was a drug raid. I innocently mentioned this dream to my girlfriend's brother who responded by saying that he knew exactly where it was and who the people were and, subsequently, went to warn them. He was not believed and within two days the caravan was raided by the police. After this, he left me a note describing the incident.

I can only describe what happened when I found the note as an emotional break up. I felt I was being singled out. Something was trying to get my attention. Trying to tell me something but what it was, what it was about, and what I was supposed to make of it were a complete mystery. Reading and studying about realities with which I was unfamiliar in no way prepared me for experiencing something like this in my own life. Such massive precognition had no place even in my new reality. I didn't know what to do with it. I left the house and walked to the bottom of the garden in a daze. I sat on the wall, reached to the sky and beseeched whatever might hear, "What do you want of me?" The question came from the very depths of my being. I truly felt lost and unable to relate to life in any meaningful way. I was truly at the end of my tether. I needed help and knew instinctively the help I needed could only come from one place. I don't exactly know what happened next. It felt like something gave me a powerful shove in the back and I ended up flat on my back, spreadeagled under an ash tree. My arms and feet felt totally earthed to the ground. The clear night gave me a panoramic view of all the stars in the heavens. I felt energy begin in my feet and come right up through all my chakras. It was a feeling unlike anything I had ever known, more precious and unimaginably more beautiful than anything I had ever experienced. I was in total bliss for forty-five minutes. Even in the cold October night wearing no outdoor clothing, I was boiling.

The answer to my question 'what do you want of me' seemed to come in a sudden obsession with astrology. I had frequently asked an acquaintance to do my chart. She never found the time. Even before this incident I'd had a deep desire, a burning need to find a way to integrate myself, with my newly discovered truths, into society. On my own I wasn't managing it very well, and I thought perhaps a reading would hold the answer. Following this incident I decided to do my own chart. Once I began there was no turning back; I became obsessed with studying her astrology books. I compulsively devoured every astrology book I could get my hands on. Nothing else in life seemed to have any importance or relevance what-so-ever. My focus was total and totally one pointed. I didn't seem to be learning so much as I was somehow remembering something I had already known and forgotten. And from my point of view, it didn't seem that I could remember fast enough. I realise now that I learned as much about astrology in the next six months as a normal person studying would learn in ten years. I say that not boastfully but as a simple matter of fact. I seemed to have no choice in the matter. I was driven. Some force within me, something almost foreign to me, drove me on. For six months I did *nothing* but study astrology. With the knowledge I have since acquired I can see that there was a window. Within my chart, astrologically, there was a very short period during which I would be able to learn, to receive the information I was being given. Unknown to me at the time I had a very short period of time in which I was being prepared for the work I was to do with Avril and the group. I had asked what was wanted of me, and although I didn't yet realise it, I had been given an answer.

Although I was given a leaflet of Avril's about this time, it was to be eighteen months before I actually followed a friend's advice and contacted her. I was still trying to find a way to live my spiritual truth within society but it was more and more difficult for me. I had saved enough money to get to India and thought perhaps I should go and live in an ashram and stop trying to fit into any normal life. The money I had saved would also purchase a computer so that I could do astrological readings. I was torn between the two and couldn't decide which to do. It was at this time that I opened a book and the leaflet I had been given earlier fell to the floor. Perhaps Avril could do a reading and help me decide. I scheduled a reading for one week in the future, but by that date had already decided to purchase the computer. I don't know exactly what prompted me to make the journey anyway, to set off to see her even though I had answered the question I was supposedly to ask her.

I had directions to her house but didn't look at them until I had ridden well into her town. The first time I stopped to read the map I found I had stopped in front of her house. Meeting Avril was unusual. I don't usually relate to people the way I related to her. We began talking as if we had only left off last week but we hadn't actually seen each other before in this lifetime. Since I had already answered the question I thought I had come to ask, I mentioned my curiosity about why I was there. We talked for hours and never found time to do the reading. I was surprised later in the evening by Joy's assertion that Avril and I had past life karma to work through. This was a new dimension of experience for me, not the idea of past life karma, but brushing up against what might be my own. I embraced it as a form of higher consciousness I was beginning to spiral into.

Before Avril and I actually found time to do my reading, I sat in on a reading she did for another client. I was very excited to find I could interpret what she was getting on many levels; astrology, numerology, Qabalah, tarot. Following the reading, Avril shared some of her first channelled material with me. I immediately realised that I was to have a part in the work she was being directed to do. For four years I had been floundering in the wilderness of my dark night, and here in one day I was being given guide and task. I thought at last I had the answer to 'what do you want of me?' It was a feeling of enrichment, excitement, and peace all at the same time.

But a further surprise awaited. Avril explained that during the reading she was about to do for me she would be tuning in to my own guide. From previous experiences I was familiar with him and knew he was a Tibetan monk. The energy present when Avril began the reading was not my guide's. It was Azzie, Avril's

Assurbanipal. I recognised him immediately. Or rather I recognised his energy. I'm not sure that I could have immediately said who he was. I felt a great love for him, as I would have toward someone who felt a fatherly affection for me. I knew I had been his student. He had taught me the astrology I was remembering. He confirmed that I had practiced astrology. I had once been a royal astrologer in Babylon.

After this reading Avril and I felt that we were to work together and for the next nine months, on a weekly basis, she sat to allow Azzie to answer my questions about astrology. It was a frustrating time because she had no concept of astrology and frequently couldn't understand my questions or Azzie's answers. There were many reasons why, on a personal level, Avril and I would have preferred not to work together. She found it very difficult to find the words to explain the information she was getting in response to my questions. I was frustrated and impatient with what seemed her inept attempts. We only continued because we knew we wouldn't get the information we both needed and wanted if we didn't. We endured the friction of our daily personal lives because the result of our combined work was greater than either of us working separately, and because of some deep affection we both acknowledged, and which held us together even at the most difficult times.

AVRIL
Accepts the responsibility

May 1994: The accommodation in Porlock cancelled. It's been leased out, of all things! Thought it meant I had it wrong, that I wasn't supposed to do it after all. My outrageous meeting with all the men. Thought I had misread the nudge. Misinterpreted the feelings. After all, why would all these men, any of these men, none of whom had any knowledge of each other prior to meeting me - all of whom have some rather indescribable relationship with me - why would they want to travel across country, continent, and ocean for some uncertain and perhaps even elusive jollity. The idea is simply too absurd. Smiles and imagery have played see-saw with reason for days. For weeks. I have repeatedly dismissed it. It won't be dismissed.

So many absurd, unlikely, unbelievable, delightful, magical events have unfolded since I began. Am I used to it all? And yet the experiences, the messages, the entities come only with my free will, my free choice. Only with complete trust and acceptance. I can look back and see that the magic happens only when I consciously make a decision and then simply trust the process to unfold in the appropriate way. If and when I manage that, synchronicities evolve. Unfathomable, the beauty of it all. The inspiration. The growth. It's simple. And incomprehensible. I know I will be guided. At least, if nothing else, I have learned that. And so with Porlock I decided to wait. Let the whole dilemma sit there to see what would evolve. Because there's the second chance. The other thing I've learned, I always get a second chance. It's as if they know my indecision and step in to give me nudges and hints toward the windows of opportunity hidden in the

The Clew

choices. Not exactly fate. More like gifts set in my path. I can see or ignore. I can open the gift or step over it. But if it's a particularly precious, beautiful and appropriate gift, they seem always to find a way of putting it in the middle of my path again later so that I have another chance at it. Not that they are going to insist on anything. But being the loving entities they are, they don't want me to miss out on anything either. They honour my choices, but always give me another chance. Give me a chance to reconsider the choice and find the gift within. And so I waited, to see about Porlock and the men.

And when I thought it was finally decided, out of my hands, coincidence found another place, same date, same rates. Another nudge? A confirmation? But the strangest thing, the strangest coincidence came later. Not at first when I actually saw the sign to the Blackdown Rings. On the way to check out the accommodation, I drove by the sign. Noticing it jogged my memory. Another nudge but I couldn't remember. Something about it seemed familiar. And then Ian asked to see the first material I had received. As I began reading it, the words blazed themselves more deeply into my psyche than they ever had before ... *the men must walk if it is to be saved*. I'd typed that four years ago in the very first message I received. The words ... *There are circles within circles that must be crossed in a spiralling movement* followed two months later in the very next message. The men - my men - the ones I've been recognising. Circles within circles - the Blackdown Rings.

Unable at first to decipher the implications, my brain dulled as my body reacted. It chilled, then prickled. Seemed heavy, then light. It smiled with excitement and simultaneously gasped in disbelief. No picnic, this. No lark. Up to that minute, it had *seemed* a lark. A treasure hunt with clues to be deciphered. With a few important events to heal the energy at ancient sites it had *seemed* all fun and games. Had *seemed* some rather circuitous method of answering my perennial question 'is this the one?' As I read my typed words yet again, *that* reality fast evaporated. Less and less a personal game of light-hearted intrigue played for trifling stakes.

I stared at Ian. For the very first time I began to sense a feeling of awesome responsibility. Gilbert and Sullivan had turned into Wagner. The photo-image. Seeing it turn into the Knights of the Round Table. I remember thinking it might be a delusion of grandeur. But thinking that - would be an excuse. A way out. Easier maybe, to think of it that way. Less frightening. No responsibility. But it's not a delusion. Fear and trepidation. Do I still I hesitate? I can't do it - can I? One moment the recognition - of what I'm being asked to do. The next moment, instantaneously the doubt, the automatic, negative, fearful response.

With the hesitation, the doubt, is the simultaneous knowledge that not only can I, but I will do what is being asked. Not sure exactly what is being asked but whatever it is, it's another of the choices. Will I choose to continue? Or will I refuse and bring everything to a stop? One reality or the other. The reality until now a lark, a romp, good fun. An operetta. It changes. No, my understanding changes. Serious. There's responsibility. Obligation. Things can go wrong. Might I mess up? If I don't pay attention, might I get it wrong? Make mistakes? I can take it seriously, be an accomplice in this work, help toward the accomplishment

The Clew

of the tasks we're given. Or I can choose not to. And someone else will be offered the chance to complete the work instead. Because the work won't stop. This is my realisation. The work won't stop. My refusal anywhere along the way won't stop the work. It will only stop my part in it. I willingly began, I have continued up to now. This is another of those places where I am being given the opportunity to choose again. Am I going to continue? Am I going to, for whatever reason, bring these people together - all in one place? Or am I going to bow out? And let someone else be given the chance? The decision is mine. It's simply a choice. To think it a delusion of grandeur would be a simple excuse. Avoidance. I thought it decided with the cancellation at Porlock. Must think again with this coincidental manifestation of Blackdown Rings.

I will do it. I reaffirm my willingness to continue. Bring them all together as asked. There is the curiosity of it, the excitement and mystery of it. And, I'm almost ashamed to say, the shear audacity of it. But is that enough? Is that the right reason to do it? I wonder what will happen if I do all the right things for all the wrong reasons.

A footnote: Ian realised he's one of the men. When I read the sentence that the men must walk if all is to be saved, Ian knew he is one of the men. It's confirmation. It helps having him along. Neither of us knows what is to be saved or what is to be walked.

Chapter Nine

AVRIL
The Devon Rings

October 1994 : It began with re-reading the earliest typed material and realising that bringing the men together isn't just for fun. It began with the increasing difficulty of trying to see the whole thing as some escapade, some romantic idea, some drama I can help orchestrate. It began. The doubts. The uncertainty. What part is coincidence that I'm supposed to pay attention to, supposed to be guided by, and what's my imagination? The cancellation at Porlock. Coincidence? The feeling I had when I saw the sign for the Blackdown Rings. Coincidence? Or my imagination? It felt significant. I'm learning to trust the nudges. All along, from the very beginning, it's as if I've been in training to trust the nudges. Trust my intuition. It's as if I've been enrolled on a 'Trust Your Intuition' course. Or am I only getting used to self delusion? Many people *are* coming forward. I must interpret that to mean something. Friends of friends of friends. Messages for us. For me. Things we're supposed to do. Rituals. Still, it's different this time. When we did the Michael Line, we were given specific instructions. This time it seems to be more about trusting our intuition. Getting information from other sources, trusting it. The encouragement to trust intuition didn't begin with the rereading or with the cancellation. But it does feel more imperative this time.

In the beginning, four years ago when all this began, I had to learn to trust the words. That they were a message and not my imagination. That they truly were telling us something to do. Easier, that trust, than this. Is this the next level? Trusting intuition? Learning to distinguish not between words, pictures and thought impressions, but between *intuition* and imagination? If it is, that's more difficult. Is it about learning to discern which feelings are from fear and doubt and which truly are intuition and truth from a level beyond what I'm used to? I don't know. I have this feeling that I'm supposed to bring these people together, that we're to do something. I had the feeling, when I saw the sign for the Black Down rings that it had something to do with that place. But if it is to come together, it will be the collaborative effort of many people, some of whom won't even be involved. Very different this level of trust, this demand for intuitive response. About giving up control? How do I distinguish between giving up control and avoiding responsibility?

Ian is a help. So is Joy. As are the others who aren't really involved but for no apparent reason will share things they are sensing about what is to happen. Ian has decided the exact time based on the location and the position of the planets. Different people in various ways are describing the rituals. Interesting that I don't get that kind of information. As if I'm to manage the place and bring people together. As if I'm some sort of coordinator through whom the information all flows. The one to see that it all comes together. But others figure out and plan the rituals. I have always had to trust others for that. So why should this be different? Because it's taking so much more trust this time. Perhaps because I feel so responsible. For suggesting all these people come from so many different places and some from so far away. What if I'm wrong? What if what I think is trust in intuition is simply being silly? What if I'm simply imagining things? Then what happens with all these people I've brought together at great personal expense to each? Is it growing any easier to recognise the knowing? Sometimes it is. Sometimes it's not and then the doubts pile in.

I seem to have memories of past lives with so many of the men involved. But if they don't have the same memories, which they don't all have, how will all this effect them? And how are they all going to interact with each other? What will everyone make of it? It's very difficult. I must simply concentrate on the work to be done. Trust it will work out. If this is larger than I can comprehend, which it feels it is, then I must simply trust. Trust others to contribute when necessary. I'm not even sure who is able to come. One or two will be coming whom I don't know well at all - others have suggested they should be there. Suggested they have some part in it. So those, relatively unknowns, will be present in addition to everyone else. Patrick won't be there. Difficult without him. Well if it's meant to be, it will happen. The difficult part is trusting. I simply *must* learn to trust.

November 1994 : Circles within circles crossed in a spiralling movement. It was about that. And the men must walk if it is to be saved. About that also although I'm not quite clear even yet what that means. And yet, it was about more than either of those. Healing the earth, but healing our karma too. The blow I'd felt when I first saw Patrick. A blow as if to the pineal area of my forehead. Finally it makes sense. And the men I hadn't met who came for some of our time together. It was about them too. Since Joy couldn't come until late in the week, she and I met before I left for Devon. She immediately sensed something was wrong. Finally realised there had been a lifetime in common. Together, all of us, in Egypt. In that lifetime the men were conducting experiments to find and isolate the function of the pineal gland. Used me because I was what was known as 'a sensitive.' In their research I had been misused and harmed. Joy strongly advised a healing, said it was necessary prior to any work we undertook together. She said they must each ask my forgiveness. That there must be a ritual for healing the injury they had inflicted. Ian agreed to plan the ritual. Patrick was unexpectedly able to join us. There have been so many coincidences, one more shouldn't seem strange. Ian asked Patrick to bring yellow flowers.

Sunday evening they assembled in a room with Ian. And I waited, nervously trying to trust. Would it be a wedge between us? Would it be silly and meaningless? Or would something enriching and meaningful come from the ceremony Ian was orchestrating? He seems to have some sixth sense about all of this. Strange this is his first experience with us and yet it's as if he takes it more seriously than I do. As if he knows things about all of it that I don't. As if he believes in it in a way I haven't managed. Perhaps it's the astrology. He seems able to see things, to put things together that don't readily make sense to me. For all our differences and difficulties, he does surprise me. As with his willingness to guide the ritual Sunday evening. It seemed a long time before he finally motioned me into the room.

The Clew

They stood in a circle, the men, each holding his yellow flower. Had I expected to see my own sheepishness reflected back to me? It wasn't. Ian again, motioning me to the centre. They stood, each of them, each of the men, stood relaxed and at ease. But serious too. Intent and responsive. Consciously I slowed my shallow breathing. To my surprise the circle radiated calm. Reassured somewhat I eased into the moment and felt the energy. For their parts, they all stood calmly relaxed and seemingly ready for whatever was to unfold. A relief to sense no hesitation or reluctance. As if they knew and accepted exactly what was going to happen. Standing for a few moments, all of us in silence, I began to relax.

Then, simply, with no ceremony, they began. Mike, young enough to be my son, the youngest of the group, "If I have in the past done anything that gave you harm, then I am sincerely sorry and ask your forgiveness." The energy changed. In that moment, with those words, the tone of his voice, the courtesy, sincerity, earnestness visible in his intent, the energy in the room changed. No longer a simple room, a circle of men each holding a single flower. Became somehow a holy place, a privileged place. Each man came forward, gave me his flower, and spoke simply. Earnestly and sincere. I was the centre of attention for a moment only. Then it changed. I was no longer the centre, but simply the place where each momentarily focused. Searching for the words, each one within himself, searching for something ... I don't know exactly. Love that finally let go the particular sorrow each had known too long? A self forgiveness that had nothing to do with me? Did they know? Did they sense it too? That it was about them, not me?

Was it love that felt so thick? And what kind of love is this? Is that what I discovered? Was that my part of it? To realise that whatever connected us in that room, love or compassion or whatever it was, is thick? There was something present that made the air feel almost solid. But not solid. Rubbery. But not rubbery. Just thick. Difficult to breathe it in. As if you'll burst into ... something. So you breathe very carefully. It unfolded in slow motion. As if it ... sparkled? A different reality. And this strange kind of love. Not romantic. All these men I love. But how do I love them? And do they ... no, not *do* they, *how* do they love me?

She was right. Joy. About the ritual. Not because of the forgiveness. Not because they needed me to forgive them. I couldn't. They had to do that for themselves. Whatever sorrow they had, whatever regret, known or unknown, remembered or in some far ancient past forgotten, seems it didn't matter. It had to be let go. Not sure I knew all that on Sunday evening. Too much happening all at once. No time to reflect. But now, now I think that's what it was. That's what was happening. Reflecting on it now I wonder if there was anything, anything at all, any of them could have done - alone or together - in that lifetime in Egypt or in any other, to harm me. Could they harm me? Can anyone do anything to truly harm another? Or can we only harm ourselves? It passes. The experience, the mood, that reality, it passes. And I'm not sure of the answer.

Monday already we were coming together. Some bond existed between us. Or perhaps we were only creating the bond anew. But my concern and feeling of responsibility for our interaction lessened. We found joy in each other's presence. Monday we would survey the site together. Spend time dowsing the circles.

The Clew

Explore. Leave ourselves open to guidance. We knew some things but not enough. We had been given bits and pieces of advice by different people, but we had no idea of the whole. We had vague ideas but not particulars. Have come to know that intuition is often enough a last minute thing, and so we continued. Not knowing for sure what we were continuing beyond turning up and trusting, we continued. By traipsing up to the site. Dark and cold and wet November Monday.

We would dowse the site. The two Johns and William. And Patrick. So many different times, in so many different ways Patrick, "You don't need me. I don't know why I'm here." And as we neared the site more and more doubting, "You'll be all right, won't you? If there's nothing there, if I don't find anything, you'll be all right, won't you?"

Patrick and William walking around, each with his pendulum at the ready. Patrick still uncertain of what he would find.. Then straightening, unexpectedly, eyes alight with disbelief. "Oh." More interest but stopping short of eagerness. Then finally, unable to contain himself, "Avril! Avril! It's here. There's something here!" How quickly from doubter to confirmed believer. Steadily he worked. Slowly and methodically. Then with doubt and mystification. Re-doing parts he'd already done. Jubilant smile turned again to doubting frown. Angry mutterings spaced between pauses, "It's not a circle." "I can't keep track of it. It goes crazy." "There's too much of it." Finally, doubtful or jubilant I'm not sure which and maybe he wasn't sure either, " It's not a circle. It's a spiral!" Circles within circles. Of course.

Steadily, slowly, meticulously he continued. Then asked for something to mark it. Couldn't keep track of it he said. Kept losing it. The gravel in the parking lot. A tarpaulin in the boot of someone's car. Loaded with the small stones, we dragged it to Patrick's spiral. Little stones soon telling a story of their own. They wound, or unwound, in beautiful symmetry speaking a mystery ancient in origin, purpose unfathomable. Transfixed we stood, spellbound. Alone in some reality we couldn't yet enter, Patrick walked, pendulum swinging it's message. Intent, we followed, dropping small white stones. Unaware of time, place, damp, cold, hunger, or fatigue we watched the spiral emerge. Finally, straightening, Patrick looked at the stones, then at us. We stood in awe.

Patrick, slowly walking the perimeter, "It's flopped. The energy is …", his brow quizzically furrowed as if searching out the right word, " … poorly." Indeed. Well, by ourselves we found it. With co-operation, by each contributing our particular bit, with only the most minimum of instructions, we'd found it. By trusting intuition. At the last moment. By continuing when we didn't know what we were continuing, we'd found it. But what to do with it? More trusting. Before we had that answer, more trusting, more intuition, and more … continuing.

And so we continued. Not yet four in the afternoon, the sun already setting, cold, tired, hungry. But our spiral teased, and so we stayed. The magical shape, somehow more present and real than imaginable, beckoned. At that moment, to give our spiral the simple reassurance that we would return tomorrow and 'do something' seemed rather like a hollow promise. Did the spiral need what unfolded next, or did we?

Solemnly we gathered outside one of the openings in the circled earthen

The Clew

bank: the west gate. I wonder if anyone will ever know the significance of what we did next. Although it unfolded naturally and felt comfortable, we are still unsure of any of its meaning. As we began, the geese came. A perfect wedge-shaped 'V', sounding an occasional honk. "The sign of Venus" Ian said. Feminine energy. Was this our sign? The women and I entered the west gate, single file, walked to the spiral, and walked around its perimeter. Each of the other women then took up a place on the quarter circle about six feet outside the spiral, still well inside the earthen banked circle. I walked to the east gate and waited for the men to enter from the west, also single file. The men mirrored the women's positions close to the outside circle of the spiral.

Ian, who had remained at the west gate, ceremoniously 'closed' the space between the earthen banks and walked to join me. He walked slowly in front of the women, behind the men, around the inward-circling white pebbles. Uncannily like the standing stones of other circles we'd worked in, human bodies loomed tall over the flat, white spiral. Arriving where I waited at the eastern gap in the earthen circle, Ian turned to face the others. As he did so the men chanted together, three times, 'Aauum.' Did I only imagine the resonance? Certainly no sound echoed off the mounds of the earthen enclosure. Did the men actually wait each time for the non-existent echo to fade before beginning the next 'AAAAAUUMMM'? Twice their silence before repeating the sound. And then the final silence, uncanny in its depth. I turned and made my way back to the spiral, walked single file picking up each of the men behind me, then each of the women, then in inexplicable solemnity, out again through the west gap. Ian ceremoniously pantomimed closing a gate. We faced the 'gate,' the enclosure, the spiral in silence. They'd been 'holding' the energy, the women said. Holding the space. Said they could actually feel the energy flow. They felt they were somehow making the whole place safe for whatever work the men were to do.

Whatever the men were to do would have to wait until tomorrow. It was dark, the geese had flown, the magic moved aside. A reality that included cold, fatigue and hunger was beginning to vie for attention.

The next morning. Candles in jam jars stood ready. Light, symbolic of cleansing - and for safety. Women placing candles, protecting space. Ian plotted the exact moment of sunrise. And the degrees of the quarters of the circle by solstice and equinox. He paired the men by birthday. Magic that their birthdays fell two to each quarter? Eight men, four pairs. The quarters of the circle plotted, each pair to stand in the quarter of their birth. We were ready.

Sunrise in November in northern latitudes takes its time. But the chill wind, the cold darkness of the not yet dawn failed to dampen our spirits. With jam jars, candles, dry matches, and anticipation, we were ready. Knowing our spiral waited, we followed the beams of our torches. Only just managing to keep their candles burning in the stiff November wind, the women slowly filed through the west 'gate.' Each found her position of the day before and stood at the ready - our signal. I entered followed single file by Ian, the four pairs of men, and finally, John. The men halted, Ian and I walked to the centre of the spiral and stood side by side. The men then took their paired positions and walked, followed by John, to the perimeter of the spiral. Each pair stood on the quarter representing the season of the year in which the day of their birth occurred.

As John walked the spiral to join Ian and me in the centre, the wind got up. Remembering the old tale about invoking the wind for sailors by walking the spiral, or calming the wind by the same means, I glanced at John. From the beginning, John and Heather. From the beginning, watching the sky, interpreting the clouds. From the beginning a part of all these moments. He sensed it too. I knew he had sensed it too. It added to my sense of awe.

Circles within circles that must be crossed in a spiralling movement ... We had decided that each pair would join hands and, rather in barn-dance fashion, circle around each other as they 'crossed' the pebbles marking the spiral. We knew there was a precedent for this kind of dancing in rituals, festivals, and ceremonies but it was usually women who danced in this fashion. This time it was the men. The men joined the three of us and we formed a line from north to south, five men on either side of me. *Carry oak leaves, hold hands, wait for sunrise ...* Ian calculated the exact moment of sunrise, good because it was overcast and gloomy. At the moment of sunrise we would raise our hands in unison. Heather faced our line with stopwatch ready to signal the exact moment. We stood holding hands waiting. Amazing. The hawk. At the exact moment Heather gestured her signal, the hawk flew straight up behind her and hovered, absolutely still but for the motion required to keep his place. Clasping each others' hands above our heads we stared at the hawk transfixed. Heather, riveted to her own spot by our pinpoint of concentration but unable to see the hawk, seemed to hold her breath in anticipation. Our arms tired. The hawk hovered looking not to the ground for some unfortunate mouse, but straight at us. With effort we held our arms steady while still the hawk kept it's vigil. Maybe two minutes. Then it dived straight to the ground and disappeared. As if on cue we too dropped our arms and, pivoting around me in a straight line, the men turned a 360 degree circle.

Patrick, his ears always his validation, shouted softly, "I can hear it! It's starting." Like a generator he said. Like a large generator starting up. I led the men out, single file. The other women, following us out, stopped at the gate momentarily before beginning their walk around the enclosure. Ten minutes we listened to their voices. Singing, chanting, first fading and then returning in a soft, slow crescendo in the growing light. Their circle completed, they turned back to face our pebbled spiral, joined hands in lifted salute, hugged each other, then turned back to us and walked out through the 'gate' opening in the embankment. We had finished. Whatever our part in this unfolding drama and whether or not we had succeeded or even had done as asked, our attempt had been sincere. And now we'd finished.

JOHN
On a mission

On a day to day basis I am careful about what I discuss and with whom. It was really a relief to know that in Devon, I could relax in the knowledge that there was nothing we could discuss that would either be taken the wrong way, or would frighten people unfamiliar with esoteric subjects. I felt a strange sense of 'family' amongst a diverse group of people, most of whom had not met before and who were not sure what they were there to do or what they could contribute.

From the time we first knew we were going to Devon, I had a feeling of impatience to continue our earlier work and a return of a strong sense of being on a 'mission.' Now we have finished, I have a sense of accomplishment, but also one of disappointment that four years of work culminating in this week is apparently finished.

Considering how extraordinary the whole event was, I was surprised that no-one expressed concern or fear about what we were doing or what we were getting into. No one wanted to do things a different way or to back out, even though we were not clear about the details of what we were going to do almost until the moment we did it! We were definitely all tuned to the same channel, if not the same wavelength.

After the ceremony with Avril on Sunday night, the centre of both my hands became extremely hot. I tried for some time to cool them, putting them under the pillow, on the walls, anywhere that might reduce their temperature. After many attempts I finally managed to fall asleep.

On Monday both Heather and I monitored the sky during the construction of the circle and spiral. We noted the huge pair of eyes in the clouds watching us, and the cloak that spread across us as we worked.

Assurbanipal had said on Sunday night that we all had a contribution to make. During the construction on Monday I assumed that mine, as a Virgo, would be to help ensure the accuracy of the marking out of the circle, spiral and all the gates, small circles and other phenomena we found.

As the men walked into the circle at sunset, I was aware of the geese flying past the site, and of the singing coming from the South near the ramparts at the edge of the site. The singing stopped when I looked toward it.

After our discussion in the evening, when it became clear that the numbers had changed and that I was now to walk the circle and the spiral we had constructed, I felt very much a part of the team. I felt comfortable that I would not be walking alone and that should I make mistakes or miscalculations they would be corrected or allowed for, as they had been for us at other events. I thought I would not be able to sleep for worrying about what I had to do and the responsibility involved. But I was unusually relaxed and slept well.

On Tuesday I was clear about what I had to do and felt very purposeful. I was aware of a sense of calm and quiet as I walked the two circuits around the circle. I experienced a sense of expectation as I paused before beginning to spiral into the centre. As I proceeded I was aware of the wind rising as I completed each circuit of the spiral, and of it falling again as I started a new circuit. Near the end of their walk around the enclosure, when I could hear the women singing but not yet see them, I felt very moved. This feeling grew as they faced the circle holding hands, and especially at the end when they hugged each other.

Heather and I needed to leave early and the group held a special 'leaving ceremony' for us. This too was very moving. I could feel an energy circling the group as we all chanted 'Auum." I found myself quite emotional and unable to chant. I felt within the group a strong sense of family. The feelings of connectedness stayed with me throughout the drive home and the following day as I thought of what we had done, of the other members of the group, of the chanting, and as I re-read extracts from the channelled material. My whole being felt lighter somehow. Something had definitely changed.

AVRIL
A stone

November 1994 : It continues to unfold. Sometimes we think we're playing. That what we're doing has nothing to do with our 'assignment.' We'll have a 'hunch' and follow it, for fun and because it makes life interesting. Only to be given what seems a sign, a clue, a nudge that we've completed something else that needed to be done. It began when four of us took a walk and found a fallen tree. The roots had grown around a pointed stone and when the tree fell over, it unearthed the stone but trapped it in the gnarled mass. "Come look at this," Tess called as she realised the stone moved ever so slightly. We took turns, Tess and I, wiggling it and suddenly it fell out in Tess's hands. Did I know it was to be in the centre of the spiral, or did I imagine it? I don't know. Does it matter? We took it to the spiral. Five of us women decided to enact a ritual, a blessing using feminine energy. We made a circle around the stone, placing our hands on it we individually blessed it. We asked Big John to raise it over his head and drop it point first into the centre of the spiral. As soon as he raised the stone over his head the hawk - the same hawk?? - flew from the ground about 20 feet from us. There were no trees there, it had been in the grass undisturbed until that very moment. It hovered as John let go the stone and it embedded itself into the ground. It hovered, absolutely still except for fluttering wings, in the sky exactly has it had only days before. For a minute after the stone was lodged, it hovered. And then left us. I suppose it could have been coincidence. Twice? And why, neither time, was it disturbed until the exact moment. Why, both times, had it been satisfied to stay on the ground in our presence and only take to the air after we'd been a goodly time in it's space? And why hover there looking, not at some meal in the bushes, but seemingly straight at us.

Was it the hawk that encouraged us to continue with the ritual? The stone was still covered with dirt from the tree roots. We decided to cleanse it, in a way to baptise it. The Rings were a good way from the river or any other source of water but beneath a lone tree Margaret found a small pool. Beside the pool was a bucket - with a hole in it. We plugged the hole with grass and managed to carry enough water to the stone to perform the needed ritual.

ANN
Reverent and intelligent energy

I had been involved in earth healing long before I met Avril. As a member of the Gatekeeper Trust I have long been involved in sacred journeys and walking the earth with awareness - in a simple, sacred way. We know Australian Aborigines go on "walk-abouts" walking the "song lines" of their land. Many of us are realising, or perhaps remembering, that this kind of reverent and intentional walking enhances, heals, and keeps healthy the energies that flow along the surface of our earth. Whether we call these 'song lines' or 'ley lines' sensitives are able to discern their vibratory health. We have discovered the ability of dance, song, prayer, and intentional attention to our earth, to help bring about healing and balance in our immediate environment and hopefully to the planet as a whole. Similar to the way acupressure can restore the healthy flow of vital energy in humans, walking and enacting intentional, loving rituals helps move vital energies through our earth. Many of us know of at least one place where we feel most alive, most in tune with the world, most truly ourselves. Communion with this 'spirit of place' is healing, for us. Perhaps it shouldn't surprise us that, similarly, communion with spirit of place is equally healing for our earth. I feel my most valuable contribution to the group working with Avril has been to dovetail the Gatekeeper Trust knowledge with the earth healing work we were directed to do.

I arrived in Devon only after the major work on the spiral had been completed. My immediate concern as I entered the earthwork was whether or not the group had asked the gatekeeper for permission to enter the site. In each of these ancient sacred places a 'gatekeeper' guards the site. If our intent is to be of service, I believe we must always be reverent and respectful of the energies present. A simple request, even a silent one, to the gatekeeper of the site, a simple statement of intent for only the highest, most appropriate outcome of our actions, is more than simple good manners. If our actions are to be valuable and positive, it is imperative.

Once I had performed this simple ritual and received permission, I entered the site. I immediately realised the area which needed work was much larger than the area marked by the spiral. My sense of the energy involved was that it very much resembled the workings of a clock. I sensed the 'circles within circles' were like the gears in a clock. They touched each other and linked to each other so that when one turned it turned another and that one turned another until they were all turning simultaneously. To the side of the spiral with which the others had worked stood a rather small stone, a standing plinth. It soon became clear to me that the circle of energy around this stone was the 'stem' for the 'watch gears.' It's energy needed to be 'wound up' so that the whole mechanism could begin to turn again. Somehow it was key. Two of the women and I enacted a simple ritual to heal and renew this vital energy.

Several in the group agreed that the energy present in the earthworks of the Black Down Rings travelled along a ley line which passed through a farm in the area. We sensed something blocking or darkening the energy along this line and sensed that in addition to the Rings site, this ley line also needed our attention. The owner of the farm was agreeable to our exploring his farmyard. He shared what history he knew of the place. A monastery had been built on the land in 1900, it had been occupied until war broke out in 1914. The owner advised us not to enter one of the buildings because it was dangerously unstable. He also mentioned that he couldn't get his dog to enter what was left of the remaining monastic building.

The Clew

I felt unwillingly drawn to the building. We had come to do what was necessary and if a building was dangerous for some unknown reason, I felt compelled to investigate, even if against my better judgement. As I walked toward the entrance to the building I felt uncomfortable. Upon entering, I felt an energy of total fear. I honestly didn't know whether to turn and leave or to stick it out. As I often do, I put a bubble of protection around myself and proceeded. At the top of the stairs I stood and intended as much healing as I could muster. Often in past healing work I have felt myself drawn to take up and wield a sword or a cross made of light. Something almost outside myself seemed to influence me to hold the glowing sword or cross in both hands and in some strangely aggressive way actually banish any darkness in the area. I called on this vision at that moment, envisioned the sword made of light, envisioned the sword sealing off the area, envisioned its light banishing the darkness and healing the area into light.

Later we found out that the monastery had lain abandoned until WWII when it was used by the Gurkhas. They stored heavy machinery and ammunition on the second floor of the building. Tragically the floor gave way killing 30 men who slept below. Deep and painful emotions, death, murder, warfare, or deep wounds to the earth as blasting in a quarry, will all cause darkening of the energy along a ley line. Our work at the Blackdown Rings would have been incomplete without attention to the ley line passing through it.

AVRIL
Receives confirmation

November 1994 : It didn't finish with our work in the circle. Or with Ann and the other women's work in the smaller circle. It didn't finish with our work at the farm, with our work on the line, or with what we felt to be our fulfillment of any of the other requests. It didn't finish until the very end. Until we were leaving. And the end, when it came, was amazing. Am I still a cynic that I need proof?

As the events in Devon unfolded, John and I both realised we were suddenly remembering things, a sentence, a few words, a description from one of the original messages. In the beginning, when we solved a riddle, found a place they sent us to, did something they had asked, we would go back to the messages and find new meaning in what they had been telling us. We would understand things we hadn't understood before. It was as if only after completing the work could we recognise the clues they had given us. We began to wonder if this was happening again.

On one level of course I had already recognised it was happening. When I saw the sign for the Blackdown Rings I remembered the reference to *circles within circles* and *walk in circles there is no other way*. Once we knew we were to do the healing we had studied the messages and included other requests in our work at the Rings. Two phrases, *Walk in circles, they must sway with the movement* and *Gather round this place with arms upraised and holding the branches* had intentionally been included. We felt we had also managed to *Cloak everything with fire and burn it on the hilltops* when, during the healing in the spiral the men had sounded the Aauum and we had all envisioned enclosing the landscape for as far as we could see in golden light. When Patrick realised he was dowsing a spiral instead of a circle, the sentence *Look for the ripples they must be counted* made sense. When he finished his dowsing and our white pebbles were in place it did look as if we had dropped a pebble in water and the rings made by the pebbles marked the ripples. Was it my attunement to these requests and our fulfillment of them that made me sensitive to further references?

Memory of the additional references began innocently enough. Paul described having to cross the river at one point. It was four feet deep and he had to hold his coat over his head to keep it dry. I remembered an image of being in deep water and holding a cloak. I found the reference *Only in the whirlpool the swimmer sits holding onto his cloak.* It did seem a bit of a stretch and certainly must have some deeper meaning. But the image *was* there. On a walk we saw cows fording across an unlikely spot. I remembered the image which accompanied *The beasts of the field must cross the water.* A simple enough statement and perhaps only a coincidence, but the coincidences were mounting. Although it was November and not particularly warm, Wendy and Margaret had played one entire afternoon in the river. They decided to collect a special stone for each of us. As they retold of their exploits I remembered *Wash in the water over the stones.* When they returned drenched from their play, they certainly looked as though they had washed in the water, and they had a stone for each of us.

John and I purposefully re-read the messages, looking for requests we might have missed. We found reference to *where the hazel wands were cut* and wondered if this were an oblique reference to where we were staying. We found a phrase explaining that *It will happen as the leaves fall from the trees and the water winds through the valley.* We were here in November, the leaves were certainly falling from the trees and the river did wind through the valley beneath our holiday home. We felt we could safely interpret nine of the message requests or clues. We listed them on a flip chart. We continued our re-reading and added five more :

1) *Turn [the stones] until the sound is made*
2) *Move sideways in line until the tops of the trees are lit by the light*
3) *Walk in line as it has been shown to you*
4) *Look back over the valley to see the signs that I have marked for you for it is only in the sunlight that the messages will come*
5) *Turn left where you began the journey and out of the sunset will come the fire.*

We compiled the flipchart because I wanted - needed - that kind of reassurance. Perhaps I stretched it a little. Perhaps I imagined a few things. Made connections where none were warranted. Maybe. Maybe not. I don't know. But finally, in the end, the sign was unequivocal. By then I had forgotten the flipchart. Forgotten there was only one item remaining unsolved. In the end I knew we were watched and guided. Our need for reassurance was answered in no uncertain terms.

By then we had already managed the other four. That began with Gray's casual comment that something needed to be done 'up there.' Only later was I

The Clew

able to see the relationship between 'up there' and the first part of one request which began *Turn left where you began the journey.* "Up there' was a small grove of trees to the left of the 'gateway' through which we had entered as we began our healing work on the Rings. But I hadn't remembered that yet. I only knew that Gray was insisting we needed to do something up there, and that up there was a stone table carved with directional pointers. We made a small procession up to the spot. Then, single file, Douw leading, carrying the stone we had placed at the centre of the spiral, several of us made a procession still higher and stood in line in order to *walk in line as has been shown to you.* From this vantage point we looked over the spiral, over the earthen bank enclosure, and over the valley beyond. We were looking at a line of trees and although it was a grey day and sky was universally grey, over the line of trees the sky glowed with a lightness. I smiled remembering *Move sideways in line until the tops of the trees are lit by the light.* At that point I remembered *Turn [the stones] until the sound is made.* We decided to fulfill this request by rotating the stone on the metal plate of the toposcope in front of us.

Once the stone was placed on the plate, I carefully turned it 360 degrees. Each woman then stepped forward and deliberately turned the stone another 360 degrees. The stone did indeed make a loud grating sound and we were pleased. It was not until the final rotation, as the last woman stepped back into line, that we heard quite another sound. Immediately we startled by what sounded like loud cannon fire. Boom! Boom! From Plymouth harbour, to the west of where we stood, came the double report. A cannon? From a ship? A salute? We never found out. But we remembered *Turn left where you began the journey and out of the sunset will come the fire.* This was the sort of handshake we had grown accustomed to. I was reassured. And forgot the flip chart, and the one remaining request. Until the very last moment.

When I woke on the morning of our departure, I sat at my window. The day seemed bleak and cloudy. I stared at the trees on the bank above the river and desperately looked for a sign. I said out loud, to Assurbanipal, to Ashad, whoever they were, wherever they were, from some desperate place inside me, "I've done the best I can, but is it enough?" then turned and went downstairs to join the others.

In the common room where we met to discuss our work and share our experiences, Gray had developed a ritual. When anyone first entered the room they lit a candle. When we left, we blew it out. It was our way of consciously requesting light, sharing light, and taking the light with us when we left. We shared the ritual one last time the morning of our departure. The day seemed bleak and cloudy. I gathered my luggage and opened the door to depart. I was hit in the face by bright sun light. My immediate reaction was one of frustration. For an entire week we had been blessed with grey, cloudy weather and now the moment of our departure, sunshine.

It was a moment before two things flashed into my consciousness. First, there was still one message left on the flip chart. *Look back over the valley to see the signs that I have marked for you, for it is only in the sunlight that the messages will come.* And second, as Jane left earlier in the week she had called from the end of the drive. "Come and look," she had called excitedly. "You can see the valley only from here." And, I might have added, from my third floor bedroom window. I ran to the end of the drive and looked back over the valley. There was my lone tree. It looked a little funny though. Hazy or out of focus. I looked closely for a moment or two trying to puzzle through and make sense of what I was seeing. The sun was shining brightly. There was no mist or rain anywhere in sight. And yet a mist seemed to be developing around the tree. Mesmerised I watched as a grey mist thickened and grew higher surrounding at first the lower part of the tree and then creeping gradually up until in enveloped the entire tree. It continued further and began to arch over the valley. The sun shone through the mist and began to form a rainbow. The rainbow grew inch by inch until it stretched over the house and onto the hilltop on which stood the Blackdown Rings. Transfixed I seemed rooted to the spot. It was moments before I gathered my wits and ran shouting to the house beckoning the others. A camera! But already it was fading. Others did see it and we did get a picture before it disappeared totally.

It was only then that Joy and Ann shared their story. When they arrived they had gone for a walk in the valley. Joy had gone up to this same tree, put her hand on it and said "We need a sign." They had shared this with no-one until this very moment.

My joy could only with difficulty be contained. When I remember Assurbanipal's appreciation, I feel a little guilty for still needing signs for reassurance. Following our work he had already thanked us.

> *My companions, I greet you for you have achieved this day that task that was set for you. As you worked, so did those of us standing on this side. The whole is complete, the sphere is constructed and waits to roll forward at the allotted time.*

None of us knows what 'the sphere' is or when the 'allotted time' will be. Invariably, the time following our work can seem anti-climactic. It's as if we expected something to happen, but visibly nothing did. Again Assurbanipal reassures us,

> *Do not be disappointed that that which you expected did not so noticeably occur. This is a problem for you in human existence. You exist just on one level and construct structures on that level. Open your eyes and mind to that which lies beyond. You have a simple sight - it is to be enjoyed but not regarded as the whole.*

Others in the group did perceive a change in the energy both at the rings and along the ley line where we worked. Perhaps this is another level of 'sight.'

Assurbanipal also reassured me about bringing everyone together. We *were* able to work together in ways we couldn't have worked separately. We *did* enjoy each other and feel a special bond. And strange as it still seems to me, others experienced healing with each other in ways similar to what happened in our forgiveness ritual Sunday evening. The time together was about earth healing.

The Clew

But there is also something else happening. A bonding. Assurbanipal described it.

> *You are not alone. No one will ever believe that again. Are these not your brothers and sisters? Do I not also stand with my brothers? When you are with your companions you believe this. I ask you to believe this when all have left your side. I ask you to be aware that we stand beside you. We have been together many times before. Nothing is changed, only in the recognition ... Reunion is a healing art. Each has been healed by having the others around. Each has returned to Source by connection to Whole. We are as One. Go out into the world and live that which you have relearned in this place.*

And now again the limbo.

> *I ask no more of you. My task is accomplished. Step forward with courage, but with faith and love more so ... I thank you. It has been a blessing for me also.*

It seems finished again. But experience has shown that what seems final, what seems like the end, may not be.

18th December 1994 : There is more work. We'll be called to do more at some point in the future. It's strange the way I know about the messages now. I know more about the words that what they say. I know things about the messages. I used to wonder what things meant. Now I have fewer doubts. I can reread something that came through and think oh yes, I know what that means. And so, although the references are rather oblique, I know there will be more work.

> *You look now to move forward. It is not yet the time. You have circles and spirals moving within you. That which you need will be shown to you in time as clearly as the candle. You know the task. You will sense it in the soles of your feet.*

That's reference to my 'knowing' to my intuition. It's the recognition when I saw the sign to the Blackdown Rings. It's the knowing that I felt about bringing all of us together in one place as Porlock and then Hazlewood. He's telling me I'm right to trust it. I don't really sense it in the soles of my feet, but he's telling me it's like that.

> *You have the power to unite. There are places which have your special power. This is important. Each group has its own colour and symbol.*

He's telling us here that we are a 'group' who have incarnated together before. There are places that it is our responsibility to heal. We are not alone and others are doing the same kind of work we are doing, but we have certain things we have incarnated to do. And we're to do them together as a group. He's using words like colour and symbol to describe the way we work together and the places we are connected to.

> *What is the purpose of matching red with yellow? Some colours match more closely together. It is always better to match each to own. See the colours which you make in areas - you will not see them but will perceive them. All will be drawn to them as a bee to a flower. You need not struggle or concern yourself with future movement. A word, a picture, a look will lead you toward the work that is yours.*

He's telling us we won't be given the specific instructions like we were in the beginning. Now it's up to us to be alert and aware, to recognise and identify and trust our intuition about what is to happen and what we're needed to do.

This next part was the most difficult part for Ian. He has been working so intimately with Assurbanipal. His 'Azzie.' Living out the roles of astrological student and master. He was literally in tears.

> *It will not be my task to lead you forward in that work. My task is completed. It gives me great joy to see its completion. I pass from this place but hold you in deep love. No one should mourn my passing for I move beyond to that place in which I must joy and delight for there I am offered that which I have long desired. It is to you that my journey forward is owed. What treasure you have given me. Receive my blessings. I thank this woman and this man also. He should not fear … I stand aside but you should welcome he who comes. I move to the great Light of existence. Follow me. Love …*

And Ian's 'Azzie' was gone.

Chapter Ten

During the ten year period that Avril was used as the receiver for the messages, the entities who gave the messages would change at least seven times. In the beginning Avril was less sure about what was happening and less sure when the energies changed, or when and if they simply traded places occasionally. However by this time Avril was clearly aware of the process. Each new entity seemed to have a more powerful energy then the one it replaced. Avril came to realise that she needed to incorporate the strength of each entity before she could proceed on to the next. Each time a new entity arrived she experienced a variety of health challenges. Often members of the group mirrored and experienced the same challenges. Those present during one of the entity changes experienced a radical shift in Avril's physical presence. Her voice changed. Her affect and mannerisms, her gestures changed. When Avril sat to allow the entity to enter, she changed consistently into a recognisable presence. When the entities changed within a single session, Avril's body, voice, energy, were clearly used in a completely new way and resulted in a portrayal of new individuality often recognisable to someone in the group. Ian had immediately 'recognised' Assurbanipal. Within moments of Assurbanipal's departure, 18th December 1994, the group's next guide arrived. This time it was Ann who instantly recognised the emerging entity.

Paracelsus would work with Avril for the next year and a half. He was a great physician and delighted in answering questions about health concerns and healing. During this time Avril continued to be available for groups who would address Paracelsus with personal health issues. Although the core group continued to meet on an intermittent basis, continued to seek guidance, continued to grow on a personal level as well as do much work toward healing their group karma, it would be several years before their next healing work.

AVRIL
Paracelsus arrives. Healing wisdom and practice

18th December 1994 :

I stand now present. I greet you, as have those who have passed before and who now pass to me the mantle of your care. I am Paracelsus - of the brotherhood of Unity. I bring you the greater strength of my being for my brother has passed from this place. I am now he who is ordained to guide your feet and give wisdom to those who seek, for I am beyond the telling of him who stood before - yet I stand before you and come with my humility in my hands ... Let us journey together. Each of you walks your own path, yet each shares the same road with brother and sister ... Live with joy and hold to the promise of that which lies before each of you. What I may offer, I do so gladly. The great Light shines and guides me to this place for there is work to do. I have accepted my task. If you would have me speak, I would answer that which is in your heart. Such commune is fair - to see and to share. There is one who grieves.

He's referring to Ian here. Ian definitely was grieving and not at all happy about this change in personnel.

> *Be calm and peaceful for you have earned as you should. It is the beginning of your path accomplished. We will be friends.*
> *Who asks?*

Ann: Greetings. May we know what your name is?
> *I am Paracelsus. Light of the Divine. I am humbled by such a position. I know you well.*

Ann: I know you too.
> *Then all is as it should be. Know my care ... I may appear strange and somewhat removed. It is so long in space and your time that I speak so. You must forgive my stumblings. My desire is great. My focus is, you would say, misty. I am not without mirth - would I choose such a ragged band of pilgrims if I were without mirth? There were more serious opportunities offered to me, but I remembered mirth. Do not fear my presence. I tremble before yours.*

Patrick: Where would the journeys of our physical beings advantage our planet? Where and when?
> *He who passed over is the one who worked and spoke of your impatience. You must understand, there are other activities undertaken by others and not yet resolved. Until they are resolved, patterns of your making are not apparent to us. It is for you to journey to those places of our need. It is complex, the structure we work with. It is most like a honeycomb. There are these patterns which fit together sometimes and open asunder sometimes and sometimes show signs of weakness. Sometimes you must connect with others. We create and also we respond. What is in our creation must wait. What is in our creation is not always free flowing. Some like you are responsive and have matching skills. Others struggle and lose focus. We must wait for that to be created.*

Marc : There are three hundred questions I would like to ask. But to keep it simple - I find that running as we are as a group - some of us are working through a process of elimination for the direction in which to go. Please can you give us some guidance?
> *Link always to the centre for there the strength is held. Look in, not out. Reach for that within yourselves which is your own security, that which you most love. Close your eyes and recall those moments when you have been entirely happy and hold to them - taste them, remember them.*
>
> *It is difficult when you are adrift to remember the times when you have been happy - and with forgetting comes darkness. Find the star within your being - remember when you understood it for the first time, when you were truly happy. However desperate your lives have been, there have been moments when you have known your own star. Make it shine through your memory. Make it shine and each point will create in the heavens that star that will lead*

The Clew

you. You seek always for material structure - that is merely the eggshell which surrounds the birth. That which is born within us and lights our way. Find your happiness and know it is and all else will be resolved.

Ann : When in Devon we were working on the ley line that passes through France and Ireland. Is this an important ley line? And is healing the earth and general healing to be our work?

You have created, what I can best describe as a whirlpool and in its movement it narrows. For those of you who work with needles, imagine that you have here a needle. What we ask of you is that you apply it in those places where needed. You have your colours and your place. You use such words which are right and true. The application of the point releases and the energy may flow. That which you speak of is part of a complex structure. It has a deep level of interconnection. Imagine an interleaved fretwork. This group gathered has the power to reach to a level of vibration which has not been freed for a long time. You are not alone, but you have a task, for so were you born, however else you have spent your time. You are the needle that must reach through three gradations. You will be shown points that relate to such structure.

Wait - it will come, as surely as the sun rises and one day you will turn around and it will be done and your searching for such a place will be forgotten. Such is the time you are living in. Simply flow.

Sometimes only one or two of you will function in such a way but never forget the whole for the whole is your safety. Always remember - look always to the centre for in the centre is gathered each of your energy. Such is the cup of your splendour. You have freedom at any time. No one is asked to do that which they do not desire.

Love one another. It will come soon, but as yet all is not secure. Your actions must follow the preparedness of others with whom you have no contact.

I must depart. The woman holds too long to the energies which are difficult for her. Know my love as I know each of you.

You walk in the blessed care each of you, with he who stands at your side. It is so. I thank you. I have returned after a great time. There is work to be done. Let us make all things whole.

February 1995 : Fascinating that it's a give and take. I sometimes get used to thinking it's all one way. Difficult to realise they learn from us. Tonight Paracelsus reminded the group not to see it that way. A good reminder for me too.

You may perceive me as some wise ancient who comes into your presence to explain all to you. That is not my role. My role is often to point out to you what you already know but have obscured from your sight. There is nothing I may tell you that you do not know. It is my task sometimes to simply draw back the curtain. But you would not seek my aid if you did not wish the curtain to be drawn back. I cannot offer you what you do not possess. I can simply clarify your understanding. As you can clarify mine, for I have purpose also in such exchange. I emphasise my learning in this place. This woman gives me opportunity to learn and for this I am grateful. We travel far together, she and I.

A sense of humour, this Paracelsus. Teasing conversations with people in the group. Bantering, actually, about 'doctoring' and his difficulties with me. A question from a woman in the group: "I spoke to you a month ago about sciatica. You suggested nasturtium, arnica, probably something else. I've forgotten" In answer to her question and by way of explaining why she had forgotten something, Paracelsus explained that the concoction had been ... *one of my richer menus*. Then later, in answer to another question he explained his idea of what he called 'doctoring.'

> *The needles would help. We have here those who work with the needles, do we not? Let them not think I do not respect their work. Needles would help. And let her bathe in jasmine.*

"It's better than going to the doctor, this, isn't it?"
You forget, I was a doctor. This, I tell you, is doctoring. Not what is too frequently practiced. There has been, you might say, a reversal of knowledge. I am not against that which is true and that which has application. I am against that which is so narrow as to be blind. That has become common doctoring practice. Yes, let her bathe in jasmine. Enough that she can scent it. She needs to take the fear away. She needs to believe herself beautiful. The smell of jasmine will help her.

"May I ask what the peaches will do?"
There is an enzyme. The woman cannot name it. I can see it. She cannot name it. We have these difficulties.

"She must read more!"
So I have spoken. But her retentive system is disrupted. We must do it through picture. She finds the words through picture you see. Sometimes you have to seek in the strangest places. You see nature has many wonders. Many of them are hidden away. Many wait to be discovered. Many are dismissed. As I said, there has been a reduction of learning in some fields. There are many secrets hidden within the centre of fruit.

Over and over he tells us of our own skills. Paracelsus told another woman in the group about her own guide.

"Recently I feel as if I've been sensing the energies of my guide. Is this true?"
Indeed.

When I asked him, through Avril, if he answered when I dowsed, he said, *'You're not tuning in to me. You're tuning into yourself.'*

The Clew

I found that rather hard to take in.
It is always easier to accept the power of others rather than the power of ourselves.

"I still don't understand."
It is your sensitivity. You pick up. It is your sensitivity. You simply translate what you acquire.

"The information I get through, I couldn't have known. It's not mine surely."
You access, as does this woman, cosmic consciousness. You have that ability to do that. Yes you have guide. Your guide guides you, protects you and will offer you advice and information when such is necessary from a source external to yourself. But you have the power to hear, to read. It is all accumulated wisdom. It is all available

"Last week I realised I didn't have the dosage for the recommendations you made. So I decided to dowse. I did get a lot of information."
That was me.

"I was going to say was it possible for me to actually be tuning into you."
That was me. I do not like matters incomplete. I prefer to deal with my own recommendations.

"I'd hoped that it was, but I didn't dare think I could …"
Of course. Have we not constructed friendship? Is not my help available to all who seek it? But you must understand that the process of our coming together in the way that we do formulates a connection which is safe. You have become accustomed to my energy. For some, my energy would be, I use this word cautiously, too refined. But you are accustomed to it. All those who speak with me regularly have become accustomed to it. They can absorb that which is mine. And therefore it is possible for them to reach out and for me to respond.
It is not easy for someone who has not had, shall we say, a passing acquaintance with me. There must be, there is a process which occurs at the time of our gathering and interaction where the energy fields recognise and adapt to one another and this had taken place in such places as this. There is as I said a matching which has occurred and therefore exists.

"So how do I ask for your help?"
Speak my name. Like you, I know my name.

"And that's all I have to do?"
Of course.

"Well I did on that occasion and I knew that I was getting a lot of help, but I didn't dare hope that it was you."

The Clew

I think it is time your grew out of humility. You have great ability yourself. You are sensitive. You know the work. You believe in the structure. That is all. You speak with me as you would with this man, this woman, that is all. I have travelled to distant places and moved in worlds which perhaps you have never seen, but I am who I am. I am not perfect. Many have seen me, you might say, become a little testy.

"You seem a little bit on edge tonight. Are you?"
I am no god. I have … a … I have those things which crowd in on me also. But I am happy to be here.

"If I have someone I'm finding rather difficult, I could ask your help?"
Indeed. But ask your own guide who is capable of offering similar assistance.

"Is he trained in medical … "
He has access to the knowledge. With me you have to cope with the personality as well as the skill.

"How do I go about communicating more with my guide? Or him communicating with me."
You need to construct a framework. You need to construct a small ritual. Observe this woman. She has an entering and a leaving. She has a process. You need to construct such in your own way so that your times of meeting are as a dear friend would call to see you at the same time every week, and you know that, and you know the shape of it and you know the kind of things you will talk about. Construct a framework and experiment and it will become easier. If you are working with information I have offered you, then feel free to ask for my continued assistance. That seems only right and just. For I have envisaged and observed and constructed and therefore I have, more easily, access to that form which I have created. So in that case by all means I am always ready. But your own is there to guide and support and has passed with you. It will be conducive to good work.

August 1995: Odd tonight, Paracelsus's answer. Not the usual herbal mix or specific colour to be imagined. No exercise or even encouragement. Seemed strange but I guess when you think about it, it made sense.

"I have a twelve year old girl I asked you about, about a year ago. You suggested lavender and that she wear green and some other things. She's no better in any way. She's in a house with five cats and she's allergic to cats. She's allergic to smoke and her mother smokes. Her mother doesn't like the smell of lavender. And I've felt recently that there's really nothing I can do to help her."
You are right.

"And having heard what you said about making a fuss about the fact that someone has a problem can sometimes make it worse, I wonder perhaps if that's

The Clew

making it worse in this case too?"

She has chosen to live that, and to do with it what she will. And it is powerful. It contains her. It restrains her. And until she breaks from within, that is what will happen and you can do no more. They are locked in struggle.

"Yes."

And you are an outsider to that struggle.

"But I was asked to help. So should I just …"

And so they will turn their joint gaze and they will focus on you. And in the end you will absorb all that, and they will go off together still fighting. And so you do not get into that fight. That is of their making, their construction, and their continuation. And they will fight to the death. Until one of them stands down. And that is what they have chosen. And they will make certain that they secure around each other that which the other finds objectionable. For that is how they fight. Do you understand?

"I understand that. Yes. I do."

And you have no part in that. You will simply become burdened by that which is not yours and it will have no effect. And you will support them in that by assuming a role when there is not role. What you may offer them is that information. That they have to clarify it themselves. They have to resolve between the two of them. Oh, it is big fight, that one. And of a deep root. They have battled so for many lives. Indeed they have. It amazes me. But there is, I suppose, some reverse pleasure in such.

"That is very much as I felt, really."

They do not wish you to take away the pleasure.

"Yes. It's their choice."

It's theirs. It's theirs. Let them battle on for a few more lives. They will eventually learn.

November 1995: Listening to the group session tape tonight, I am again comforted by Paracelsus love for us. His love, his care, his gentleness, and sometimes his ability to confront when needed. But in a humorous way. Like the woman tonight. After his introduction, her question, and his answer. Fascinating.

There are some here present who know me as I know them. There are others to whom I may appear very strange. But remember you appear strange to me also. So we must exist in the kind of harmony with one another's differences yet seeking to reach always a point of clear communication. I speak through the courtesy and love of this woman. Yet I may not speak without your desire. Each of you is a portal to the door through which I enter this place. It is the woman's power which summons me, but you are the door. You each have power. Seek to understand it. To understand your own and to use it to enact

The Clew

your vision. No one has the same. Each is different. Some match. Some divide. But there cannot be a single focus. There must always be the mirror. There must always be the opposite. How else can all be held. So let us begin our purpose. There are those who wish to speak and I welcome opportunity to offer what wisdom is mine to give. I have travelled some distance and had a little learning. What is mine I willingly share. I learn so, never doubt that. That is my purpose. We have the same purpose. To learn and to grow. We help each other. So let us begin. Who speaks?

"Humble greetings Paracelsus."
I do not wish humble greetings. There are those greater than myself.

"But I'm not one of them."
Do not lower yourself. I see the light.

"First of all thank you for sharing yourself to me. My first questions becomes unnecessary because it's already been shown to me."
Strange is it not?

"Very strange actually."
Learn of your gift through such means. Do not hide from it. Those who may, must see. What else?

"I would like to ask for your advice in a way I would like to change. I have a very beloved friend who seems to store up lots of anger and find reasons to push the anger at me. My feeling is that if we look for reasons to be angry at another person, we find it. And he finds lots of things to be angry at with me. My response is to withdraw like a hurt child, get very hurt and withdraw and cut myself off. I don't seem able to behave any other way actually. What else can I do?"
What else can you do. Well you can be yourself. And to be yourself you must learn to accept your whole self. Where is your anger? (On the tape there is a very long silence at this point.) *Tell me where it is!* (Still silence and no answer.) *Don't be afraid of it!*

"I don't really want to be angry with this person because … (interrupted)"
"Where is your anger? His is his own. If he speaks, I will speak. But we speak of you. Where is your anger? (Another long silence.) *Do you know?"*

"I don't know, really. I just know I don't want to be angry with him."
Shall I tell you where it is !!?

"I was hoping you might." (nervous laughter)
It is under your right foot!

Under my right foot? Where? I must be really stupid. (In a sing-song, little

129

The Clew

girl voice.)
>You're not stupid.

"I must be." (same unusual, mockingly little-girl voice)
>Why will you be stupid?

"Well he keeps telling me I am. I must be." (same mocking voice)
>*He keeps telling you you're stupid?* (Paracelsus laughs) *There is only one stupid person in such relationship and it is not you. But you do have your anger under your right foot and so if that is stupid, then you must own it. For it seems a strange place to keep it. Why do you keep it there?*

"I think possibly I didn't know it was there. If I'd known it was there I would have taken it out and had a look at it." (She's really mocking Paracelsus now, but he continues to be patient and supportive toward her.)
>*I recommend it. It has become somewhat weakened under your right foot.*

"I think it must have done. I mean … "
>*You placed it there a long time ago.*

"I did wonder how long ago it was because … "
>*You were a child. You were a child. You hid it there. For so you were taught. And so it hides. It has become pale, a little worn, and in need of energy. It has power. It has as much as the other. But it is, you might say, hidden from the light. So you must bring it out into the light. And as you say, you must look at it. And see what colour it is. And own it as yours.*

"Do you know what colour it is Paracelsus, will you tell me?" (still sparring but more serious now)
>*It is deficient in colour.* (In a very serious, loving, and sympathetic voice, no longer teasing in any way.) *It has been in the dark a long time. But it may obtain colour. It has a thirst for life. A sense of adventure. And an ability to project. And it has great forms. Put it in your heart, my friend. And let your heart couple with it and see what it makes. Do not be afraid to put it out into the world. But put it out with love. But the love may be for yourself. There are times when we may use our anger for love of ourselves. When it is truly righteous. Examine it. Do not fear it, it is a friend. But as a friend, it must learn its boundaries. Must develop communication. It must express with love. Anger may express with love. If it is right so to do. Do not fear shadows for if you do, you become one. Take the anger, put it in your heart and feel its power. And if you must express it in the world, then express it with love, but use its power. There is no purpose in hiding. Not when you have tasks to achieve and matters of moment to accomplish. No one can hurt you if you will not allow it. You have all power to keep the barbs of others at bay. You are no different from all else. What you invite you receive. What you do not*

live will be given to you. When you live your power, you will not need to suck it in from others. When you own your anger, it will not be offered to you.
"Thank you." (only sincerity in her voice at this point)

January 1996 : Tonight a woman asked Paracelsus about a panic attack she had suffered at an ancient site. Her experience sounded a little like my initial experience with the energy. Paracelsus even mentioned it. I guess I didn't panic because I had the earlier experiences or something. Strange how some people come to this work.

"About eighteen months ago I had a massive panic attack which I really still haven't got over."
What occasioned it?

"I really don't know."
Where were you?

"In Brittany, in France."
Ah.

"And for no reason, I was terrified."
Yes. You would be. Had you been there before?

"No."
And you will not return, I suspect.

"No."
Good. That is sensible. But you have yourself in such a sentence recognised something important. And that is that it was related to place, that it is not related to this place. And so what you have within you and what you suffer from is acute memory. Understand that. It is a memory. It is not here now. It is just that your body remembers and holds that fear though the cause is gone. Let me see. Why the fear? (Long silence) *Were you near the stones?* [Carnac]

That morning we had been to see them.
Yes. That was the fear. You see you do not understand your sensitivity. With time you can learn. But you do not understand it. And what happened in that place was that you were overwhelmed. You absorbed too much. Too quickly. You need to take great care if you visit such places. You have a high sensitivity to the energy there. That you find in those places.

"Yes."
Did you know that?

"I did."
Well then you were foolish.

The Clew

"I didn't know it before I went there."

Then I accept that. But you will not be foolish again.

"No."

It is possible for you to visit such places. There are few that have the power of that one. But you must always, always encircle yourself before you go. You must always put up some protection. Then you will be fine. You must shut off. Until you have learned enough and lost the fear Then you may use the light for it is considerable. But you have to learn how to get hold of an electric cable. And what you did was, you took hold of a very large cable. It was as if you climbed ... what do you call ... one of your ...

"Pylons."

Thank you. You climbed one of those and grasped hold of the power. That's what you did. Now you can see that was unwise, can't you?

"I can, indeed."

But you survived it. So remember that. Instead of the fear, remember that. You survived it. You have such protection. There can be none stronger than that and so you are safe. Turn it on its head. You are safe. You survived it. And so you must learn and seek to learn a little of your own energy. A little of your own sensitivity. Something of your skill perhaps. But you cannot do this until you lose the fear. That is all. You have no need to fear. You simply have a need to understand. Understanding dispels fear. Do you see that?

"Yes, I do."

What you experienced, you might say was normal. For you. But it taught you, showed you. And you can use it to begin with. To learn from. To grow with. If you had experienced it to a lesser degree perhaps it would have passed without your attention. You simply had a somewhat large prod. And can you see there is no need for fear now? It came and it went in that second. It is simply your body that remembers. The electrical functions of your body went into override. And so there are those you know who can drain that down and you must learn to protect yourself and when you feel safe you may then begin to access the sensitivity which can understand the nature of such places. You have electricians, do you not?

"Yes, we do."

Surely they must first have to understand the danger of their trade. But it does not stop them working.

"Is there any reason I was drawn to that place then?"

The reason I have spoken. You discovered yourself.

"I had to learn about that."

You discovered yourself. It was your beginning. Did not this woman also begin with a shock? For some it comes that way. As I said, if it had been smaller, you would have taken no account of it. Go for the positive. And not the negative. Why did this happen to me? It didn't happen to him. It didn't happen to her. Why did this happen? How did this happen? It happens because I am who I am and so who is this? What is this? Why did it not happen to him or to her? Do you see? It should inspire curiosity, not fear.

"It certainly does."

Good. Curiosity will dispatch the fear. You have, for want of a better term, very sensitive circuits. Learn to protect them. Learn to insulate yourself. And you may be amazed. You will be able to go to such places and understand their purpose. And identify the different nature of energies passing through them. In time you can do that. But you must first learn to insulate yourself. And you must learn. And you must read. And you must study. As does anyone who embarks on the development of a skill.

"It was interesting because on the morning we went to see the stones, I was talking to them and …"

Well they spoke back, did they not?

(After group laughter subsides) "They did speak back to me, with the words 'You have ears to hear and eyes to see.'"

I have just spoken the same.

"And it was very moving at the time."

It is for you to learn the controls. They cannot do that. They simply have their power. It is you that must teach yourself. You can speak with the stones. There is great work for you to do. There must be a return of understanding. A lot of them, others also now live in such a way and begin to spread understanding. It is not to fear. You have full control. If you are foolish, you will suffer. If you are wise, you will not. There is no damage. I can see none.

"Thank you."

You're very welcome.

Chapter Eleven

AVRIL
The arrival of Ishtar. Past-life recall.

17th April 1996 : So many people on this journey. With so many talents. Strange, indescribable talents. Talents that shouldn't even exist. Why am I surprised? Joy has known things. Told me things. Ann sees things. Tells the group and me things. About the entities. And the entities themselves - in many ways they are certainly inexplicable. And the energies they seem to trigger in all of us - how to explain that? After all this, why am I surprised? Maybe it has been this trip. Bless my mother for her encouragement and for leaving me the financial means. This trip. Around the world. Maybe it's all of these experiences. And being so far from home and totally out of context. Perhaps that's why it was so surprising. And it *was* surprising. Totally unexpected and not like anything I'd experienced before. So, after Ann and Joy and all the others, why was this woman a surprise? Perhaps it was the information rather than the woman herself. The information she helped me access. Said she worked on the chakras, balanced them she said. And intuitive massage. No longer a foreign idea, the chakras. And the massage certainly sounded like a good idea, intuitive or any other kind.

She said I could ask a question. And so I asked my question. There've been so many men. I keep meeting them. I know it's in my chart. I know now all about my moon in Libra in the twelfth house and all the astrological reasons for this obsession I have with finding 'the one.' And I know about my Uranus and my Venus, the push-pull of that conflicting energy. I *know* it all but it doesn't make it any easier to live with. It's like being on edge all the time. Constantly looking over my shoulder and always wondering if he's somewhere around, if I'll see him, if he'll see me. So I asked her. Am I to meet him? In this lifetime? Is he incarnate on this planet somewhere, now? Or have we somehow missed each other this time around and that's what the searching is all about. Because if that's what happened, then I'd like to stop right now. Simply stop the search and be finished with it.

She worked for a little while before the voice began. My voice. Not exactly like the other entities. More like I was speaking to my self. Like my own voice from a past life time. While she did her balancing, her massage, the woman asked my voice, "Who are you?"

And my voice replied "I am the priestess. Servant to Inanna. Daughter of Marduk. This woman remembers." I was speaking. Or someone I had been in another time in another place was speaking. I said I remembered. But I didn't remember.

The woman continued to work. We were both - or all three of us - were silent for a very long time. Then the woman spoke again. Asked this voice of mine my question. "Will she find her partner?"

"If he wishes." When it said that, when I said that, when the voice that was me from some other time said that, I felt a vast sense of relief. Finally! To know that he was alive. If he wishes. So it isn't totally up to me. The woman continued her massage and balancing and I experienced a sort of floating sensation. Floating above the earth somehow, looking down as on a school globe. It seemed as if I were seeing parts of it in rings, in circles of light almost the way a spotlight lights a circle on a stage or a searchlight lights up a circle in the sky. Most strange. A bird's eye view as if I were trying to find the energy of my partner. I could see bits of the globe in these ring formations. Examining this aspect of the globe and then another. Sensing the energy to see if he was there. From my vantage point above, I continued searching. As if I knew he was there, it was only a matter of finding him. I lay still as the woman worked, and seemed to be in two places at once. On her table, under her nurturing hands, and high above the school-globe earth, searching. Totally relaxed, I floated up farther and farther, higher and higher until I could see the entire globe.

She was almost finished. Instinctively I felt it. She was about to finish. My voice sensed it too, gave a sigh and spoke again. "She can live my freedom. They will come together and the gods will sing."

And the strangest thing happened. The circles of light I had been seeing, examining, hunting through for some recognisable energy, intensified. They seemed to signal something. Then there were two circles of light, of energy and they came together. Still, from my vantage point high above the earth, I'm not sure even where on earth it was, but the energy belonged to some particular place … I felt like I found him. Like I found his energy field. It was a very unusual feeling. One of letting go. Of relaxing. Of knowing that it will happen. I hope I can remember. The feeling. I hope it makes it easier. I hope there's less urgency from now on. Ashad. I remember that feeling. Perhaps I *will* know it again.

3rd June 1996: Only one day back from my trip and already it's strange again. It's as if my life will never be quite normal again. Ian had spent time with a woman in Wales. He recognised almost immediately that she was a very powerful psychic. He found it rather uncanny, actually. She told him that she believed that in a past life he had been the Russian composer Scriabin. She took him up to her attic and gave him a photograph of the composer. It was an exact likeness of Ian at the age he was then. Ian also subsequently found out that Scriabin's last composition was to have been premiered in India, that he was to go to India for the premiere but he never made it. He died only a short time before. Ian wonders if that explains his own near obsession with getting to India.

He'd had the passing thought that she might have been his mother in that past life. For some reason I asked Ian what he knew of Scriabin's mother. He said she had died when Scriabin was 18 months old, in Austria, of TB. In that moment the memory, the vision flooded back to me so vividly. After the accident, when I was staying with Douw. Lying on his couch, my chest hurting from the accident. Difficulty breathing. And the flashback. TB - I had TB. I was dying of TB. And I was in Austria. And in that moment, the memory even more vivid than when it came as I lay convalescing from my accident in America, I knew. Unequivocally I knew. If such a wager were possible I would have wagered my

The Clew

life on it. The woman in Wales hadn't been his mother; in that lifetime some part of me had been. I knew. And I had known from the very beginning. From the first moment I saw him balancing his bicycle between his legs, looking at his map. Standing there, dishcloth in hand, looking out of the window, I had known. I had known we had some very strong connection. It explains the strain between us.

And Douw. Interesting that in that lifetime in Austria I felt he was caring for my affairs. In some way a steward. And after my accident - it was as if he stepped into the same role. Again he was caretaker. He even helped me with some financial arrangements. Repeating the old relationships The old ways of interacting. So. Ian and Douw and me. The connection. From some other time. The feelings, the memories, the inherited patterns of interaction. And the love - always the love returns. And who else? And what other patterns? And how many lifetimes? And where? Perhaps life was easier when it was lived on only one level. When I didn't have to know all these unknowable things.

6th June 1996 : It happened again tonight. It seems from no where, with no warning, one leaves and another comes. And the energy is so different. I can feel it. Can remember it once the session is over and I am back to normal. Can remember what it felt like, how different each was. The others notice it too. My voice changes. My mannerisms, gestures, voice inflection, all change. So now, with these words, Paracelsus has left us.

I greet you my friends. We have shared much together have we not? It has been my delight to work with you all. I admire such commitment as you have shown. We have made a good journey together, and each alone. Now there are many changes in your lives and in my being. I follow those who have gone before me. I am freed from certain bonds. You have assisted me in this purpose. I owe you much ...

You must journey forward. Carry those responsibilities which are left to you to perform. There will be a great gathering of those you know and those who are yet to come. You are returned as one being of light. Each of you merely a point of radiance in the whole pattern. Is it not a wondrous thing? I tell you, you are all greatly loved, however much you struggle, however much you have forgotten, however much you obscure through your deeds and through your forgetfulness. Remember this. Remember each of you, that without your willingness, your patience, your learning, there can be only insufficient light in the whole. You each have a beam that lights the centre. So are stars made. Do not forget that in your struggles. Whatever besets you, the greater lies beyond. You have, each of you in your form, the power of the gods. You must tie it to the love of the universe and not to the love of self or any one other. Life is to be shared without doubt, but the task is greater.

So, my friends, I leave your side ... I am called home and I am joyous. You are called again to your task and reminded of that which has always been yours ... You have done well. I give you love and hope. More precious than jewels are these. I fade to the life beyond and to the service which calls me. In my place comes one who bears the dream, who brings the memory, who creates the future. I bow before such power. I leave you and this woman who has been my benefactor. She moves forward also into new being and new life. She has learned well.

It is enough. We are parted. Wait, for the door opens …

I wonder when this great gathering of *'those we know and those who are yet to come'* will be. And I wonder how we find those who are yet to come. More men? More recognition and knowing? How will I know which are which? Which are to do the work, and which is the one? Will I ever know? I thought it would be easier, after the voice in New Zealand. Perhaps it will be. We are called again to our task. What will that be? And when? More earth healing?

It's always a little sad when such a friend leaves. Seems less strange than it used to, to think of him as an actual person, as a real live friend. We're changing. Beginning to redefine 'normal.' It wasn't as sad this time as when Assurbanipal left. That was so difficult for Ian. This time, when Paracelsus left, wasn't so difficult. There was a very long pause before Ishtar arrived. When she spoke her name, *"I am Ishtar,"* Ian laughed. I suppose he would rather have his Azzie back. Ishtar took him to task immediately. *" … and you laugh, my friend! Beware foolishness!"* Perhaps we were too used to Paracelsus's teasing sense of humour. How did he put it? *"I am not without mirth,'* he said. I remember. *"Would I choose such a ragged band of pilgrims if I were without mirth?"* Well! And now we have Ishtar. Quite a different energy this. She spoke so slowly in the beginning. It was as if she had great difficulty coming to terms with where she was. I felt her off to one side, some way from me. She spoke somehow from a distance and slowly came closer. She seemed to have difficulty settling in - or whatever it is they do. She didn't seem as comfortable with us as the others had been. Hers is certainly a more intense energy than I have experienced before. No need to record everything she said. This will serve:

I come … I am commanded so. I do not know my place, for it is strange. I acknowledge your beings … My purpose is your care. My task is your guidance. My faith is the living light. My memory moves from the darkness into being. I join this woman and she becomes myself. Is that not a remarkable thing? Wait, I will accustom myself to old movement … My knowledge is beyond that of him who came before, yet it contains his wisdoms and the wisdoms of those who were his predecessors … What is mine I offer … You will feel my presence, it is not the same as those before. Stay firm and committed to truth. Love as you have been taught. I may destabilise your beings for a short time but I could not have come so if you could not receive me. I thank you for this … I am truly both your guide, your companion, and your servant. Remember the power of love and you may grasp hold of it …

2nd July 1996 :

I greet you and acknowledge your commitment. Without this I could not be present. You must understand I come to few, but you have worked with diligence and skill, each in your own world. I acknowledge this …

The Clew

> *You have all served me well through many lifetimes. Do I not recognise such love? Are you not again gathered in my name? We are joined, but you see, my dear friends, we have never been parted.*
>
> *Do you not recognise each other? Do you not feel within this shared space a sense of belonging you have yearned for, and that yearning comes from your memory? You are returned together but remember also that you walked and breathed and loved, but you also quarrelled, you were also hurt, you were also rejected. These memories return also.*

Quarrelled, hurt, were rejected. And abandoned, killed, went off to war. As Scriabin's mother I abandoned Ian at 18 months. And in some other lifetime, evidently again as his mother, I killed him. And, in Devon, one of our number had turned pale and faint on first glimpsing one of the men who had gathered there. She had to be helped to a chair. "The last time I saw you" she said, gazing at him with such intensity, "you went off to battle and you never came back." Whatever she was feeling, whatever she was experiencing physically, was clearly very real. And what of Patrick. In that monastery on Iona, how did I love Patrick? And that other lifetime, seeing him being led away as an old man. Knowing I was to take his place. Memories indeed. Yes, these memories return also.

> *You, my friends are changed ... For many this process has been painful. I regret that. Such has been necessary when the lives between have created disturbance ... And there are others who now hear my voice who will come to your side, and you must begin to focus on this.*

We're to focus on those who are to come to our side? To help with the group? Be part of the work? There are more of us? I'm to find still more? This goes on and on.

> *You are not just some small group of people who enjoy themselves. You are a band of those who have come to serve. Not only the individuals, but the land; not only the land, but the very globe you stand on. This is no game. This is your oath realised, made flesh, brought into being at the time of its need. And so you are drawn together and as we speak in times to come I will show you the way. For now, consider, plan, construct. There are these others who will come. How will they be recognised? How will they be secured? How will you all be connected? How will you work? In your small band you have built connection, but you must have structure to absorb the whole. For the time comes when all will gather. You cannot pass beyond into the new light unless such occurs. You are not alone. Others of my companions work with those of their faith. You, my children, are of my faith, and hear my voice. It is your task to bring love into the world, to focus its power, to live its being. But we must get to know each other again. What I speak of is in time to come. It will happen slowly and with care.*
>
> *Each of you will be as this woman has been - a magnet for many ... Each of you will centre and draw to you those that will gather and as such the*

The Clew

construction begins. You have here the one web. Each of you begin to make your own pattern around you. And those will unite until the structure reaches out and many join with the others who work so. You have this land in your care. Such is your memory.

There are those of you who must live elsewhere, for your light must shine in such places, and must gather to you those who are gathered there ... I ask you to shine love, for it you fail and the connection is not made, then the weakness may cause the whole to collapse. This is your task. This your memory. You might say, this was your training. There is nothing more important in your lives than this, for it builds your life on firm foundation. When you live my love, love comes. When you live my rage, you destroy everything around you. Such is my power and you are the vessels of such. For so you began.

So, who wishes to ask of me?

Ian : I came out [from a beach in Wales] with a lot of angry spots on the top of my head in a circle and came back feeling very ill. Was there any significance to this and if so could you tell me what this was and is this part of the process of memory?

You confronted your anger, my friend. And you did not like what you saw. But it is changed. You do well ... You had choice and you have chosen well ... Use my colour, my friend, and the sound of water, but do not let the anger lie there. It will destroy your talent if you do. And you have great skill. Were you not also my servant? Did you not chart the movement of the stars? Did you not give auguries to the people? They remember you so. For you were their teacher. Reach for the heavens again, for the earth still hangs about your feet ... Step onto dry land and reach again for the stars. Your wisdoms are needed.

John : Is the anger you have described Ian dealing with also applicable to me and the difficulties I have experienced?

Indeed. But you have lived differently to this one. You have contained yours ... Anger if not acknowledged, festers, becomes a volcano, that lies below, bubbling seething. This one [Ian] knows how to seethe. There is perhaps a point at which you could come to common understanding as you appear to have lived at opposite ends. I suggest you both move to the middle. It is for the same reason. You too have memory and power which comes now into being, but if you were not cleansed as this one you would be destroyed by it. String music you need, and the hands of your friends.

There is no one here who suffers who cannot be healed by those amongst you. For you have great power and strength and skill in your beings. You know many wisdoms, many lie forgotten but they will return. Others will add to them. You were once my priest. I acknowledge your power and your devotion as these remember your goodness. Hold to that, for that is not removed.

Who speaks?

My name is Heather. My eyes have recently changed colour, back to blue. Is this necessary?

The Clew

You wished it. It has come with your memory. So you stood before, and you are returned to such being. Do you not feel new power?

I do.

Then you are gathered to her who was before, and did she not have the bluest eyes?

I'm getting there.

You are indeed. You begin, for now you know your being. Before, you were divided. Only half. You, amongst all these, present were most conscious of the missing half. You did not know what was missing. But now you are whole and she who stood before, whose power was light to many, is within you. Now you may begin. And when you look into your glass you may know yourself.

Thank you.

... Even those who are not conscious of their being will eventually pass through the door, if their intent is loving. Faith, faith first, love always, memory follows. For is not memory wrapped inside faith and love? So all of you have lived. For some it has been the smallest kernel, but it has survived. It is to these I speak. For it is your faith and love which have given me entry.

It is changed she said of Ian's anger. *You do well ... You had choice and you have chosen well.* It's the same for all of us. We're making different choices. I'm more gentle with Ian knowing I abandoned him when he was 18 months old. Knowing he has those memories of me, that experience of me. Knowing we have that between us to heal. Mark and Ann's relationship is different with that memory between them. And when I realise Patrick and I are again sparring on an intellectual level, I can smile with memory. And make a different choice than I might without it. It is changed. We *are* given new choices. Not new choices. Rather a chance to choose again. *Such has been necessary when the lives between have created disturbance.* And now we have a chance to heal the disturbances. By making different choices. The anger she talked to Ian and John about, it isn't only Ian and John. We have all these other, unknown memories to settle. I don't *understand* it. But somehow I sense this is what's happening.

23rd July 1996 :

I am Ishtar. We recognise each other, my friends, although our time together has been short. You are each now known to me. I see your pattern clearly. It is a pleasing sight and like a constellation of my memory ... Others work too, I tell you this always. Trust in that, for one day it will come together and there will be understanding. And you will be amazed how many have sat so as you do here, thinking themselves removed from the world and from those who live in it. You will be amazed how many are guided by those of their faith. You, I have told you, are of my faith and of my being, and we are joined in love and by

The Clew

love, if you will live it. So, let us speak together, for there is much to share. Who asks?

Patrick: I have no memory of my service with the others, with yourself. How does this disadvantage hold me back?

It is no disadvantage for you live it. It would be so if you did not. But you live love and give it to many, and this comes from your memory ... Let me look, for I remember you well. You are less bowed than before. Before you carried great burdens upon your back. They were, my friend, the burdens of statehood. I know your name ... Once you held all knowledge and were yourself held in reverence. For a short period you were the leader of a nation. Mighty indeed ... You have feared your power. That is memory. Fear it no longer. For with love it forms a great light that shines from you. You have indeed transformed self ... They know your presence and have waited for your footfall at the time of the new year's birth. You are once again amongst these who were your people ... Each will come to his own as before. For each must be in his or her place as before. For there are moments in the earth's turning when form must be replicated, colour remembered, shape restored. There are those amongst you with such knowledge, as are there others who now sit in their own places. You will form the lock in which the key must be turned ... I am that power which manifests in many forms and under many titles. This you remember and for you to begin your work, you must first have memory. Such is my purpose. I am of your past but also will lead you to your future. That which was once our light is restored here in this place, in this land. There is task but first there must be stability, and as I have spoken each of you still balances with the joining of the new to the old. When all that is achieved we may move forward ... In my being you become one with those others who have walked with you, and who walk with you still, although not apparent to your gaze.

The 'stability' she speaks of, the 'balancing and joining of new to old' is the healing we are doing with each other. The different choices we're making in our relationships to each other. She tells us it is in her being that we become one with each other. Something happens to each of us in her presence. It's provoking. It provokes things within each of us. Things we need to look at, need to heal. There is task, she advises. We'll be doing more together. But as a unified group this time. Not as the separate individuals we've been before. I don't know how it will be different. But I sense it will be.

So now she too is speaking of ... *moments in the earth's turning ... form the lock in which the key must be turned ... light is restored here in this place, in this land.*

Ian keeps saying it has something to do with astrology. The age of Pisces and the coming of Aquarius again. We thought the Arbor Low work was connected to that also. Arthur's Excalibur turning the energy off, and the Dragon Sword carefully crafted and used to turn it back on? This is all coming around again on a different level. We were told this in the beginning. At the time of the Kuwaiti invasion we were told *Your land will once again be the knot into which the power lines converge*. We were also told *The power will be finished at this place* (in the East) *and the centre will move to your own land*. Is Ishtar speaking of the same thing? They also spoke of our role *to retain the sounds that would be needed when the earth moved into its next cycle*. The earth's turning and the earth's next cycle - is this about the coming of the Aquarian age? And there was that mysteriously important sounding sentence I received on 18th April 1991 : *Your task and those of many like you will be not only with communication but also in locking on to the correct frequencies that will be needed to move the generator pulse of the prime energy to your land and then to secure it in place.* Ian says it's probably even more important than the move to the Age of Aquarius. There's something about the precession of the equinoxes which seems to have something to do with the time it takes for a cycle of the constellations of the zodiac to each go through appearing on the horizon at sunrise, something that actually takes 26,000 years. He thinks it has something to do with that. The energy changes each 2,000 years as now when we go from Pisces to Aquarius. But also within that 26,000 years there are other, stronger energy shifts. He explained that somehow this is one of those times - of stronger energy shift. And that perhaps whatever we are to do has something to do with that. Perhaps this too we've all been part of in the past and we're all here now to do it again. Doesn't make any sense when you think about it, but then what does?

Patience. It's difficult. I wonder what we're to do. When? How? How will we know? How will we manage to bring it about? Who else is to be involved? Was it easier in the beginning? It seemed our guidance was more clear then. Patience.

> *What I speak of is in time to come. It will happen slowly and with care ... for one day it will come together and there will be understanding.*

8th August 1996 :
> *I am Ishtar and I greet you, my friends. Once more are we gathered ... There are changes still afoot and I acknowledge for many of you this is disturbing. I do all in my power to assist but there are some changes that must take place within your energetic structures, for they must be rebalanced. You must return to a purity of being before your work can be undertaken. Your lives are short but your memories, and those particles which form your being, have no end. It is with these I work. I repeat, we will undertake together the task of cleansing, but first we cleanse yourselves, and for each this is a separate process, and will bring to each of you a confusion between present and past. There are those of you who must learn to contain certain aspects of yourselves, and there are others who must learn to free certain aspects. So is balance achieved, and each of you, within yourself, knows.*
>
> *I am not that one who will bring you to the place of conclusion ... I restore you to yourselves, for only in your whole beings may you undertake that task which is required of you. Only in your whole beings can you connect, can you grasp that which is above and join it to that which is below. It is true that all do this to some degree. You cannot live in physical being if you do not do this, for*

the current which vitalises you cannot function without such connection. Illness comes when such connection has been dismembered, misaligned. For this task of yours, all such misalignments must be removed, for you must channel pure light.

I can't help but wonder how one channels pure light. And how are we to grasp that which is above and join it to that which is below. When I'm thinking about these words of Ishtar's or about the channelled messages, or about what's happening to us personally, about our interactions with each other or with the earth, when I'm thinking about any of that it seems the one word 'energy' isn't enough. Ten words for energy, all with slightly different meanings, would be helpful. It's interesting about the 'current which vitalises' us. The early entities spoke of the energy of the earth, how we are to work with it, tune it, strengthen or change it in some way. But I don't remember a reference to our own 'current.' I don't remember mention of any above/below 'connection' that we all have or do to some degree.

You may think my stricture hard when you feel pain. It would be as nothing to the experience that would await you if we had not done this work. I will see no harm come to you ... I prepare you as others also are prepared ... I have told you your love and memory secures you and you must hold to it. Nothing can stop what lies before, but you will change it, as will those others. For if you do not do so, then it will stop. So you have worked before.

So we have worked before. In some other age, when the energy of some other age was changing. We are to do something we have all been a part of in the past. And Ishtar is teaching us to work together, to trust each other again. She is teaching us to connect with these past memories and heal them so that we function together as a group.

You are a small cog. Let us not over-estimate, there are others who work, whose power is far greater than your own. But you have the power of love and you have remembered it, and there are only few who have done so, and this is your strength and this is your task ...

Our strength. And our task. And the power of love. All these men I love but none is 'the one.' It's about the ways we love each other, the women too. All the many kinds of love. It's as if we're all being given opportunities on a personal level, opportunities to look at things about ourselves we might rather not look at. Anger, doubt, disappointment, fear, resentment, physical challenges - it's all there. All the barriers to love. On a daily basis we're being given the opportunity to make different choices than we may have made in the past. This is not an easy time for any of us. Something is going to happen that none of us can stop but we can change it if we succeed in remembering something about ourselves that has to do with love. Well this is certainly different than our previous work.

The Clew

October 1996 : So many changes since Ishtar arrived. I knew straight away her energy was very different, but how different, and how it would affect us - I couldn't know. I remember in the moments after she arrived, my head swung from side to side. It felt almost like a snake's head weaving back and forth. I remember the sensation and thinking about the snake and thinking 'how odd.' She had two heads and my head went from one to the other, back and forth. Two heads, love and war. The goddess of love and the goddess of war.

She too prompted us to read. Study. Go back and remember. We did. We found her history. Inanna. The voice - my voice from some other time - the voice during the massage. "Servant to Inanna." The name of the archetypal energy Ishtar grew from the name Inanna. In Sumeria, Inanna, later to be Ishtar, was gentle, soft, very much about love. The Venus energy. After the Assyrian conquest and the beginnings of patriarchy, she became Ishtar, the goddess of love but also the goddess of war. The first time Ishtar spoke to us she said, " we have known peace and war, love and hate." And she said her power was transformed in me if I could hold to the light of gentleness. It was my test. I didn't understand then, but I think I do now. Her energy was profoundly challenging. We even made light of it at the time. John said he felt his hair singe whilst she was speaking. Wendy said she levitated. Paracelsus was gentle, humorous. Not Ishtar. It's as if I have to constantly choose. The message she brings can be interpreted in one of two ways. Ian explained that it has to do with my sun in Aries/Mars and my moon exactly opposite in Libra/Venus. He explained that Ishtar's words about my test being to hold to the light of gentleness has to do with whether I will choose to interpret her energy from my aggressive Mars energy or more gently from my Venus love energy.

Interesting how the groups have changed. When Paracelsus was with us I was holding three or four groups a month. People liked Paracelsus. There was much demand for his knowledge, his help with health related issues. He helped many people. I tried to continue meeting on the same schedule but people found Ishtar difficult. I remember one group session soon after Paracelsus left and she arrived. One of the women asked about a headache. "Wait, I must seek knowledge," she said, and then she left. I could feel that her energy had actually departed. I remember thinking to myself she had probably gone off to ask Paracelsus for the information the woman needed. When she finally came back she seemed really amazed by the fact that someone could have a headache and even more amazed that there might be an aid for it - rosemary. She didn't seem quite sure what rosemary was. "How strange," she said. "My energy through a plant." She clearly found our world strange and weird. She apologised to the woman because evidently her headache was actually caused by Ishtar's energy. It had unbalanced her in the same way we often found the entities' energies unbalancing. Ishtar was always quite surprised when someone asked her help in some health issue. It was clear she had to work at being sensitive to a question of this kind. She actually said more than once that she was with us to learn to be sensitive. Clearly aggression was her more natural mode. I have also had the insight that had I interpreted her message in this aggressive manner, the entire experience would have ended. Our work as a group wouldn't have continued. I may have even ceased to received the messages. It truly was a test.

But the groups have changed. I do fewer of them because people don't find Ishtar as nurturing as they did Paracelsus. They find her much more challenging. Even within our own group, the core group involved in the earth healing work, some have found her energy so challenging they have decided not to continue. But even with all of this, there is a group cohesion that is different than before. Somehow she is challenging us in ways that force us to work through our individual differences. It has something to do with vulnerability and trust and self reliance and mutual support. I can't point to any one thing, but the feeling is there. We're different. All of us. And as a group - the group is different too. Indefinably so, but so none the less.

2nd December 1996 :
> *I am Ishtar and I speak with you now for the last time. We part my friends ... My task was to journey with you along your path for that short space, that space in which you might draw to you that knowledge without which you could not progress further. You have acquired such.*

This is very strange and doesn't make sense, but we think we may have surmised the knowledge she refers to. We read about Sumeria and Assyria but we also seem to have 'remembered' things. We have put the pieces together. In these ancient times in this area there were many city-states. Each was independent and had responsibility for nurturing, caring for, supporting, worshipping a certain energy. Personified as a god or goddess, the energy seems to have actually been described in ancient astrology. Based on the energy of a particular planet or solar body the energy would have been seen as the love energy of Venus, or the more warlike, aggressive energy of Mars. One city-state would have a temple to Jupiter or the Jupiter energy of faith and optimism. Another to the energy of Saturn which has to do with converting energy into form, into matter. We suspect we were all connected to one of these city-states and its temple. For we were all together. With song, and dance, and prayer, and festival and celebration, and who knows what else, together we nurtured, cared for, and anchored one of these archetypal energies. It's difficult to put into words because we have nothing like it in our present day reality. Maybe it was something like beating the bounds. Or pilgrimages. Or maybe May day dances or something like Beltane fires. Maybe if we think about these remnants of earlier worship we can get an idea of how these ancient peoples nurtured their personally appointed archetypal energy. Who knows. We don't. But we know that we were all a part of some such indefinable relationship. And we think that somehow we had to remember this, discover this, in order to continue on our way to our next task. We think that's the knowledge we have acquired.

> *Perhaps as I speak now you begin to understand for the first time the nature of purpose in life, the nature of your true being. You have been sheltered from such knowledge for, without security, such knowledge destabilises. But each of you in your own way, and in your own world has applied learning, reached for*

The Clew

> *wisdom, secured instability. It is all a little new, is it not? Yet I tell you, you may trust it for it has been my task to weave such.*

We've slowly come to our knowledge of reincarnation and that we've lived lives together. We've slowly accepted that we have loved and hated each other. That we've helped and hurt each other. That we've nurtured and deserted each other. That we've worshipped together, grown together, but also fought with each other, killed each other. That somewhere in our memories these loves and hurts remain and we must heal them. And yes, had anyone insisted I believe this ten years ago, I would have been destabilised, just as Ishtar says. And the group? Had we remembered these sometimes rather violent and certainly very deep and strong feelings we have remembered toward each other, I doubt we would have stayed together as a group. In the beginning is was fun, detective work, a lark, shared camaraderie in the most jolly way. No, in the beginning we couldn't have healed these hurts we've discovered. They too would have been destabilising.

> *You are all joined. Do not forget that such joining is made by the heart. Without love you are all as nothing. If you lose love, you lose your entire journey … Where have you each journeyed inside yourself, in my time with you? Each of you has confronted thoughts and images which you have never shared with other, for it has seemed too strange. Did I not come to bring you memory? … Live love within the world, with each other, and with your fellows and with all who draw your focus. Whatever passes before you, give love.*
>
> *You are come to task for the light must seed and fruit again as before. I am content. I do not see perfection before me, but I observe adequacy and can ask no more. Do not fear responsibility. You are not asked to give all away; you are not asked to change form; you are not asked to lay down your lives … You are asked to love and encompass those who that light will draw in. You are asked to shine … We are divided for short space only. Let us remain as one, in love and joy united, with peace at the heart of our being and harmony as its shape. Do not waste your gift … I give you my blessings. My gifts are yours. You move onwards and I also. You are in and of my love; that is eternal.*
>
> *I am Ishtar.*

Chapter Twelve

During the evening session of 18th December 1994, Assurbanipal 'stood aside' and asked the group to welcome 'he who comes.' Avril paused for several moments during which time Assurbanipal departed and Paracelsus arrived. The voice of Paracelsus then spoke telling the group the 'mantle for their care had been passed to him'. He also said he brought them the *'greater strength of his being and that he was beyond the telling of him who stood before.'* Then, one and a half years later, on 6th June 1996, Paracelsus bid the group farewell by saying that he *'followed those who had gone before.'* Of the one who was to follow he stated, *'I bow before such power.'* Again Avril paused several moments to allow the two vastly different energies to trade places. Within moments Ishtar spoke to the group telling them that she was now responsible for their care and guidance and that her knowledge was beyond that of him who came before but contained his wisdom and the wisdom of his predecessors. A short six months later, on 2nd December 1996, Ishtar too moved aside for *'the long awaited-one who would bring* - within Avril and the others - *the spark to flame.'* Once again after a long pause, the group's new partner had arrived, *I am Merlin, servant to the Lord and servant to you.* It would be almost two years before Avril would hear yet another, and the last voice, who would speak the words *I am Lord of one power alone.* Almost two years before she would realise that each of the entities had been as an individual strand all of which together made up a cable, and that finally, and one time only, she would actually bring through the energy of the entire cable. She was being prepared. The group too, although not yet complete, was simultaneously being prepared.

A pattern of similarities seemed to be emerging for the times when one entity left and another arrived. Avril's voice timbre and inflections, her mannerisms, and her speech patterns changed to fit the personality of each entity. While all this returned to normal as soon as the entity departed the session, the physical challenges she and group members experienced lasted longer. Avril and various members of the group sometimes experienced mild respiratory ailments, flu-like symptoms, or a general malaise following an entity's arrival. It is interesting that the entities voiced sympathy for what the group was experiencing. Ishtar told the group :

> *I may destabilise your beings for a short time but I could not have come so if you could not receive me. I thank you for this.*

Merlin explained

> *... my light has entered your beings. There will be a response, act kindly with yourselves ... Each of you gives out my light. You must adjust to this as those around you must adjust ... You will not suffer permanent pain, damage, disablement, but you may suffer temporary pain. But your adjustments have taken place, you are lighter and may therefore absorb light more intensely than before.*

Avril is very clear that the energy of each new entity was more intense and more

The Clew

powerful than the energy of the preceding one. She affirms that had she been asked on that first day in April 1990 to bring through the level of intensity present during the message preceding their last work, she couldn't have managed it physically. She simply wouldn't have been able to withstand the physical strain the later energies put on her body.

Upon arriving the entities also stated their purpose, as if sharing with the group the agenda for their tenure. Paracelsus, who made available information primarily of a personal level, said :

> *The great Light shines and guides me to this place for there is work to do. I have accepted my task. I bring many wisdoms. If you would have me speak, I would answer that which is in your heart.*

Ishtar explained that she would be helping the group remember,

> *My brothers and I have come merely to remind you of that which you know, of that which has sustained you through many lifetimes ... My purpose is your care. My task is your guidance.*

And Merlin, who would guide the group to their final task said,

> *I come to re-build, to re-form, to make anew that which is old and beyond its use. We build again. There are those who have worked to make foundation - you amongst them. Now we will rise above the surface ... Know my voice for I am Merlin and will bring this land to its true being and form.*

In these ways each entity, in the beginning of their time with the group, reassured the group and spoke of their own appointed task and of the tasks of the group. Additionally, and - perhaps most heartwarming of all - they spoke personally of their own difficulty with this reality and of their gratitude to the group. In order to come into this reality, they seemed to undergo some shift in awareness or being. Ishtar pondered the strangeness of this new experience :

> *It is a strange being, I must accustom myself. It has been so long since I have spoken ... I must find my way again ... I come. I bear the light of being. I am commanded so. I do not know my place, for it is strange ... Wait, I will accustom myself to old movement.*

Merlin spoke in a similar way,

> *I am confounded by this change, yet I am drawn hither ... I have task and am commanded.*

Without fail, each entity expressed gratitude at the opportunity to have been of service and explained they owed the group much. Assurbanipal explained :

> *I move beyond to that place in which I must joy and delight for there I am offered that which I have long desired. It is to you that my journey forward is owed. What treasure you have given me.*

Paracelsus said :

> *He who passed has great wisdom, yet you taught him those matters which*

were his to learn and without you he could not have learned such things. He goes forward into greater glory ... I am freed from certain bonds. You have assisted me in this purpose. I owe you much.

Ishtar thanked the group,
I am well satisfied for you have returned also to me great gift ... You have given me great joy, for you contain such within all of you ... we work as you work, for without you we come to nothing.

On 2nd December 1996, after six months with the group, Ishtar moved aside for Avril's penultimate guide to step forward.

AVRIL
Merlin arrives. Preparation for the final task.

2nd December 1996 :
Love goes. I come ... I greet you and offer you my blessings, for does not my light shine now here? ... I am the Wizard. I come to re-build, to re-form, to make anew that which is old and beyond its use. We build again. There are those who have worked to make foundation - you amongst them. Now we will rise above the surface ... Know my voice for I am Merlin and will bring this land to its true being and form ... And with this woman's help I will speak to the world ... Yet we have serious work, much to do, much will be worked within your own beings ... You are secured, you have listened, you have changed, you are ready. Secure each other, each one within the whole - that is the pattern. Do not hold to littleness ...

Ishtar said *you are come to task for the light must seed again and fruit as before.* Now Merlin speaks of another task. Ishtar prepared us. And now Merlin continues. And we too continue.

23rd January 1997 :
All will be summoned to their business, will sense responsibility - not that which burdens but that which is a joy of creation. For all who have heard, have task, and there are thousands of you. What is this task? You are as small lights. You are as beacons linked together as are the heavens at this time. You will all link. Imagine your globe covered in small lights. To be sure there is darkness but so much smaller than before. You are like a glistening net wrapped around your globe, and now we may begin to use it. You must wait to discover our purpose. Simply hold your space and your light. Confirm connection to others. When you are reached for - respond. Imagine that all the inhabitants of the earth stand arms outstretched and touching another with their fingers. This we have worked to achieve, and I am Merlin, and know the plan. Has not

The Clew

my magic repaired? Are not wonders in my gift? Do I not make whole, in order that all once more may be secured? I prepare ... You will come to task in your own space and with companions. For all who are now conscious will join together ...

I thank you. I am companion and move now amongst you and many others who know my name. I bring magic, pattern, the weaving of colours, the working of design ... Seek to become the best of yourself. Know yourself now to have moved out of the old shell. My friends, the chrysalis has broken apart. You may come to as much glory as the butterfly. Shine your colour joyfully.

6th February 1997:

... Many, like you, sit so. But we do not come simply in this way into your presence. Many alone in their own spaces hear our voices and begin, for the first time, to understand their place in the whole. Many are led to task they do not understand, and yet they do it. We cannot teach you to hear. There are those who are born with our sound within their ears. Many others will come to have their ears opened. But the desire must be within you. I cannot impose my will or my nature upon you if you do not wish it. I and my brothers must be invited. I am within your being but you must wish to speak to me. And yet, after great time many do so wish. For those born with sight and hearing begin to educate. You may say there are those born who come to switch on the lights. With light they may see clearly. They may choose action. Does this woman not switch on light? But she is not alone, she is one of many. And now do all of you not also have such knowledge that you may switch on light for others. If you choose, if you choose ... You have not yet fully understood how to live your whole. Many will be born before that occurs. And so you will interpret according to your experience, and so there must be limitation.

Your sun, your source of light, is not the source of light, but for you it is the centre. For me, not so. For there is a greater light beyond your knowing, beyond the worlds of time and space. There is the heart, the pulse to which all are connected ... The whole of which you are a part is itself merely a very small part of the whole ... We cannot convert you to light, we can only work through those who can. There are enough but, you see, does not your planet teach free will? Enough there may be, but do enough choose to do the work, that has been the question. Yet we continue, we are encouraged. And so you travel to light but it is not the light of destruction. Remember this, for many will teach it ... Interpret through ... memory, for have I not spoken that this has occurred before. And do you all not have memory of such, however faint. For there is only one memory. There is only one ... Those with [memory] will pass the light through them into the earth and you will remain as one. Those with no [memory] will ... not recognise their task - to be the conductors. The light must enter your globe; if it remains outside it your globe perishes ... That is not our desire, and increasingly not yours either.

You must understand we may only act when there is hope ... I think it important that you discuss this ... consider it, educate yourselves, and see yourselves as beings of light and as the switches. There is much now that goes well ... I am come and could not have so done if it was ended before my being. I prepare, am servant to that light of which we speak. Not your centre, but the centre.

Are you referring to God?
Such word imports to you the closest understanding you may yet reach. Such word imparts to you a power and glory beyond your understanding and in such case that is correct. You may only grasp the merest hint in that word, but you do grasp it, you do have sense and awareness of such. There are no words in this woman's being, for she herself stands amongst you ... I spoke of that source of which you are a part and I a part, of which every atom, every particle of existence stands in knowledge of that power and is formed from that power, and is fed from that power. How can one conceive of love which loves all that? The flea to the cosmos my friend. That conceived, that made, that loves, that nurtures. The flea to the cosmos. If you can encapsulate that within your words then you begin to have a sense of it ...

The teaching widens, must spread beyond yourselves. For you must be emissaries. Your moments of pleasure and interest, fascination, your moments of exchange with my brothers have not been purely for entertainment. You have been taught; many others also. But now that teaching moves beyond, into the greater realm, for you must reach out and touch each other, and all those others who have been so prepared. There must come a wider knowledge and learning to your globe. You are grown, my friends, and therefore must act so ...

20th February 1997: Tonight someone in the group asked a very interesting question, and solicited a very interesting answer.

How can we improve our ability to communicate with our guides?
A wise question, my friend. Would others ask it also, my brothers would find their existence easier. Firstly, accept. That is difficult is it not? How many have sense of awareness and yet question, disbelieve. So firstly, accept. Secondly, seek some structure of meeting. It is as if you arrange to meet any friend. Where will you meet? Such place might be a chair in which one may be still, but I think in the first instance it is wise to have such structure; it may be in the garden beneath a tree, it may be with a light, but create structure.

What too often occurs is that you place yourself, or yourselves, in positions of, for want of a better word, I will use servitude, student to master. You have power. It is our task to nurture your power. It is not our task to ignore it. It is not our task to prevent you living your life. So take your power and ... meet as equals friends. One who wishes to draw close may simply make their presence known, as if they stand on the far side of a field and wave to you. You invite. And so at the beginning of consciousness it is easier perhaps, if you establish a framework, if you establish the place and the time. And then invite and observe what happens. Acquire recognition skills. Such recognition may come in any form. Sound, colour light, form. A whisper of the wind, a breath in the ear.

The Clew

You alone will know, but do not dismiss the small.

22ⁿᵈ February 1997:
> *... For as you have journeyed you have left behind you imprints and patterns and you must return through them all. So where you have left anger you must face the ghost of anger; where you have left cruelty you must face the ghost of cruelty; and where you have left love, you must face the ghost of love. For they are all yours. And so I tell you, you face nothing that you did not construct. No great teacher or punisher constructs these for you in your life. No-one has said 'I will do this to him or to her." They are your own, and must be defeated by you alone. And yet remember, you stand in line with each other . . to make this journey back. And you will not come back to the laurel wreath, the crown for the individual pride, you will come back because you have all confronted such apparition. You left alone, but you return together. That is the difference.*

Our understanding of this is growing. Each time one of us has a memory, or we have a group memory, this understanding grows. Ann said it well. She said it's as if any thing we've said, something like "I'll remember this" about some thing we've been hurt by or upset by, if we've said it - or perhaps even intended it - then we have to come back in a lifetime with that person and heal that. Perhaps it's easier to recognise feelings like "I'll get him for this." Perhaps those we can recognise and let go easier than situations. I'm reminded of the mother/daughter couple Paracelsus spoke about. How they came back in lifetime after lifetime and set up the arguments. What the daughter needed for healing, the mother prevented by her own choices. And, he said, it had ever been thus. Did the mother know, on a conscious level, that she was creating the situation she would have to come back in another lifetime to have a chance to heal? And would continue in this way until she did heal it? Did she know that? I don't think so. Perhaps those are the most difficult of all. The unknowing ones. The unconscious ones.

We have great difficulty among ourselves when we know what needs to be healed and we've been shown what it will take to heal it. I'm beginning to think that's part of what the entities have been referring to when they say 'remember.' They're talking about the skills we have and can only access once we have the memory of another lifetime. But they're also encouraging us to remember the physical and emotional hurts we've caused each other. Remember so that we can choose another way. Choose again. Forgive and choose a different way.

> *There is great knowledge available now to many. Those who have been prepared may receive ... And there will be imbalance, oscillation, for you cannot change so without causing such instability. Much that has been solid will be seen as cloud. It is not only the enemy that appears so, all that has sustained you will appear so. For so it is. And therefore those who have learning, true learning, must hold their place, for they secure the Being that is your life.*

9ᵗʰ April 1997 :
> *Do you enjoy the joys in your life, or do you think they are not to be enjoyed?*

Do you think you should turn from pleasures perhaps for the sake of others? Don't be so foolish. Think how can you truly serve others if you have no joy of self? For it is only with joy of self that you can offer love to others, and when you have no such joy then your service is constructed of pain. You are born to live joy in the world. Such I teach and such must be remembered. You have lived too long in darkness. Many have preached of self denial. If you wish to deny yourself, then deny yourself bitterness and regret, but don't deny yourself delight. However you may summon it, it may merely be the light of a flower, but ask yourself what is it that delights you and go in search of it. All may be happy, perhaps only for a moment, but once decided then reach for it - not on the backs of others, for such happiness is false. I speak of true joy.

You have a task, and that task is to become yourself - the best of yourself, and to shine out in the world. Don't waste your energies on attempting to change others. Put your whole strength into changing yourselves, then you may change others as well, for when they observe the light they may be drawn to it. I don't ask you to lay aside service or responsibility. I ask you to judge your use and need of it, and the truth of its being as you live it. If you use responsibility and service to others as an excuse then such action forms no love. First come to love yourself for you are, and contain, everything. And know that you are born with light to shine it out in the world.

17th April 1997 :

All know the call that summons them. All are drawn for all know their task. And you come to task. Have I not spoken of hope, of joy, of love, of manifestation? You must begin to live such, firstly in your own lives in small, gentle ways. Live it with those around you, those who share your space. Lighten their lives and in turn they will learn to lighten others. Do not attach yourself to them. Do not say "I will teach you this. See how I live my truth. This is what all must believe in." Do not do that, for such I do not teach. I teach you to live your light purely and simply; to know your power and to respect it. I teach you not to inflict that power on others. Power is not directed such; only by those who do not comprehend. Your power is a light within you; a flame of being which shines out. It is not a firebrand which you hold in your hand and charge forward to clear all before you.

Imagine a table in a room with a single lantern upon it. See how its light extends beyond its frame. See how the echo of that light fills the room. Perhaps there is still darkness, but there is a fraction less in every corner than there was before that light was lit. Now place another, and another, and another. Now do you understand? This is your task. Mine is simply to bring the light to flame, but I do not make the lamp. I did not form the wick. I come now merely to light them up, and when the room is lit, what may enter?

19th July 1997 :

And there must again be new form. Not all departs, I do not speak of absolute or total destruction, far from it, but I speak of some. And how may you survive this, or should I say, how may you assist the survival of others?

The Clew

And you assist this by recognising and identifying this work, and by inviting it into yourselves, into your own lives. For if you do this, then you reduce the potential for, what we might say, could possibly be catastrophe. For you invite in gently and gradually ... For the doors stand open and that which waits may be invited to enter. And if so, like any good guest, enters gently, calmly, companionably. It is only if locked outside and resolutely refused entrance; that the anger builds. And then the door is broken down. Change approaches, change stands outside the door, change seeps in. You do not stop that, you may not stop that, but you may open the door willingly with open arms. You may loose those parts of yourself which have been too rigid, too attached to earth, too fixated on structure ... You may invite courteously, you may invite gentle change, you may welcome flow. I hope, I trust, that many do.

23rd September 1997 :

There is no difference between us, merely, you might say, that I have studied a little longer and have met those teachers who you, as yet, may only view at distance. I have conversed with the wise, but my small wisdom I may make available to you if you will share yours with me ...

There are many unconscious of our being, unconscious of themselves. But that changes. Much now changes. We speak as once before. You might say, the volume is turned up a little. And so, more hear than before. And we speak because we must. For these silences you have bred within yourselves have brought us all to the edge of disaster. Such isolation you have lived. Such isolation mankind has believed in. It is not true. And so, there must be powerful change to change that concept, that belief, that thought.

For some, such change may take the form of simply believing that there are other beings on other worlds. That is how they will perceive it. And yet see how many turn even that first stretching out into fear. It in itself is a limitation. You are asked to believe in far greater than that. And what image will each of you call to mind. If I say to you 'You are not alone. I tell you you are not alone. No single one here, not one of mankind stands alone. That which you have always longed to be at your side is present, exists. That which would always end your emptiness, your loneliness, is here, is true.' What would you each see I wonder?

... all are connected. Each of you, had you so desired, could hear any of these others present before this gathering, before you had ever met. For all are connected, and you must come now to such an understanding. There has been time long past when such was known and understood and was practiced. But there was pain and division, a pulling in of boundary, a separating out. A downward spiral, a solidifying.

... Do not fear these new skills, do not seek to isolate, shut out. Seek to live your connections with all life so that you are enhanced and may live your whole being. You touch each other, you touch everything that lives, as they touch you. Welcome such, for with such welcome will come the end of aggression. For when you know yourselves as one being, who is there then to fight?

The Clew

30th September 1997 :

I am Merlin and I greet you. It is a blessing, friends, to gather so. Do not fear my presence, I speak with this woman's assistance. You see merely one aspect of my being. Understand, for do you not look to understand the nature of such exchange. Imagine in this woman the stem of a funnel. I must pour in all of my being and it must be reduced to that which you can perceive. It must take on shape and form and colour that you can understand ...

I come to prepare change. I come to tie change together, for you move now into other worlds, of understanding, of knowledge, of action, of connection. You, my friends, and those who live now stand at the beginning of a new order. But have you not stood at the beginning of others, for do you not so travel as I do? All moves forward toward completion. Ah, but that still lies long before. But you must make those changes now which must be made in their time and in none other ...

There must come a greater love of one's fellow man, but above all else there must come a greater love of your earth and of that which it moves amongst. You have not succeeded entirely in the love of all. Such was the lesson you were presented with long ago to begin this learning ...

I and my brothers offer you wholeness, but I offer you learning also, with a light touch. Can you not enjoy lessons? Is there not an excitement in knowledge? If you will only access hope, expectation, and loose hold of fear there is nothing that may not be opened before you ... If you shine light, you will draw it to you. Lay aside darkness, it has no purpose any more. We are well met, friends, you and I, and may yet come to greater understanding if such is your desire.

18th October 1997 :

All exchange takes place between all. So is learning stimulated, encouraged. Each has its own identity, each lights lifts, interprets. And each interpretation is individual. And so there is always much to learn, is there not? What one perceives, another may not. What one experiences, another may not. And it is only through the sharing that knowledge is deepened, understanding broadened.

You come together now for such purpose, although you still make a lone journey, but now you may join together if you choose. For you must bring your own individual knowledge into a concrete awareness. You must learn from others, share with others ... But do not shine where another needs to shine. Do not expand your light to such intensity that all others are blinded by it. For they have equal light to you and must live it in their world as much as you live yours in theirs ...

What you will make of all this lies in your hands. Do not ask me future for such I do not decide, nor any of my brothers. We may offer you seed but you must choose where to plant it, you must remember to water it and you must decide when to harvest it. We have no jurisdiction over that. We may only pray and hope that you will nourish seed; that you will bring to harvest. Each their own harvest, and then each to serve to bring in the harvest of the greater realm. All is one.

Chapter Thirteen

AVRIL
Healing group karma

January 1998 : It's interesting the way things happen now. We used to be told so much. Instructed. Given clues, hints, and then rewards and treasures when we found something or got it 'right.' It seems now that process was a learning device. Training wheels. More and more we're asked to trust our intuition. To go with our own insights and feelings about things. When we heal something, release old energy, make wiser choices, we're aware of their pleasure. We're thanked. We're told how much it means to the universe. But there's less overt guidance. As with Gray's forthcoming visit. As soon as he rang up to say he was coming, as soon as I heard his voice on the phone, I knew we were to do something else. I didn't know what or when, but I knew we were to do more. And I knew it would coincide with his visit.

I waited to see when that would be. Ian waited too. Trusting that Gray would be directed. Gray would know the time. Would pick the date. The Buddha. My sense of him in Devon - the Buddha. Sitting silently. Walking silently. Moving quietly. Almost non-actively involved, and yet as active as any of us merely in his presence. An anchor or something. Solid. Grounded. Yes, wait for Gray to tell us when he's coming. Then we'll know. November. So it will be November again. Beginning of November, same time as Devon four years ago. Ian checking the planets, checking the things that Ian checks. Yes. That's it. That's when we're supposed to do it. And then more knowing. I knew it was to be Cornwall. Even more or less knew the place in Cornwall. But not *exactly* the place.

And then I found, re-read the words Merlin had given us more than a month before.

> *I may be form to you, I may be name, I may be colour, I may be sound, whichever you perceive. You may reach for me by any means, I know mine own when I am called.*

I knew what he was telling us. He was telling us that we didn't need always to get the messages through my voice. That we didn't always need to show up in the form of a group, that I didn't always need to sit and have his voice come through me in the way we had traditionally received messages. That we are to learn to recognise the information in anyway it came. That any one of us may see something, or hear something, or interact in some way with someone or something that will prompt the knowing. The intuitive sense that there is a message. We're all more open to it. It's a skill. We're learning, perfecting the skill. Not long before Gray's phone call we received those words. Was he advising us that we needed to go with what we felt? Reassuring us even then? I think so.

And so I have continued. Maggie takes a holiday three times a year. All the brochures she collects. All the information she has. Sitting at her table, the

The Clew

brochures spread out in front of us. She pointing to this one and that one, dreaming of the next holiday. My joking comment 'so find a good place in Cornwall.' Moments later she handed me the brochure. A picture of holiday accommodation. Of the room where we would meet as a group. And I knew again. Yes that was it. That's where we were supposed to meet. Where was it? Yes, the same area where I had intuitively thought we should be. It's unfolding. I don't know specifically where we are to do our work. I don't know yet specifically what we are to do. But I know we are to do something, I know it will be in Cornwall and I know it will be on 8th November. From this point I will trust in the process. It will unfold. We will be shown task. We will be shown.

January, 1998 The 'king' has come. 'King' is as close as I can come to the feeling. The word isn't quite right, but I don't know a word that's right for the feeling. So 'king' will do. I remember when I first realised he was coming. Maybe there is something about doing the washing up. Washing up four years ago I 'saw' the knights of the round table. That began the process of the Blackdown Rings. I wonder if this will begin some equivalent process. This time, standing there, hands in warm soapy water, I suddenly sensed 'the king is coming.' I don't know what I was thinking prior to that thought. Nothing of any consequence. And suddenly there it was. I might not know who the king was or what his coming signified, but I was certain of one thing, he was coming.

I turned to Ian and explained my inner knowing. A kind of buzzing in my head and then the knowing. I couldn't answer Ian's question. I'd no idea what it meant. I'd no idea when he was coming or from where. I knew it had to do with the group but that was all I knew. I knew the king needed to arrive before we could do the next piece of work. I didn't know what 'king' meant in this context. More than likely another of 'my men'. But king? I'd no idea what it meant. I think now that I know. It's in his chart. Ian can look and see something about where Jupiter's position or the sign of Leo is in a person's chart, and somehow in this case he knows that in some past life kingship played an important part.

Meeting him was another of the coincidental processes. After I moved here to Devon to be closer to Hugh and his wife, I called a friend to update my address. I mentioned that Hugh wanted someone to dowse the energy of his new home. My friend suggested we contact Colin because he did remote dowsing, could do a reading and mail it and not have to actually make the trip to Cornwall. Arrangements were agreed and after we received Colin's reading, I eventually managed to ring him to say thank you. I spoke my thank you and then became aware of a long silence between us. It was most unusual. Finally I asked Colin if I knew him. With only this connection over the phone, without being able to see him, or see into his eyes which is usually the give away, still I felt we knew each other. This again! But stranger still, when I asked him that, after the silence I heard him begin to cry. Obviously we knew each other. Was it coincidence that the very day I called was his late mother's birthday? I haven't been *his* mother! At least I don't think so. But there it is again. The mother thing. Same as with Ian. We arranged a meeting which, when it took place, was disconcerting.

I knew him instantly, but didn't know him. I knew that I *had* known him,

The Clew

that there was a connection. And knew even that he is to be in the group. But he wasn't who I had expected. It's as if I'd been expecting the king, but he wasn't the king. When he walked beside me, I knew his energy. But when I looked at him, there seemed to be a mismatch or something. It wasn't that I had any particular image of him prior to meeting him. It wasn't that. But something wasn't right. Why or how I had expected any thing in particular I don't know. I can't even say exactly *what* I expected that felt wrong. I only knew that something was not quite right. He agreed to have Ian look at his chart, and Ian discovered that kingship has played a role in his past. At some point he was a king. Or had the opportunity to be one. I'm not quite sure exactly how it fits, but Ian understands these things and said there was that factor in his chart. I guess I didn't get this one right. He is to be in the group, he agrees with that, he senses that. So I made a mistake about his not being the king. I feel now we are complete. November. I can look forward now to November.

April 1998 It began weeks ago. Ian and Colin. Colin asked Ian to do a chart for Sara, a woman he had recently met. Astrological charts prompt memories for Ian. It's a very powerful skill and one all the entities have encouraged him to develop. We've been told before that members in the group have all incarnated together many times. That we have both loved and hated each other, and that we all have much to work through in this incarnation if we are to work together. That somehow healing amongst ourselves is important to the healing energies in the universe. That was Ishtar's lesson. It seemed with Ishtar's energy all sorts of issues needing healing erupted.

If we needed any proof that Colin, joining us at this late date, is part of the group, we certainly found it. When Ian saw Sara's chart, he 'remembered' that he and Colin had 'bad blood' between them in a past lifetime and that Sara had been the cause of it. Instead of confronting Colin, Ian continued to seethe. The group gathered to meet Colin, but Ian didn't arrive. For a while we thought nothing of it, he's sometimes late because he has a problem being in the group anyway. Finally we realised he wasn't coming and decided to do a healing ritual. We each spoke our feelings for Ian and what it felt like that he had decided not to come. We had completed this ritual before Ian finally did arrive. Because we immediately sensed his seething emotion, we decided to share with him some of what had been spoken during our ritual. As each person spoke, Ian had a rebuttal.

After listening to several of these, Colin abruptly turned to Ian and hissed, "I would actually think you heard us if you stopped saying 'yes but …' "

It was Ian's turn to hiss. He turned to Colin and spat the words, "I didn't come - because of you!"

Ann immediately picked up on what was happening at a level none of the rest of us could sense. "Two brothers. They're brothers and there's been a feud. Over land or inheritance or something."

Colin then did what Colin does, "Wait, I'll try and get it." But he couldn't get it. Usually he would have been able to figure out what the past life connection was. He's very good at that. But this time he couldn't get it.

I turned to Ian and shouted, "Stop it, Ian! You're blocking!" I knew from the look on Ian's face I had it right, he was blocking.

Colin kept asking, "Who? Who is it?"

By that time I had seen more. "It's a wedding ring, a dowry!"

Colin insisted, "Who is it!?"

Patrick asked if it was me. Colin, confused and struggling, said "Is it someone here, who is it?" Ian bent toward Colin so totally absorbed it was frightening. Leaning forward, close to Colin's face and in the most malevolent tone I think anyone could ever be capable of using, Ian spoke - distinct and separately - two syllables, "Sa-ra." Full of venom and yet barely audible. Colin seemed to go into shock and fell forward in his chair. Margaret ran to Ian, frozen in his chair. Patrick and I went to Colin. We had often joked about Patrick's ability to 'zap' people whilst, at the same time, acknowledging a deep respect for his healing abilities. Right now it was no joke. He 'zapped' Colin whose heart began beating. It had, terrifyingly, stopped at Ian's words. He began to recover.

Ann spoke quietly from the corner, "There was a death." His piercing gaze fixed on Colin, through clenched teeth, Ian agreed. "I killed you. And I could have killed you again now." Jarred sober by his own words and calmed by Margaret's presence, Ian sat back and audibly took several breaths. "I never want to be in that place again. I felt not one ounce of compassion." He seemed confused, troubled, and more than a little bewildered by the depth of his emotion.

Eventually, after much work from and with all of us, Ian and Colin managed to half-heartedly hug each other, and it felt like the crisis passed. The result was some kind of truce, a sort of healing between them. And so we continue to find our links with each other. We continue the healing, the memory. We continue.

19th April 1998 :

> So what will you send forth? Will you send out that light which is the best of yourselves or will you send out that light which holds to grievance, reduces all to the physical level? ... You do not see that that which leaves you contains you within it, and changes you in its journey and continues to change you.

What we think, what we say, the actions we choose - that which leaves us contains us and changes us. We are our thoughts, words and actions. By choosing, we become. And by re-choosing, we can re-become. We're all being given this chance to choose again. Ian and Colin, graphically, given a chance to choose again. Recreate the old energy, the old words, the old actions. Or choose again. And change that which they sent out.

> And as you are changed all else are changed. And as you gather, such effect is multiplied many more times than the number of you here present. What we give birth to is ours and part of us forever. So take care what you loose upon the world.

These words, this paragraph after Ian and Colin's experience. Gently chastising? A warning for all of us? If they had to confront that, had to heal that experience, had to come back together in the same incarnation in order to make

The Clew

amends - is it also true for everything we're doing now? And everything we'll do in the future? I remember the ritual at Hazlewood. The yellow flowers. The feeling that I was not doing the forgiving. I was not the one being healed. They were. The wound had not been mine, but theirs. They needed the healing, not me - and the ritual was about their healing. They were being given a chance to choose again. Any time we hold grudge or grievance, do we have to incarnate with the person against whom these feelings were held? So that we have a chance to heal them? To choose differently? No wonder we're admonished to live with love.

> *Our task is to live hope, to weave magic, to create anew. But create new thoughts, friends, do not simply replicate the old. For have you not lived those and have they not constructed for you such pain as you have all suffered, life after life? And that is ended if you choose so. But you must choose. I come to offer you the opportunity of new construction.*

There was more. Much more. The messages are long. Many levels, too, of understanding. But these words jumped off the page! *You are one and almost whole again together, but each stands alone within that.* When I spoke the words *You are one and almost whole again together,* I *knew*! I knew. You are *almost* whole. I continued with Merlin's voice. I continued to the end of the session and the end of the evening. Usually I have to reread the messages to prompt my memory of what was spoken. I didn't need prompting to remember those words! I knew immediately what they meant. But I couldn't do anything about it. It was already too late. I'd missed my chance. I comforted myself that if it was meant to be, it would be. It would come around again. I would get another chance. But I knew. I had made a mistake after all. The king *had* come, but I hadn't recognised him! Because I thought we were already complete. Because soon after I realised the king was coming, Colin arrived and I accepted that he *was* king. Even when it didn't feel right. Even when something felt mismatched. Because I thought. Because I thought! I didn't trust. I didn't pay attention. I wasn't listening. I was making assumptions. I was thinking!

Two weeks ago. The conference - Mystics and Medics we teasingly call it. I met him there. He's the one I was expecting. I think on some level, I even knew it at the time. Certainly the recognition was stronger than with any of the others because it was shared, we each recognised the other, at exactly the same moment. That's why Colin wasn't familiar in the way I expected. Colin is a part of us and I did recognise him. That part was correct. But he wasn't who I expected because I was expecting the king. I don't know what 'king' means in this context. Not king in a sense of ruling. More like 'king' in the sense of the one who makes it all work. The linch-pin. I don't know why it seems like Jan is to have some role like that within the group. But for the remainder of the channelling session, for the remainder of the evening, I carried around the knowledge that I've made a mistake. And comforted myself with the knowledge that if it is meant to be, somehow Merlin or one of the others will manage it.

So another one. Jan. At the conference I went to the front to ask someone if we could speak after the session. Jan stood up in the row ahead just as I arrived.

The Clew

Our eyes locked immediately into one of those 'where do I know you from' looks. It *was* powerful. I *knew* I knew him. And I knew he knew it. But I thought the group was complete. I thought finally I had found them all and my task was finished. I thought I had the king and that ended it. I wasn't looking for anyone else. I didn't pay attention. We stared at each other long enough to recognise embarrassment before we both looked away. Later found us walking to the same session so we walked there together. A class on Sufi dancing. At one point we dancers finished a dance holding hands with a partner. At this point Jan and I were partners. Neither of us realised when the dance ended, or when the others sat. We stood holding hands, in some totally different reality, seemingly transfixed. Finally when we opened our eyes that too was a little embarrassing. Afterward we talked. I told him what I did and gave him one of my cards. Then he explained that a woman at the conference had been pursuing him all weekend and I think for that reason he left the conference early. I might have known, I might have recognised, I might have taken the opportunity to make some contact with him. I didn't. Now I must simply trust that it's not too late.

May 1998: And I arrived home to his message. He wanted to come for a reading. I'll have to wait on this one. This one is not clear. I know he's to join us. And I'm certain he knows it too. Yet he seemed so ambivalent about everything. On the one hand he's drawn to this alternative reality. Fascinated by it. On the other hand he finds it too, too strange. And crazy. And irrational in all the worst ways. He thinks we're all probably a bunch of weirdos. And at the same time he's curious. The curiosity is there, it shows, it comes out in the questions, in the activities he chooses to become a part of. In the workshops he attends. In the fact that he came to me for a reading. He's truly conflicted about all of this. And so it was difficult to ask him. But he stayed overnight after the reading and so that evening I took the risk. I talked about the group. Talked about our work. Explained our group meetings, how we pool our resources and talents. How we've been guided in the past. Finally, the next morning, I spoke my truth. That I thought he was one of us. Not of my intuitive knowing that somehow he was 'king.' I didn't speak of that. Not that somehow he was the linch-pin and the work in November depended on his being there. Not of that. Not the words Merlin spoke *You are one and almost whole again together* and my immediate knowing that to be whole he must be with us. I didn't speak of any of that. Only that he might wish to join us. Might wish to be with us.

Was I surprised by his answer? Or was I surprised by the doubt he continued to express even after his answer? "I wondered when you were going to ask me. I woke up in the middle of the night and I knew immediately I was part of it all. I don't know what it means, but I know I belong." So that much at least. That much recognition. But how will he be a part of it? He thinks we're all a bit spacey. Out of touch with reality. At some level he doesn't really welcome involvement with us. He resists. So *how* will he become a part of us?

June 1998: Where to begin? So much has happened. How to sort it out. How to make sense of it. He wasn't coming. Jan. Couldn't make it, he said. Still the

The Clew

doubts. Still unable to see himself involved in something like this. Said he was *unable* to come to our meeting in May. That was puzzling to me, but I let it go. Nothing I could do about it. If it's meant to be, usually, somehow, it manages to happen. There are windows of opportunity, Ian says. Times within which the possibility for something happening is greater, or lesser. He understands it that way. I see merely that it always comes around again. I have free choice but if it's something that is a gift meant for me, it comes around again. And so I had to trust. If this was a gift for Jan, it would come around again. He would get another chance. If he missed this opportunity, a time would come when he could choose again. I let it go. And then the call. The morning of the meeting. He was coming could we pick him up at the station at noon. Yes. So, he decided. Don't ask what was responsible, how it was managed. Don't wonder, accept. It happened, that's enough.

And when did the problems begin? With his arrival? Or was it before that? Perhaps they began with the coincidence - except that Merlin said it wasn't a coincidence. I'm sure I don't understand. And yet I do. My figurine of Merlin breaking. Ian and I deciding to stop in Lower Slaughter, my beloved village in the Cotswolds. I opened the back door of my car and my Merlin figurine fell out and broke. 30th May at 6:30. Strange that we knew exactly what time it was. And that I remembered it when Jan spoke of his decision to come to our meeting, 6:30 the night before. 30th May. Coincidence? I wondered, Wendy decided to ask. Perhaps I expected the answer. It was still a surprise.

"Merlin, this is Wendy. We were talking of your image breaking. Maybe you could tell us more about that?"

I have changed ... and such is no longer image ... I am changed at the moment of your wholeness ... that was the power you could contain ... but you are changed now for you are whole and I have waited for such a moment. I and this man, this one who comes, have business with each other. And I have waited and am glad of his presence, for we are long known. But he has feared memory, almost feared me ... He, more than any one of you, possesses my power, and yet cannot use it without your form. We are well met, friend, well met indeed ...

Rather graphic example he made for us I'd say, breaking in that way, at that time. So this is what 'king' meant. Jan more than any one of us possesses his power. Ironic that in the moment Merlin says we're whole, we split. And that the cause of it is this man - the one for whom he waited. Wendy and Heather and John and Patrick on one side, if you will. Ian, Colin, Jan and myself on the other. Others somewhere unknown, in between. There have been problems before. But this was different. Quite different. I'm not sure whether what's happening is from this lifetime or some other lifetime. We went for dinner after the meeting. After Merlin spoke. Jan is like a flame to moths. We women did strange things in his presence. Petty jealousies erupted almost from the moment he set foot in the door. Rivalry. Competition.

A phrase came back to me. Merlin had spoken following Colin and Ian's altercation.

> *If, for one second of your life, you can gather so in total unity and harmony with one another without grudge or grievance, in that moment you change such a multiplicity of being. And so you are called to task for one second.*

'Called to task' are the words he uses to describe our next assignment. It refers to November and of course I saw *that* - knew *that* was in the future - was our next assignment. But the other, 'without grudge or grievance' I certainly thought past. I thought we had already managed it. The ritual at Hazelwood. Ian and Colin. Patrick and I. Ian and I. Discoveries by the others, healing there too. We had discovered already so much past karma. Healed so much. Forgiven each other so many times, so many things, so much already. Ishtar's legacy. The 'work' she prompted. The loss of some people after her arrival. We had accepted that too. All of it - without grudge or grievance. I had already dismissed the phrase. And now this.

Colin suggested he and I combine efforts to try and tease out what was happening. Whether or not it was related to the group karma we were growing so familiar with. I'm not sure what to do with what we discovered. It takes a while to grow accustomed to these things sometimes We worked separately, but both were getting much the same story. Colin is very good at karmic recall and I found his agreement with my discoveries validating. We both picked up a lifetime of strong attachment and deep hurt. Wendy, Jan, and myself. In the Mediterranean. Once Colin picked up the Mediterranean, I knew it was Corsica. But I didn't know why. We dowsed a map of Corsica. Bonifacio.

It was beginning to fall into place. On my travels in Devon I frequently passed a church in Crediton, St Boniface. My eyes turned toward it every time I went by. Each time I passed it I thought I must stop. But I never did. If something is important, if I'm supposed to see it, I always manage to do it. It happens in unexpected ways, but I always manage it. I never stopped at St. Boniface. Felt drawn to it, felt the mysterious pull, but never quite managed more than that. So. It wasn't meant to be because it wasn't the church. It was Bonifacio. In Corsica. Stronger than any feeling I had ever had about the church was this new feeling, this new pressing need that I must go to Bonifacio. We continued our recall, excited by what we had discovered so far. Only to be jarred by what came next.

In Corsica in the late fifteenth century. Two branches of 'the family.' The Mafia. Mine in Corsica. Jan's in Naples. Not allowed to marry because 'family' feuds, Jan and I had a long-term relationship and were very fond of each other. We had two children. Jan's father died. A conflict then, between my father and Jan. And Colin, in accordance with the norms of the brotherhood, the 'family,' the Mafia, arranged the marriage. A very advantageous marriage. Jan inherited his father's shipping business, but this marriage, to the daughter of a much larger, much richer shipping man brought him connection. Wealth. Power. Wendy. Enter Wendy. And exit me. In one stroke my family rejected me, Jan turned his back on me, my daughter died, my son was put in the church and I became a nun. And I wondered at the tension in the Indian restaurant following Jan's first meeting with the group? His first meeting in this lifetime with Wendy and the others who

The Clew

had also played parts in that other lifetime? Perhaps it is strange we were able to act as civilly as we did.

That is strange enough, but there's more. Ian had been doing astrology for Jan. He had been to London and visited with Jan and his partner. She actually had invited Ian to visit their summer home on Corsica. Patrick has an expression for what happened next. "As only happens in the very best of fairy tales." Jan extended the invitation to Colin and me. We have free choice, free will. But sometimes the coincidences, the synchronicity makes the gift in the choices quite evident. I don't know what Corsica will bring. I don't know what this visit to Bonifacio will bring. I do know that it has to be made. And I know somehow, it has something to do with November.

30th June 1998, Corsica: We decided on Cauria, where the Dolmens and Menhirs are found. We asked Merlin for guidance. The answer was specific and puzzling, and we only made limited notes.

This is a strange place, yet we are well met and for a fine purpose. I feel more than gratitude for you - recognition. We need to discuss the matching of the light. There is much to be done.

Ian: With reference to tomorrow's visit to Cauria, do we make two triangles (referring to the interesting way the candles were arranged on the table)?

You have received the image correctly. Yours is a serious purpose, because there is a serious cause - of construction. You must stand

Ian - east   Colin - west   Jan - centre   Avril - north/entrance

The light enters via the woman - connects with her field - then you are activated - receive your power - you might say, it manifests, at one level.

Why were you chosen? You may not know. You have shown faith. To bring power takes many lifetimes. The task needs the sum of your powers. It brings you replacement, and brings reform elsewhere. I give you the image of a laser pointing to the sky. You are responsible for reforming a small but crucial aspect of the heavens. There are several places like this which have been switched off. These are mirrored on the ground. The light on the morning needs to be brought in, in sequence.

You are each accustomed to working by yourself. You will be working as a team from now on. It will require adaptation, sensitivity, balance and listening. This is a real task, not just an exercise. I will be with you tomorrow: Merlin's light will be shed … This is a test, for you to stand and think together.

I am reminded of something Merlin said the first time Jan was present at our meeting.

Enough of lessons, now we may live in partnership. That is very different. You are out of school. Now, you might say, you must learn on the job.

Merlin's words today said this is a real task. But he also said it is a test. For us to stand and think together. This feels like training. I think he told us that so that we would take it seriously. And yet he began by saying *This is a strange place, yet we are well met and for a fine purpose.* This is not the task. That is in November. This is learning. On the job. We're to practice. Standing.

2nd July 1998: Jan went straight to the centre and stood. The Dolmens were not a circle as we were used to, but Jan found the centre and stood. I went to stand directly in front of Jan only to realise there was a standing stone completely blocking my view. I could see nothing of Jan. Colin and Ian then took their places on either side of Jan only for Ian to decide they were in opposite places. Two interesting things than happened. Once they had traded places Colin dowsed to see if they had it right. They did, but his dowsing reversed direction. That had never happened to him before. There was some jostling around as they attempted to get in a straight line with Jan. This was the base of the triangle - as Merlin had directed. Jan was surprised that when they were in a straight line he could sense the geometric shape of the triangle - between the three of us - Ian, Colin, and I. When they were as much as six inches off centre, he could sense it. He was quite surprised by that and had never experienced anything like it before.

In the meantime, I was puzzled by the stone I faced. Once they felt they were positioned I began doing something I had never done before. I opened my crown chakra, in a way similar to how I do before I begin channelling, and invited the energy in. Then I pulled it down to my heart chakra and began sending it to Jan. As I did so for some reason I instinctively cupped my hands, one atop the other in Buddha fashion, just below my heart. Within moments I became conscious of an aura around the stone between Jan and me. I don't see auras very often. And I realised the reason for the stone. I couldn't sent the energy to Jan directly. I needed to send it to the stone and somehow the stone sent it on to Jan. The stone was a relay transmitter or something. I should have known. Nothing is ever by accident. As I sent the energy, I could see Jan's arms begin to rise. He was picking up a sound. He vocalised up and down a scale and when he found it, he vocalised it. After a few moments, he stopped, and lowered his arms.

So - Colin's dowsing switched direction. I held my hands in that unusual position and saw the stone's aura. Jan experienced the geometric shapes. If indeed we were learning 'on the job' we were quite satisfied with our day's lessons. We returned home to a message from Merlin.

What change do you feel after working under yesterday's sun?

Ian: "more exalted, at peace … losing fear"
Colin: "losing separation"
Jan: "feeling togetherness, the force, in the triangle, losing restrictions"

Moving from the seen to the unseen? Letting go of isolation? These are powerful wounds. Yet the work you have done goes further than you realise. It is to understand Power, its size, its implications. We are trusted with it … It is more than simply a 'letting go.' [The wounds] *were attached for a long time …* [It has been] *for you to witness the magnitude of the process … which reflects not just the mind but the entire self … the body must reflect also. As*

The Clew

you let go of what you have long carried, others did also. You must communicate the result to the others.

3rd July 1998: When I think I'm getting used to it, when I think I've accepted enough so that there won't be any more surprises, when I begin to relax into it and feel it's coming naturally, something new always challenges me. There have been so many unusual, difficult to assimilate, powerful experiences. And now today, so intense. So driven. Obsessed. I can't explain it or know where it comes from. I could only follow it. Go along with it. I had told Jan that I needed to go to a church in Bonifacio. I didn't know what church or where it was or how to find it. I knew I had to be there at 11:00. We drove to the old part of the town. We left the car and began walking. I never walk fast. I'm unable to walk fast. Before all this began eight years ago I didn't walk much at all. Walk now, but slowly, carefully, purposefully. There was nothing slow or careful about my walk this morning. Purposeful yes, but a driven purpose. I noted the time. 10:00. A sort of panic set in. I must be there by 11:00. *Must*. I strode out in front of the others, driven. From behind me "Avril! Wait! Where are you going?! How do you know the way! Avril!" And Ian, sensing me, as always, "Just follow her. Just do as she says!"

On and on. Through narrow streets of buildings three stories high. A maze of endless streets going nowhere and yet on I pressed, going *somewhere*. I could feel it, I would know it, I would know how to get there. And I must get there. I must. By 11:00. They said I passed by a church and didn't even see it. I was racing up the street when a priest turned the corner into my path. Black robes. I felt sick. Not sick - terror. Absolute terror. And faint. They dragged me, Ian and Colin, to the edge of the precipice, where the city overhangs the sea. Concerned for my condition they tried to administer healing energy. Frantic, I hardly noticed. I must go. There was no time for this. The pressure to be up, to continue, was unendurable. I couldn't read any signs, I didn't know I was heading toward the town centre. Abruptly I turned left and shouted "There it is!" We stood by a Romanesque church. Tourist information advised it was the oldest church in the town, the only one there in the late fifteenth century. I had made excellent time, we had more than half an hour before 11:00.

When the time arrived I entered the church, went straight to the candles lit one, and put it in front of some figurine. I didn't pay attention to where I put it. It either didn't matter or I did it so automatically that I didn't have to pay attention. I walked to a seat, centre front, and sat alone. Then, strangely, I automatically reached for the black scarf I had packed and covered my hair. My childhood spent in the Church of England certainly didn't teach me to cover my head in church. Mystifying how automatic it was, and how imperative. Briefly I remembered standing in my bedroom packing for the trip and wondering why I was packing a black scarf. I was alone at the front of the church. The others lingered at the back. There was no one else around. I knelt to pray for the release of the karma connected with this place. With this island, between Jan and me, between all of us. I prayed to heal and release any grudges or grievances I might be still carrying. When I opened my eyes a small boy smiled at me. He was alone. His parents must have been somewhere else in the church. He looked at me smiling,

The Clew

pointed to the candle I had lit, looked back at me and laughed. I followed his outstretched arm to the figurine where I had placed my candle in front of Mary, the mother. I turned to leave the pew, saw Jan, hugged him, and heard myself saying, "It's alright. It's over."

I thought it *was* over. I felt so relaxed. The urgency, the enormous pressure was gone. We decided to go to a convent I had been drawn to. A convent. Only it wasn't a convent any more. It was a cemetery. And I remembered something I had said in the car on the way this morning. I had said, "I shall find my name." Colin had responded, "Yes, I think you will." And I knew that I had been buried in *this* cemetery. I spoke it out loud, knowing it couldn't be true because it was not an old cemetery. All the vaults were post-war. But Colin responded, "Yes, about five feet from where you're standing, Avril. You've come straight here. You were buried on this site." As he said it a strange feeling of peacefulness flooded me. I could feel the experience of having become a nun. After all the trauma of Jan's desertion, my family's treachery, the death of my daughter, the loss of my son - I could feel the release. The contentment I finally found. Being a nun had been a very positive experience for me. Standing there, I knew it. I felt it. But there were no stones from the late fifteenth century. How was I to find my name. I let it go. Finding the site, experiencing the positive feelings of being a nun, that was enough. I asked no more.

Bonifacio had been oppressive. The tall buildings let no light through to the narrow streets. The church was dark. The heaviness had been palpable. I had sought release, to leave as soon as possible. This was different. Here in this cemetery, on the sight of what had been a convent building, high on a cliff, open to the sun and fresh air, I could have stayed here forever. Walking slowly among the vaults, alone to soak up the sunshine, I saw a plaque. As I approached it, it seemed to glimmer. And as I looked one word seemed to shine at me. 'Serafina.' Yes, I thought. That's it. Serafina. I caught up with the others.

"I think I've found it. I think I know my name."

"What was it?" Jan asked.

"Serafina."

He stood very still, was very quiet for a moment, and then slowly turned, smiled, took my hand and said "Serafina. I do believe you were."

And that should have been it. The day should have ended there. That was enough for one day. But it didn't end. And there was more. We went on to another spot, La Hermitage de la Trinité. Walking in a garden there we saw a large, prostrate stone. Since in both Britain and Scandinavia (where Jan was born) kings are crowned on a stone, I jokingly told Jan he should sit on the stone. He would have none of it. He noticeably avoided it. I couldn't coax or tease him onto it. I left the others to walk among some trees. Only to hear Jan call my name some time later. He was lying on the stone with his eyes closed. Colin stood to one side and Ian to the other. In a straight line. When I was within 30 feet of the stone Jan suddenly began giving me directions still with eyes closed. A little forward, a little left, too much, a little right. Until he had me exactly, exactly opposite him. We stood in the same pattern we had stood at the Dolmans. Opening his eyes he laughed and sat up. He could 'see' where we were. Much like an

The Clew

infra-red camera I suppose, he could sense our energy. In geometric shapes. He experiences it as geometric shapes. He played with it. Not *exactly* accepting it, or his role in it, or the 'weirdness' of it. But playing with it.

We returned home again, to another message.

> *There has been a change of energy, has there not? And learning. You begin to absorb what approaches. You begin to feel true power. Remember - never forget - what you have been taught. You are prepared: remember stability.*
>
> *I speak with the three. From now on, when you work, summon the others. Lay aside these small arrogances, what is left of hurt, doubt, defence. What you seek only operates through a greater form - brotherhood. You can work without it, but to truly become, turn now to each other.*
>
> *You have come far - to understand the nature of balance, the linking of power not connected to self. You are no longer hermits ... hiding away ... behind closed doors, shut windows. You must live your knowledge in the world - separately and together. The self is small compared to the whole. You three need the others - such is the structure. In this way light is brought in and change wrought.*
>
> *From now on there will be always enough of you to stabilise the whole, and there will always be those who hold.*
>
> *So, now I ask you, what have you left behind?*

Restrictions, limitations ...
> *What form of these held you back?*

Not believing ...
Not trusting ...
Not allowing ...
Being too self-critical and critical of others ...

> *Are you come to faith? You perceive the journey exists. You have strength. You have love. Love is the gateway. You have tried to control love, yet it is that which contains all ... You feel it now. You lost sight of it. You structured it. It became form, ritual, forgotten. When you truly understand that you are love then your power will live in the world ... love is the most skilled builder of all. That which is ended is not love.*
>
> *Enough. You are become companions. Companions respect each others' silences and space, share pain, reflect our true selves to us from loving kindness, know our innermost being without offence, sit in silence at the end of the days without words, never leave us alone, isolated. Let us each go to our own journey, yet with common cause.*

Chapter Fourteen

AVRIL
The final task

November 1998 : There has been time to reflect, time to allow for understanding. Immersed in the process, in the accomplishment of our 'final task,' I was too close. I understood and didn't understand. Now it's finished and I look back, reread the messages, remember. And some of it begins to make sense. It must have made sense then also, before we were 'called to task.' But I couldn't see it, couldn't have written about it. I was too full. It was too pregnant with meaning yet for birthing. I've needed this time, this space, this distance. To begin to understand. Not only the final task, but the final entity. For in the end, it was he who guided us. The memory of his energy and our relationship to *that* which allowed the work.

> *Here are the men of my being, summoned so ... We stand in our place, friends. Remember this, for you are called back ... so that you may repair that which together we once formed ...*

We remembered the entity, that power. And somehow intuitively we remembered what to do that would manage the repair. But that which we together once formed is still a mystery. I know that it was a very, very long time ago. I know it had to do with earth energies. I begin to think I know the questions to ask. And then even the questions elude me.

> *Know my voice. I am beyond that of your previous substance. I stand now in wholeness, as do your beings. I am beyond name, yet possess many.*

He meant beyond the named energies we'd already known, meant he encompassed them all. This voice, this energy was the 'cable' in its 'wholeness.'

> *In this woman each aspect of my being has lived, has presented itself, has woven itself into your own tapestries, has stirred in you memory, has inspired in you, fire.*

The others, the earlier entities - had each been an aspect of this being, one separate strand of the cable. But in the end, for the final task, we would need the whole cable. Would need to be able to hold *this* energy. In its entirety.

> *So you have learned, so you have invited me into yourselves, a little by little.*

In our journey we had absorbed, adjusted to, accepted one strand at a time,

The Clew

each beyond and encompassing the strength and knowledge of the one before. Until, finally,

> *I am the light of that which was once your being. I am incarnate in your very selves.*

We had managed this far. We had gone through the energy changes, we had puzzled through the clues and finally learned to follow our intuition. To intuitively know and trust the information we would need. We had acclimatised to all the energies. The cable was present in our very beings. We had managed to come this far and now, apparently as in some other far off time, the final task was once again up to us.

> *See within yourselves the unity of your being, of these strands of mine. For all life exists so. All Lords of such being as myself are formed of parts, and it is only to few that whole may be revealed.*

For this one time in our journey the 'whole,' the 'cable,' spoke through me. I'll never forget my physical reaction from those minutes. Never be able to separate 'my' physical problems at the time from the strain caused by bringing through this energy. In any event my weakened condition certainly made incidents unfold in an interesting, if not confused and distressing way. And in the end the knowledge that even that - the confusion, the distress - even that was part of the learning.

> *We are come, we are returned. Hear this, my voice, as you have heard it in aeons past, not once, alone.*

Strangely, this was a voice we knew. I had recognised Ashad. Ian knew Assurbanipal. Ann recognised Paracelsus. *This* voice, Colin knew. Said he froze when he heard it, that he remembered it in some elementally inexplicable way. And when it ended, when the voice had gone, Colin said he felt a sense of desolation. A sense of being alone in a way he hadn't felt alone before in this lifetime. And now the voice, the cable, this archetypal energy of ours, was telling us that although we would only hear him this one time in this lifetime, we had heard him before in aeons past. And whatever we had all accomplished before, whatever we were all gathered now to attempt to accomplish again, it had been and was again under the guidance of this voice, this energy.

We *did* recognise it, and it *was* from aeons past. From Sumeria? Or Assyria? This was the energy we'd been responsible for. We had intuitively known we had all been connected to a particular temple, a particular energy in one of the ancient city-states. To this particular 'cable of energy,' we had been connected, had been responsible for nurturing, for anchoring. Merlin called him "Lord." *I am Merlin, servant to the Lord and servant to you* he spoke so many times. But already he had told us another name. The archetypal name. Long before we knew this energy, long before we could have known the outcome of our task, nineteen months earlier,

The Clew

in conversation with a workshop group, Merlin had coaxed Ian and I to the name, to the identity. *How may the light enter if there is no temple to receive it?* he had asked. *And so you must build the temple. You might say, how do you say, you lay down the red carpet. Do you take my meaning?*

We knew he didn't literally mean build a temple. Not a building. But prepare something. Prepare a place, or come to a place, or find a place to honour 'the light.' Later still 'building the temple' would be described in equally metaphorical terms, 'Stand in pattern.' 'Turn the key.' Already, metaphorically, Merlin was explaining. *And so you must build this temple,* he had continued. *And how will you do that? Who knows how to build?* 'Capricorn,' Ian answered. *Which of my brothers, friend? Who is the life within this form, this goat of yours? Whose power builds it, who rules it?* To this Ian answered, 'Saturn.' *Indeed. And so we know, nay honour, who builds. And he must build again.*

After I received this message, a year would pass before I met Jan. Longer before he came for a reading, asked Ian to do his chart and we learned he was a Capricorn. With his Ascendant and three other planets in the same sign. A year before Merlin would tell us that Jan, *more than any one of you, possesses my power, and yet cannot use it without your form.* Had we been able to understand, we would have already known, nineteen months earlier. Even then Merlin had been preparing us. But we couldn't know. Slowly, very slowly, we would begin to understand the references to form and structure. But without all the pieces, without the final voice, without the unravelling of the mystery of the final task, we weren't able yet to know. If, indeed, we know even now. Capricorn then. The archetypal name for the final voice, the final entity, the energy that guided our final task, had to be Saturn.

This voice I managed at the end, this structuring energy, also spoke words of bringing into form, building, laying foundation, repairing.

> *I stand here remembered, so you may repair that which together we once formed ... Know this my strength, but know also this my love, and my power is love. Yet love in structure, love in form, love in the building of it all. I am such Lord, and so I manifest here, for it is time to build again ... the shapes must be restored, renewed, adjusted. I am come to restore with love and to rebuild with love. But we must lay foundation, friends, and such has ever been your task ...*

But still we couldn't know. Not until the very end. Not until after the end. Only in retrospect are we beginning to fathom what little understanding we have managed.

> *This alone, this time, this space alone, we speak. No more, until again. For in its time there will be again ... This once, for this moment, until again ...*

This task of ours - this building, repairing, moving the pulse - we have performed this task before. Once every aeon or so it seems. It has to do with the precession of the equinoxes and the changing of the ages. From Pisces to Aquarius,

The Clew

but something much, much larger and further apart in time than this change of 2,000 years.

And what exactly were we asked to do? Stand. Remember our places. Long before, I'd typed the words *You are the conductor, the force must pass through you into the ground.* The second message I received, in June of 1990 had described us as conductors. We'd understood our function in these terms from the beginning. And we'd been groomed for this last task, prepared from the very beginning. So many times we returned to the messages and found a reference that we had thought we understood, only to understand it on a deeper level ...

> *And therefore I am come to ask of you, for I do not command, or demand. I am come to ask merely of those who know me, who remember me, who comprehend my being within their form, their structure, their work. You, friends, choose. But if you will stand, then you will restore that which may build anew, in such form as your Earth has not seen before. For you place and turn the key to begin anew, to restore the pattern. You are the pattern ... And so you are called to task friends, those of you who remember your places ... We stand in our places ...*

We were simply asked to stand. So simple it sounds, that request. To stand. So, without knowing it, without realising it until the last, we'd been practicing. Eight years of training. The Moon Grove. The Michael Line. Arbor Low. The Blackdown Rings. Corsica. Each time different, each time more complex, more involved, each time requiring more of our own intuitive memory and remembered skills, but we'd been doing it. We'd been training. This time, this final time, we were required, almost entirely, to do it of our own free will, from our own intuition, from our own memory. With the Moon Grove, the Michael Line, Arbor Low, we'd been given specific instructions. The work at the rings had been more intuitive, but even there others had given us messages. Unknown to us we were slowly being weaned: from specific instructions, to trust. In our own intuition. In our own inner knowing. In our own memory and skills. In this final time, we were on our own. And the outcome was unknown. Earlier Merlin explained

> *when we come to stand in that place you are summoned to, I also am tested. ... we wait to measure your accomplishment. For at this point we may not. We stand nearer ... but we cannot measure until the precise and exact moment of enactment. Only then will I know, and only then will you know.*

We were given encouragement, we were coached in many other ways, but at the actual moment, we were on our own, and the outcome was completely unknown. And we stumbled. We stumbled.

Seven months ago, in April, Merlin admonished us. We didn't recognise the warning.

> *If, for one second of your life, you can gather so in total unity and harmony with one another without grudge or grievance, in that moment you change*

such a multiplicity of being. And so you are called to task for one second.

He was telling us, already able to see, what would make the difference between success and failure. We thought it was about the interactions of the group through to that point in April. We thought we had already managed it. We had already healed so much. We could be in each other's presence without rancour. But that was before Colin. Before Jan. Before the final entity. And so we didn't recognise. Didn't realise the one second we would be called to task was the final second. Didn't yet know, couldn't yet conceive, of all that still lay ahead.

I get ahead of myself. Skip over events. Important events. We came so close. After all those years, we came so close … In Corsica, Merlin admonished us *Lay aside these small arrogances, what is left of hurt, doubt, defence … You need the others - such is the structure.* We were told so many times, in so many different ways that we needed to work together. Merlin defined our journey, our purpose as having been *to enable you to stand together with shared wisdom.* He told us that he did not deal with egos, but that because we are human we do. He advised we must lay aside *these small issues of yours.* And we thought we had. We met in September, following Corsica. We healed the divide. We listened to Merlin's message together. He affirmed our work toward forgiveness, the 'lightening of our loads.'

I spoke once before that you must all return and face that which you have left behind. You have been confronted by these shadows … do not think it all dispersed, but there has been lightening of such loads. More for some, less for others, but there has been lightening. And that, perhaps you might say, is my requirement …

And so let us speak of this space where we wait to measure our accomplishment. [For] *summoned to place we are. And you may ask me, why this place? … This place is of your being. It stands in your air, it roots in your ground, it flows in your blood, it speaks in your ears. All of you will recognise this place. And you are called to redress that which occurred long ago. You are called to lighten that which was created by pain. You are called to release that which was trapped. But beneath that, beneath all of those, there lies something of such power that only few may stand there safely.*

And so, you see, we have reason for these journeys of yours. For I would not take you to danger. Have no fear, you will not be struck down by lightning, you will not be crushed by falling tree. I do not speak of danger such as that. I speak of such power which disorganises patterns. Such, if you remember, occurred before, in your previous place. One experienced such. In this time there is not the same concern, but I speak of such disruption of pattern that that which is, to use your term, sensible, is distorted.

For such places of power create these realities of yours. You might say, they beam the picture. Many pictures, in fact. And you may move from one to the other if you are not secured. And so how do those amongst your beings, amongst mankind, how do they view such? They call it time travel. They know its existence but they complicate, they confuse, and such they must do, for to have

The Clew

> *such power yet is not allowed. And yet without such energetic foci there would be no picture at all ... And so, such place serves so. Merely one beam. It alone cannot make picture, but without, picture may not be made.*
>
> *And so you are called, as others, and as you before have been called, to recharge such. For there is a pattern of advance and decline. You might say, it is time to turn the key. There are many keys to be turned, you merely have one. And perhaps that is enough of explanation beyond that of which you have personally dealt with. Except to say that I remind you that this task has been performed before, and that all of you have stood in such service at such times as that is needed ... Not necessarily each and every single one ... you may say there is selection, and next time you may not be present when others will. What matters is your pattern.*

Time travel? Does this have something to do with vortexes or portals or something? In Corsica Merlin told us

> *I give you the image of a laser pointing to the sky. You are responsible for reforming a small but crucial aspect of the heavens. There are several places like this which have been switched off.*

This sounded like science fiction again. What were we being asked to do? This recharging, this turning of the key. This switching back on again. Even without understanding, we could sense the awesome responsibility of it. In Merlin's words

> *And so you see, therefore, how perhaps that which has occupied you so intensely is quite small compared to that.*

We thought we could heal our petty differences, forgive our remembered hurts and injuries. Ishtar helped us. Merlin continued to help us. We reminded ourselves to heal, to forgive. Confident, we helped each other. Encouraged each other. This part at least, we thought we understood.

> *What I hold to with you, in love and gratitude, is that, apart from the occasional hesitation, you have moved forward, of your own choosing. I value that beyond price and as such you have invited to you that which you invite. How could I appear if there were not those who worked for my presence when they did not know me? And those who began consciously this journey did not consciously know that, could not see me stand waiting, or my brothers. Yet listened to that within themselves, within yourselves, reached for it, heard it, yearned for it, trusted it. Oh, such are possessions indeed. Many falter, many falter.*
>
> *If you stood in this place and remained so, I would commend you. What I ask of you is beyond that which, perhaps, might have been expected. For I did not, nor others, know of the power of your memory, or your willingness to connect to it. We may only stand in love at the sight of it, and to offer you such*

The Clew

in return.
　　I am Merlin, servant to the Lord, and servant to you. I thank you. Even I have no words for that which I would wish to express.

Merlin spoke those words in September. We were encouraged. We were excited. And we were awed. And, in preparation for November, we reviewed the message Merlin had given us in May.

"Merlin, It's Ian. Is the work we are coming together to do in November a separate piece of work or is it connected with something we have to do at the major eclipse which will come across southern England after that?"
　　You prepare for such, and have prepared from your beginning for such. For you are attuned to that which requires entrance and you must make the way. And so have you worked, and so have others worked, in their space, in their light. But you are called to place itself. You might say, how do you say, you lay down the red carpet. Do you take my meaning?

"I do."
　　Such is the task. Such you prepare.

"Is there anything we do on the day of the eclipse, or have we done everything that we need do?"
　　Oh, always hasty friend. That, you know, I may not answer, for I must wait to see all gathered. How do you know what to build when you do not know what materials are available?

"I was hoping you'd tell me that."
　　I know your brick is available. I wait to see if it is present, as the others. Who comes? How much? Of what texture? Of what strength? There is enough to build, for certain. But we may advance beyond that. But, to be sure, as I speak of change and possibility then be certain that this light you will greet enables that. Beyond your imagination. For it may bring such change.
　　For there is task, as we have spoken before, not just for you as individuals, nor for you as family, clan, group, but for this land there is task. And as you have distant memory of your past, this land, also, has distant memory of its power. And as you have come to re-attunement, to re-direction, it too has the same possibility. But what it lived before, in conquest, how will it live it now? You begin to see how you play such part in such outcome? For are you not, and your land also, one whole? And are not your thoughts linked together? But without doubt, it has task, and will have power, after the light comes. You live in moments, friends, these lives of yours are merely moments.
　　I am Merlin, servant to the Lord and servant to you ... Well done. I have long hoped for such, and stand with all those others of our being who have worked equally so. What blessings are ours, in our gift, are offered to you. We have come far. It is a fair journey, friends.

175

The Clew

You might say we breathed deeply at this point. We squared our shoulders. We were ready. November. We would not meet again until November. We knew the where and the when. We thought we were ready for the what.

And November came. And we arrived in Cornwall, and again, so did the problems. I'd had severe bronchitis for a week and I couldn't speak. I had waited until we were all together to channel any last minute instructions. I was simply too sick to manage it and couldn't have spoken anyway. Normally the first day would have been one of planning. I would have channelled our final message, we would have undertaken any last minute instructions. It would have been a day of bonding, of excitement and readying ourselves for the task at hand. The reality was very different. Some went off to a church in the area to see if any healing was needed. Colin and Patrick worked with dowsing and intuition to find our site. Gray wondered off on his own and found a remarkable grotto-like place.

Mid-day the following day, wrapping as warmly as I could and feeling absolutely miserable, I accompanied the others across the little bridge into the field which had been determined as our site. Jan, Colin, Ian and I went straight to our places. Gray went to the top of the field immediately and sat, Buddha like, as always, the ring master, watching while others found their places. John, Heather and Wendy went to the bottom of the field. Marc chose to stand near the bridge, and Margaret moved to a place below Jan. Virginia didn't come into the field but chose to sit on the bank of the stream. Nothing happened - and very much happened.

We stood, each separately in our chosen place. We stood for the allotted time. Each dealing with our own thoughts and feelings of isolation. For me, they were overwhelming. Normally under such circumstances, I would have been intellectualising every why, what, and wherefore. Trying to figure out what was happening, what was wrong, how to fix it. But it took all my energy to breathe. Physically - and emotionally even more so - I was exhausted. As if re-enacting the relationship from fourteenth century Corsica, Jan and Wendy were being close again. The feelings of rejection I experienced when I saw the two of them together certainly felt like a re-enactment of that old tableau. To that, Jan and Ann seemed to have also recalled a past-life connection, and I watched their happy exchanges with a feeling of intense emotional pain. I felt shunned. Utterly wretched and deserted. In that other lifetime I was the rejected mate. In this lifetime, again rejected, I was back in girls' school, on the playground, everyone was pointing at me, making fun of me, gossiping about me. Totally innocent and totally unable to defend myself, self pity in large dollops.

Over and over in my mind I repeated *If, for one second of your life, you can gather so in total unity and harmony with one another without grudge or grievance ...* without grudge or grievance ... I couldn't do it. I knew I had to. With all my heart I wanted to. I tried to force myself to. But I couldn't do it. Feeling sorely mistreated, misunderstood and maligned. Didn't I need sympathy, understanding, care? Didn't I need nurture? I was getting the exact opposite. Endure this without grudge or grievance? Too much to ask.

I watched myself. Human frailty. This was about something larger. We'd

The Clew

been told. Merlin didn't deal with egos, we did. I must get beyond it. Move outside myself, outside my inner struggle, to the larger. Eight years of training. Eight years of choosing to continue. Eight years of being entrusted with this responsibility. And now this moment, I couldn't fail. I could. And I felt like I did. So it had come to this. No wonder Merlin said *We cannot measure until the precise and exact moment of enactment. Only then will I know, and only then will you know.* I didn't know, couldn't know and really didn't care what the others knew. I knew I was failing. Perhaps had I not been physically and emotionally exhausted ... but in that case the present scene would not be unfolding the way it was. It was too late. There was nothing I could do. I could not stand without grudge or grievance.

John was the one who remembered. He had heard the words so many times. As we poured over the early messages for clues and understanding, read and re-read them again and again. He remembered and spoke the words: *Men stand like corn stooks in the field and the life is draining from them.* He saw us, standing in the field, and saw the vision. We stood like corn stooks, the life draining from us. I knew those words had been about humanity. They were meant for something larger than the sad, disjointed 'standing' we had managed. But it so aptly described us, the isolation and dejection. For a moment I was able to believe this too had been foreseen and those words foretold this moment. That even this aborted attempt wasn't totally unexpected. And I managed to convince myself momentarily to trust that something would happen. That nothing was ever futile. There were windows of opportunity. Perhaps we'd missed one. I must trust there would be another. I must manage the trust. For a brief moment I could manage that. For the brief moment that I did manage it, I stood, perceived everything falling apart, and reassured myself that everything was unfolding exactly as it was supposed to.

I left the group and went to stand under a tree. This should have been a time of celebration. Should have been joyful. We'd arrived at the final task. Anticipated, offered and accepted, responsibility assumed - a pact. We'd made this pact. With each other. With the entities. With the universe? And it had come to this. That it was such a mess was incomprehensible. It had been about healing and unconditional love. What went wrong? Jan came to join me, stood beside me. But physically we were as separate as if there had been a wall between us.

I knew this whole mess was about Jan. It had been my task to continue until I had found him. I had continued. First I had found all the others. And then, finally, I had found him. It had been about finding all of them and the work we could then do. I had found them all, found him, only to have him mess it up. Make a charade of it. Unforgivable. Without grudge or grievance? Impossible. And if I had messed up, I had messed up because of him. Because of the way he was acting. Because of the way the others were acting with him. A wall between us. As separate here as we had been in the field.

We were supposed to stand opposite each other.

The light enters via the woman - connects with her field - then you are activated.

Merlin had told us specifically. Ian - east. Colin - west. Jan - centre. Avril -

The Clew

north/entrance.

In Corsica it had been so simple. It had been fun. In Corsica, because of the standing stone between us I hadn't been able to see Jan, and yet we had been connected. There had been a bond in Corsica. What had gone wrong? In the field here I had been able to see Jan but we were isolated from each other. There was no bond, no connection. We weren't opposite each other. Corsica was supposed to be training, supposed to be about where we stood. Learning on the job, Merlin called it. So what was *this* about? We hadn't stood in the same places at all. We had each gone to a place intuitively, and it wasn't the same as Corsica. What had gone wrong? What!?

We began to straggle back. We had our photo taken. Jan came up the field, one arm around Wendy, one around Ann. I stood on the little bridge and suddenly the sun came out. I asked for the light to be positive and go forward. The light. *You might say, how do you say, you lay down the red carpet.* I asked that it had been accomplished. That we had managed somehow to prepare the way. And felt totally abandoned. Felt no response. Felt nothing. Virginia and Gray approached and walked with me. As we passed it, Gray pointed out the little grotto he'd found yesterday.

We arrived at our cottage resigned to it being over. Disappointed. Bemused. Jan avoiding me. It was too much. I lay on a couch in the corner and rebuffed any attempted approach. An hour later, in the loo - why always the mundane places? Soaking in a bath. Doing dishes. In the loo. I was in no mood to appreciate the humour. My mind a soggy mass of wet cotton wool, I felt the merest little electrical ripple. There's something else. From the stairs I saw Ian hurrying toward me, always Ian. We both spoke at the same time. "There's something else." Ian said, 'You've got to channel!' "No, I simply can't. I can't." I took an antibiotic and went to bed. The morning would bring what the morning would bring. I would not get my hopes up. I didn't think it possible.

Following breakfast the next morning, at Ian's insistence, expecting nothing but hoping with every fibre of my being, I took a deep breath and the coughing stopped. To my astonishment *that* voice came out. Not Merlin's voice. The other one. The last one. The one Colin knew. I spoke for 15 minutes without once coughing or pausing. And then I stopped. And began coughing and couldn't stop coughing. Margaret worked with me until I began to recover. I opened my eyes to see the men leaving. Where were they off to? And then the women left. Margaret and I were alone. He, the voice, the Saturn energy, had told them

> *Now you may comprehend the nature of this woman's task. For it was hers to find the pieces to make the pattern, and you are found and she is healed. And so, you must undertake such task, if you wish.*
>
> *There are, here, two tasks. One old, one new. You must first journey to memory, to that place where you once stood and understood your standing, where you once practiced art and craft. That place that you arrived at after long journey. Return, remember, and heal. Yourselves first, your whole second, the ripples third. And when you have restored such, and walked in your places, then return ...*

The Clew

The men had left to return to a church nearby ... *where you once practiced art and craft* ... The men knew they had been involved together at some time with the Templars. A church nearby was known to be a Templar church. *That place that you arrived at after long journey* made reference to the crusades and the Templars sojourns in Palestine. The men knew they were again being *called to redress that which occurred long ago.* John and Patrick worked outside the church, dowsing and healing. Jan, Colin and Ian worked inside the church. At one point Jan searched for the particular tone that would resonate with the place and knew he'd found it when one of the bells in the tower began to resonate loudly with his tone. Merlin had spoken similar words in September.

> *All of you will recognise this place. And you are called to redress that which occurred long ago. You are called to lighten that which was created by pain. You are called to release that which was trapped.*

Ann intuitively knew what this might be about. She and the women worked at a different church. She immediately sensed the church had been misused. Some of the entrances had been closed off and the energies couldn't move as intended. She sensed being drawn to one particular spot because the energy there was so dark. Holding candles, Wendy and Heather held a positive, safe place for Ann to work. She felt herself being draped in the mantle of the Knights Templar, recognised it as the beginning of the familiar ritual, felt the sword-cross in her hand. Moved to enter the space of dark energy, the cross-sword moved ritualistically in her hands. Held first in her right hand, swung over her head and grasped with her left, the imaginary sword-cross plunged from the force of both her hands holding the hilt, into the ground. At the moment of thrust and, apparently at the moment of Jan's bell sound, she 'saw' an opening actually open up, and saw figures of humans floating through the opening. Quickly, as if in a hurried rush, as if going up a ladder, they ascended into a larger opening in the heavens. As soon as they were all through, the heavens immediately closed. She instinctively knew she had, in the entities words *released that which was trapped.* The voice of the last entity had continued.

> *And when you have restored such, walked in your places, then return to that place which awaits its instruction. For, you see, the centre of the pulse is to be moved. It is to move from pain to light. For that which is of this place is that which must be emitted to the world, and no longer pain of the other. You know your workings. Together you are become as before, and memory will be restored.*
>
> *It is enough, until the time of consideration ... I am come to restore with love and to rebuild with love. But we must lay foundation, friends, and such has ever been your task ... Loose hold of that which brought you pain and grief and suffering because of it, for it is gone, it is ended ... Know merely now, for a moment, that which restores your memory. For I am Lord, of all you once were and are now. And I am glad of your service, and remember your loyalty and your learning, and bless your legacies.*

The Clew

> *Go about your task. The Earth waits, there is much to do, and without you, how may there be beginning?*

With those instructions we knew there was more. Not only in the churches. The churches had been the first of the first of the two tasks. *One old, one new.* The other task, the one about which the Saturn energy said *And when you have restored such, and walked in your places, then return,* this task still lay ahead of us. Odd the words I spoke to Ian before we left to attempt the 'final task' again. "I can't do this. I feel castrated." Odd that choice of words. Odder still his reaction. Reassuring. Don't worry, he knew what needed to be done. He would do it. My surprise must have been visible. So unlike Ian. To take charge that way, to be so confident. "I felt it this morning," he said. "A power coming in. Leave it to me. I can do it." For once I was willing to leave it to him. More than willing. I only wanted to hide. Literally. And I did. Behind a tree. I smile now remembering it. There was nothing humorous about it at the time. I remember my thoughts. "I am doing absolutely nothing. I cannot do anything. I am helpless in this situation." Was this what Merlin had been referring to when he said *Whose wisdom is followed? You still have that one to overcome, and I tell you that one comes at the last moment.* It was Ian's wisdom, or guidance, we trusted at the last moment. Prior to that moment, I wouldn't have believed he would assume the responsibility of it.

It is only now, in retrospect, fitting all the pieces together from a place of distance, that I can accept the failure of the day before. It wasn't a failure. What happened on 9th November couldn't have happened without the day before. We were still in ego the day before. Still doing it our way. Still attached to the outcome. Still in left brain. It took the seeming failure. The absurdity of it all. It took the frustration of seeming defeat, what seemed a fiasco, a debacle. It took that. To move us into a space of readiness. To move us into a space where we were no longer attached to any particular outcome. We had already failed miserably. What worse could happen? Malleable, eager but in a pliant way, finally truly receptive, only now could we do what would be necessary. Only now, having seemed to fail, could we leave our egos behind long enough to stand ... *for one second ... in total unity and harmony ... without grudge or grievance ...*

We walked, not to the field where we had stood like the corn stooks, but to Gray's grotto. And we did know it. For each of us in our own way it did 'stand in our air, root in our ground, flow in our blood, and speak in our ears.' John was first. His bold stride to a spot, "This is my place, no-one will move me from here." Patrick, "I'm here!" Gray to his spot, sitting, always Buddha-like, on a stone overlooking us all. Each with authoritative certainty, no questions asked, to their place. And me hiding behind my tree. In the next moment Patrick, John, Colin all calling at the same time, pointing me to my place. I went and stood. Exactly opposite Jan. I glanced at him. Nothing. What had I expected? He looked miserable, fed up. With everything. As if he hadn't known what to expect, but certainly this wasn't it. He seemed infuriated, as if he wanted only for it to be ended. He looked indignant - with me, with the process, with the lot of it.

At that point, "Why does Avril always get to stand in the middle?" And I knew I had been right. It *had* been about petty jealousy. Who gets the man. This lifetime or some other, it didn't matter. One was as real as the other. It didn't help. This was validation. I had been right. It didn't help at all. In that other lifetime I had been powerless - to keep my family, my partner, my children, my place in life. In these days my powerlessness had returned and, try as I might, I knew myself unable to forgive.

All in our places, Ian started flipping tarot cards. An urgency about his actions, his presence. Were we in our places? Pull a card for John - and he recognised the answer. Another for Gray and another answer. Ian looked like a magician doing a card trick, only he wasn't a magician and this wasn't a trick. Serious, deadly serious, as rapidly as he could manage, on and on. For each of us he pulled a card, for each of us an answer. Slap a card, slap another, slap again, and again. That simple, that quick, that certain was he.

The women took up their places and I'm reminded again of Merlin's words in Corsica. *From now on there will be always enough of you to stabilise the whole; and there will always be those who hold.* The women. Other times. Singing. Holding candles. Protecting and guarding the space. Holding the energy. *There will always be those who hold.* In a diamond shape around the rest of us. Stranger than knowing our own individual places, for we each did *know* where we were supposed to be, we also felt each other's energy. John, Patrick, and Colin had known where I was supposed to be. Margaret, standing behind Gray, moved away from her place to better hear Ian as he pulled the cards. Gray ordered her back, he was so conscious of where her energy needed to be. Heather and Wendy, two sides of the diamond, lit their candles. Margaret high on the bowl of the grotto, Ann at the bottom.

Unaware of it then, only later would Ian tell us - when he'd had time to draw the shape we made as we stood in the grotto. Had time to compare each of our birth charts with where each of us stood. Only later would Ian tell us we were standing in the shape of the Qabalistic Tree of Life. We each instinctively knew our place, but didn't know what Ian, by studying our charts, would later discover - that somehow each of us embodied the particular energy of the archetypal Sefirah on whose place we stood. For now we only knew, instinctively, as we had been trained to know, that we each recognised our place within the whole.

Finally satisfied we were all in the correct place, Ian stopped just as Wendy called out. "A figure eight! Around Avril! Gray and Jan need to make a figure eight around Avril!" Leaving our differences behind, we simply followed each other's wisdom. Walking quickly the two men each made their two loops, crossing in front and behind me, making form of Wendy's intuition. A figure eight. The sign for infinity? Or the eight representing Saturn? She didn't know. Only knew that it needed to be walked.

Ian kept looking at his watch. Urgently, almost frantically he insisted Jan's spot still needed healing. Automatically Jan stepped aside. Together (together? These two? Each of whom finds the other equally mystifying? These two?) Patrick and Colin rushed toward Jan - and collided - stomach to stomach on his exact spot. After a moment of shock, simultaneously threw up their hands, "Oh what the hell!" and embraced each other. Still frantically watching his wrist, Ian ordered the three back to their places.

Jan was absent. His body was present, but *he* was absent. Disconnected.

The Clew

Clearly he didn't know what he was doing, why he was there, didn't feel a part of any of this activity. Ian, picking up on his distant presence, spat the question at him. "What's wrong!"

Jan, uncertain, was sloppy with his answer. The words stumbled, lagged, excused. Impatient, Ian fairly ripped a card from the deck and slapped down the Hanged man/Wounded king. "Jan needs healing! He's got to be healed!" he shouted.

Without anyone saying anything, the men all left their places and ran to Jan. Colin in front, Patrick behind, the others enclosing the gaps. The two who had only now healed themselves, Colin and Patrick, put their hands opposite each other on Jan's back and chest. The others seemed to be hanging on to him. I remembered Corsica. I remembered sending Jan love and light. Open crown chakra, invite in light, lower it to heart centre, beam it to him. I remembered. I tried forcing myself to do it. I couldn't. Grudge. Grievance. Grudge. Grievance. Mind insisting, heart not responding, feeling instead its own opposite insistence. The men zapped Jan.

There was a change. I became aware of a change. Energy coming up out of the ground, coming up Jan's body. It reached his neck, his head came up, his eyes met mine and suddenly ... it was as if his eyes switched on. In that moment he became at once that one I had searched for so long and so far. Now I knew! ... A priest-king, a priestess and a sacred marriage - the ancient ceremony of the cyclical renewal of the Earth's abundance. It was all so clear. *This* was the memory I had had to reach for. *This* the final recollection that awaited us at the very heart of the labyrinth that we had all journeyed through. *This* the ritual which, in some strange, energetic way, we now had to re-enact. 'Destruction', 'Destruction', my first voice had said and, later, *'You are the people of the memory who know the old ways. Your task is to pray and to make the journeys through the light of time.'* And now, not dead those eyes, no longer dead, but steady and looking straight at me, finally serious, present and, also, remembering. "I'm ready". Such simple words for such a vast change in energy. He was indeed ready. And, finally, present.

Ian shouted the men back to their places. Eyes on his watch he shoved his cards into their bag, into his pocket and in that moment, eyes still on his watch, shouted "NOW!"

Easy. Open crown chakra, invite in energy, lower it to heart centre, send it out to Jan. And my hands. A mind of their own. One atop the other, Buddha fashion, below my heart chakra, making a cup to receive and from which to send. Both of us remembering.

Then Jan began the sounds. Up and down a scale until he found a certain pitch. And held it. Only a moment or two but I could hear the sound circling around. And then Jan stopped the note. I know because I could see that he had stopped. But Margaret heard it long after he stopped. Sitting high above us she heard it circling up and up. So early in the messages Ashad's words *our voices spiralled along the circles of power.*

Eight years earlier, in the first message we'd been told that if it was to be saved, the men must walk. And only the night before the Saturn voice spoke *For you place and turn the key to begin anew, to restore the pattern.* Tumblers in a lock,

The Clew

moving forward one rotation as the key turns ... "Move one place!" Ian's urgent order. Jan and I stood still. The women stood still. And as we'd planned the night before, the 'men walked' one place forward in a clockwise direction and 'turned the key.'

"That's it! We've done it!" Uncharacteristic excitement and delight in Ian's voice.

We stood for a moment. Unable to believe his words? Or not wanting the moment to end? Then slowly, spontaneous movement. Toward each other into something like a group hug. And at that moment, as we stood all touching one another, we heard it again. As we had at the Blackdown Rings. There it had been a gun in Plymouth firing a salute. Boom boom. This time it was Concorde arriving from the west over the Atlantic. And another, almost identical boom boom. *And out of the sunset will come the fire.* Their signal. Their handshake. Their wink. Their 'well done.' And we knew. We had indeed done it. We'd found each other. We'd healed enough to stand one moment without grudge or grievance. The men had walked and turned the key.

We'd done our part. Whatever happened now, we had at least done our part. The 'coincidence,' the 'synchronicity' of the 'fire out of the sunset' told us we had succeeded. Even without Merlin's words which would come later and confirm our knowing, we knew we had managed to do as asked.

We stood around talking. Relieved? Proud? Awed to have managed after all? Grateful?

Except for Patrick. He went looking for a wall. Not a real wall but the energy of some old wall long since gone. He does that. Looks for old, no longer existing walls. And finds them. And he found this one too. And called to Ann.

"Ann! Ann! Come and feel this wall!"

"Leave it alone, Patrick! That's my wall". And only then did she tell us. She always put up a wall of protective energy around our work. To keep us safe and to keep anyone in the area unaware of our work safe. But none of us knew that before. Only Patrick could have found it. All this time she'd been holding the energy, protecting the space, putting up her wall. Trusting that it worked. And now Patrick showing her it was real. Showing her that someone else could feel it. Another wink. Another coincidence, We might not be able to put any words around this, might not know what it was all for or had been about. But within each of us we heard the faint echo of Ishtar's voice. *'This is no game. This is your oath made flesh, brought into being at the time of its need'.* We had kept our word. *No more, until again'* that last great voice had said, *'For in its time, there will be again.'*

Epilogue

Merlin's message, 10th November 1998 :

Greetings friends, friends indeed. I am that brother who has walked long time with you. I am come now to rest of spirit. For that which was task has been achieved, and I now hold this piece you have created. Feel it move within your own beings, for such is joy. Look at it now, observe its light, observe its texture, observe its flow, for you have not witnessed such for long time. You have been misformed by its absence, you have been shaken by its disconnection, and it is now restored.

What will you do with this gift? What will you do with the gifts of yourselves? What will you do with the gifts of each other? These are now your choices. This journey is ended, and you are come now to these journeys of your own beings. You may tie them together if you wish. You may walk alone, or together, if you wish. But you are now whole and therefore must choose.

What have you learned, what do you now comprehend that before was absent from your knowledge? How are you changed by that knowledge, that wisdom? How will you live it in the world? Will you share it in speech, or convey it in action, or offer it through your hands? You may choose, for it will flow as you direct it. For do you not feel it now? Do you not feel it now, turn, for turn it does from this place, and I ask you to listen, and I ask you to feel this turn, this spin that you have created. Only I know, and perhaps this man present amongst you, how far it goes. But you may feel its pulse. And I ask you now, each and all of you, to feel this pulse, to hear this hum, for when you leave this place you take that with you. And when you are alone, whenever that may be, if you become silent, and attune, you will hear it again, for it pulses now in your being. It has changed your structure, the pace at which all of your selves now move is altered, adjusted. Such is aspect of the work you have done. Even with your learning it is not possible for me to explain the full extent of that which you have achieved. Know only by my voice that it is changed.

There is much time to consider these journeys of yours. Not now, not in this space, for you must each reach back to the beginning. And that beginning you alone can identify. When was the moment you turned, for it was in that moment that this woman heard you. It was in that moment that the drawing together began. I ask you to find that moment and to look now at its reflection. What did you seek then, what did you yearn for then, what dissatisfied you then?

Look now, and look now also at the size of the gift you possess, for you possess wholeness, but you possess also each other. There are few who come to such relationship, few who are able to stand in new beginning with such clarity as you now have the possibility to do. For those which were old bonds have been freed. You are all redeemed through your actions, all free of that which has long bound you. And that is through your actions, and your decisions, and your struggles. I stand in wonder at your being, and joy in your delight.

Whatever you choose will have purpose. No one thing is asked of you, only potential offered to you. Remember, my friends, the dream. Are you closer to it now, for it is yours, each and every one of you, it is yours, if you wish it. Small change occasions a certain insecurity. There will be moments, short only, when you will be disturbed by your new beginnings. Although you are disconnected to the old, vision of it remains and may sometimes draw your eyes. Yet I ask you to turn them forward. To know that that which has been your service has earned you, each and every one of you, that which will be your reward. And if your eyes are closed, how will you see it?

Now you journey, away from this centre, back to the points of light which we have often spoken of. Remember, you are those points of light, wherever you sit, whoever you meet, whatever occupies you. You are those points of light which vibrate from this being, and this being from its connectedness, its flow with the whole, for so, without doubt, it now flows. Live these lights of yours. Know also, that that which has been our past may be changed. That which has been this woman's service may be adjusted. For you have no need of her, yet consider this, or perhaps you do, if it is not for the voice, then why?

We may speak, I speak, of change, not of dislocation, but that which has been journey is ended. Some of you have travelled far on this journey, from the beginning. Your faithfulness has allowed this to happen. Some of you have entered almost at the end, yet your powers have allowed this to happen. Each of you who has joined this journey has allowed this to happen. You have made pilgrimage, friends. You have made pilgrimage of the heart. Feel that, and reverence it, for that is your discovery, that is what has waited for you at the end of the journey. You have come to love. To feel and understand it and use it beyond the possibility of many, that is how you are changed.

How do I express to you, in this my being, in this the being of all those who have walked beside you, all those who also stand in service to that name you served? How do I express myself to you, when I have such joy in my being that I may hardly express at all? For know also that I am come to wholeness, as are my brothers, through your actions. And we are come to change, to movement, to new possibility and potential. Look around you as you return. Observe changes, for the changes have begun.

So it is time to end. I have spoken of my gratitude. I may not depart without such gratitude to this woman who has been faithful above all else. She hears my voice, she knows my love.

So, go forwards with blessings in your hearts and in your hands, for you are laden with them. Be bountiful in your generosity, courteous in your speech, and loving in your justice. Practice that which you have come to embrace, and stay with each other in thought and love.

I am that Merlin, servant to the Lord, master of that which has been mine to fashion, and you are my friends and companions. I journey with you in your every moment. We have never been so well met as we have been here in this place, at this time, for this purpose. Well done indeed. You have wrought great miracle here. Hold that in your lives and you will make many more.

You live in love, friends, be certain of it.

The Clew

Part Two – The Rationale

The Search for Understanding

*

The Astrology of The Clew

*

The Tree of Life and the Turning of the Key

*

The Story Told, The Challenge Made

*

Final Wish

The Clew

The Search for Understanding
Avril Newey

Reader - the strange, intuitive, cathartic story you have just read, demands explanation. At the apparent end of, at least, this part of our journey, has it been possible to find any answers which satisfy those of us who lived it and may satisfy those who have read of it?

It is an astonishing experience to find oneself, without any warning, the recipient of 'voices' The Old Testament Prophets certainly heard them, Joan of Arc was burnt at the stake for obeying hers and celebrated mystics have written of the bliss their 'voices' invoked within them. Countless others, over centuries, have been tortured, maimed and killed for attesting to the existence of such phenomena. Countless others have been, and are still, drugged/locked away to protect themselves, and others, from the terror and the brutality of the particular 'voices' that intrude into their every waking moment. In modern times such an experience as mine has come to be known as 'channelling' and, judging by the number of books of channelled material appearing on booksellers' shelves, is manifesting to a quite extraordinary degree at the present time. It appears, for the most part, however, that in the Occident world, outside of spiritually and esoterically based groupings, any objective assessment of personal intuitive reception has, in the past, been rendered almost impossible as a result of the fear, superstition and prejudice which years of critical scientific focus, medical pronouncements and religious extremism have occasioned in the Western psyche. There are, however, hopeful signs that such attitudes are beginning to be broken down.

Yet, in the ancient world those who could 'hear' were accorded great respect, their needs were provided for and their counsel regularly sought. The oracles of the Canaanites, the Assyrians, the Phoenicians, the Egyptians, the Greeks, the Romans and the Celts, amongst others, communicated the messages they received in the shape of warnings, blessings, rhyme, riddle, song and story. These people believed that those with gift to 'hear' were the interpreters and communicators of messages from those gods and goddesses whose names might change but whose powers sustained and directed life, as long as humanity continued to gift them reverence through prayer and offerings.

I can in no way deny my experience. I 'heard', or perhaps, more accurately, 'sensed' words. These consecutive 'voices' announcing themselves as guides to myself and the group, greeted us, when they each arrived, with careful explanation of their skills and purpose, gave notice of their impending departure and, at their departure, spoke of their own changed being - the result of our exchanges and described the essence of the 'guide' who would follow them.

Who were these 'guides', these 'voices'? I hope that as you read on you may acquire enough insight to answer that question to your own satisfaction and, also, who knows, perhaps enough memory to return to these communicants the names that somewhere, deep within you, you remember them by. For the names I gave to these voices came, without hesitation and in such a manner, at the very moment

The Clew

when they first entered my consciousness.

In the pages that follow we can only outline the information and insights we have acquired along the way and which have succeeded in answering at least a number of our own questions.

In 1992, with the arrival of my second guide, Assurbanipal, the group were encouraged to study astrology, however, at that time, we did not understand the message and, therefore, did not consciously act on this instruction . Although around this same time, I did meet and seek personal advice from the astrologer Jeffrey Morgan, who gave me the most fitting date for the Devon gathering. It was only with Ian's arrival in May 1994, interestingly still during the period of Assurbanipal's guidance, that I became aware of the contiguity between events in my, and the expanding group's, journey and corresponding planetary movements in the heavens.

All past and future, expected and unexpected, events, viewed through the lens of astrological knowledge took on a meaning and significance that could not be ignored. The more that we examined, the correlations, under Ian's guidance, the more open we became to the concepts that 'above' and 'below' were inextricably connected; that humanity's actions and experiences are responses to subtle energetic influences from within the cosmic frame and, most importantly of all, that planetary energy patterns stimulate events and create pictures in our lives, in the same way that electrical impulses create our television images. We perceived, however, one major difference, in humanity's case, we ARE the picture, we ENACT the image, we EARTH the intent, we live INSIDE the story.

Such a realisation then demands the question, who's intent? We cannot answer that, other than to point to those words that all societies across the ages have constructed, to name that which the ancient world believed was unspeakable. We can only bear witness to the fact that what we sensed, in both the interchanges with the guide voices that I transmitted and the moments of group ceremony we constructed, was simply an essence. The underlying sensation that we all experienced, in the many and varied guide exchanges, was that of an accepting, and compassionate love. A power and warmth which we all felt within our very beings and that these feelings alone were sufficient to encourage us to continue our journey together.

During the eight years of our shared journey, astrology was not the only esoteric concept that we were guided to examine. My first-ever message had said, *'There are secrets kept inside great books in the care of hooded men. The secrets are to be unravelled, the story told.'* As the worlds of channelling, astrology, healing, reincarnation and finally, Qabalistic structures opened up for us, we all began to grasp a much deeper, richer and more forgiving perception of ourselves and others and an increased awareness of our personal potential. As well as a growing consciousness of the inter-relatedness and inter-stimulation of all that exists and an awareness of the patterns of growth and development that both individually, and corporately, mankind enacts on its journey through the aeons.

Two months after our final ritual enactment in Cornwall, Ian's knowledge again provided answer. Through astrological interpretation, he had arrived at some considerable understanding of the previous earth-healing gatherings, at Somerton,

The Clew

Arbor Low, and the Blackdown Rings but this final one began to take on a very particular shape in Ian's mind.. Now, as he was musing on that event, he suddenly 'saw' the structure the group had formed and, for the first time he recognised it. It is very difficult, if not impossible, to do that at a time when you are inside the picture! That, no doubt, is the reason why humanity, much of its science and some of its religions have not considered that we are the actors in the continuing saga of the expanding and contracting circles of life.

My last and most powerful voice, the one that had spoken in Cornwall had said, *Now, you understand the nature of this woman's task, for it has been hers to find the pieces of the pattern, and you are found and she is healed ... You are the pattern.*

John had said, on entering the grotto, "This is my place, no-one will move me from here." Patrick, "I'm here", Colin, Jan and Ian had recalled and duplicated their places in Corsica. The men had called out, "Avril, you're in the centre" The great voice had said, *"Here are the men of my being, summoned so ... you know your places."*

And their places? Each one of us had taken up a position which formed a part of the diagrammatic pattern of the ancient, Qabbalistic, map of creative process, 'The Tree of Life'. The four outer women, about their own work, instinctively standing in the shape of a diamond protecting this inner shape. Were they remembering, and recreating, the roles of priestesses who once served in the long-since forgotten temple ceremonies of earlier civilisations ? So many women at different times throughout our journey contributing their crucial presence, always nurturing, informing, healing, securing. Yet, only now, with Ian's recognition, could we understand that each man, in his personality and life experience, had been living the essence and energy of the spot (or Sephirah on 'The Tree of Life') on which he had chosen to stand. They had indeed known their places and known that I should stand at their centre, with direct connection to each and all of the points that they made. For I had indeed found, and recognised, one by one, each man who stood in his place, *'For it was her task to find the pieces of the pattern'*.

Now, all these men, in that place re-membered, both in memory and in form and one man, in particular, Jan, sought and found to act in partnership with me at a singular moment in time - but for what reason? Ancient myths speak of other partners, other seekers. The Egyptians told of *'ISIS'* who searched the world to find the dismembered parts of her husband/brother Osiris's body, in order that their love-making might restore fruitful life to the Earth. In Assyrian/Babylonian mythology we learn of *'ISHTAR'*, goddess of both love and war, who journeyed to the Underworld to bring back the lover of her youth, *TAMMUZ*, the vegetation god, who had died as a result of her love - so that he might again play his flute upon the Earth and return Spring to the dying world. In Greek mythology, the story of *DEMETER*, whose daughter, *KORE*, had been snatched from her and taken to Hades, leaving Demeter bereft and searching for her and, in her grief and pain, denying the Earth its harvests. Scandinavian myth honours the VALKYRS, or battle maidens, whose task was to choose the bravest of the human battle slain, the Einheriar, and carry them to Valhalla to await their task of fighting alongside Odin and his fellow gods at the Ragnarak - the great battle at the time of the ending of

The Clew

the world when the old gods will die and the Earth will be changed. Whilst, in British legend, *'ARTHUR',* the beloved king, sleeps in a hill in the care of great queens, who will restore him to life whenever devastation threatens his land. All of these stories detailing the re-membering of energies by the feminine in times of cyclical Earth decline.

The men, myself, all the women - '*... and you are found, and she is healed'*, the great voice had said. Is it possible that I have also through enacting out these archetypes in my own life, truly healed some deep, ancient wound within myself and even, perhaps, beyond myself? As the work of the great pschoanalyists tell us, the stories of love, greed , anger, loss, passion, death, re-birth etc. that myth records and humanity enacts are not many, but intensely powerful and always the same, generation after generation. Yet can it be that in living these patterns of emotion we all of us effect action and reaction far beyond the spheres of our personal lives - perhaps even as far as the stars?

So, the whole group found, drawn together, each to play their unique and essential part in the enactment of an immortal story, as the ancient world had witnessed performed in so many places two, three, four thousand years ago - Erech, Philae, Eleusis ... A story of healing and the restoration of the Earth's abundance, cyclically initiated through human ritual enactment by those who, in some instinctive energetic way, can recall both memory and pattern, now, once again, remembered at the turning of another age. '*Destruction, destruction'*, that first message had said, '*The men must walk if it is to be saved'* and later, '*you must place and turn the key'*. 'The Tree of Life' known in esoteric literature to be a key (or a number of keys), the men, these men, had walked, had indeed remembered ... walked and turned the key.

Before the Second World War, Alice Bailey, a renowned channeller of spiritual material (whose work is continued by The Lucis Trust), wrote of the seven cosmic Rays of Influence, whose individual interactions with the energy fields of the Universe, the Earth and its inhabitants, manifest specific behavioural responses. In her writings she detailed specific ray influence on the astrological constellations. For the sign of Aries (my birth-sign) she noted that the influencing Rays are Ray 1 (Will and Power) and Ray 7 (Synthesis, Ceremonial Order, Magic). Certainly, it is true to say that my determination had contributed to the enactment of the ceremony in Cornwall and the others that had preceeded it.

Alice Bailey also wrote that Ray 7, itself, is particularly associated with three constellations, Capricorn, Aries and Cancer. Fascinatingly, Jan, myself and Gray, who stood along the centre pillar in the Cornwall pattern, were each born in one of those three signs and were totally unaware of this correlation at the time of the ceremony.

Another quotation from the writings of this powerful mystic has come to light since that November afternoon in the far South-West of England and, with hindsight, appears to be of particular relevance to what took place then. Referring to the activation of the Seventh Ray, Alice Bailey, in her book 'The Seventh Ray: Revealer Of The New Age' wrote, "Let the Temple of the Lord be built" the Seventh great Angel cried. Then to their places in the north, the south, the west and east seven great sons of God moved with measured pace and took their seats ... The

The Clew

work of building thus began. Thus shall the Temple of the light be carried from heaven to the Earth … God has created in the light. His sons can now create … Let the sons of God create."

'Seven great sons of God moved with measured pace' … 'The men must walk if it is to be saved'. These two phrases, channelled by two very different women, their words divided by a gap of 60/70 years, without any doubt at all, contain the same resonance.

I had certainly found more than seven men on my journey. Three had chosen not to become involved. Ten had stood in their allocated places at the Blackdown Rings but only six stood in their, self-chosen, places in the particular pattern on that final day, with myself taking up the seventh position. Five men had walked - Jan had remained stationery in his place, opposite me, as did the protecting women, all of them somehow certain that that is what they should do. Masculine and feminine energies, interacting with each other in a particular shape and movement forming a 'lock' and turning some cosmic 'key' in the process.

On 1st November 1977, an American astronomer, Charles Kowal, discovered an asteroid in the heavens and, subsequently, named it Chiron (*'No thing is named by chance'* - Ashad). In Greek mythology Chiron was the half-man/half-horse, chief of the Centaurs, the son of Saturn/Kronos and was teacher to many of the gods. He taught Hercules, warfare; Asclepius, healing; Orpheus, music and was the guide and mentor to Jason on his great quest for the Golden Fleece. One day, he accidentally wounded himself in the foot with Hercules's poison-tipped spear. It was an agonising and mortal wound but Chiron could not die, because he was an immortal. To end his agony Chiron gave up his immortality to Prometheus, who had been condemned by the gods to eternal torment, for giving the gift of fire to humanity, unless one of their number gave up his immortality to him. Consequently Chiron has become known as The Wounded Healer and represents the concept of healing ourselves through healing others.

Fascinatingly, the Moon (memory) was exactly conjunct (the same spot) Chiron's position in my birth chart (14 degrees Cancer) at the moment when I began channelling, exact, again, on that same degree at the moment when I met Jan, and exact once more on that same degree, the day before completion, when I had stood with the others in the field with such a personal sense of pain and suffering. Equally fascinating is the fact that the astrological sign for Chiron is written so,

⚷

and, in the astrological world, is popularly referred to, for obvious reasons, as a 'key'.

How had I found and recognised the participants for this most ancient of plays? Ashad was once asked the question, 'Who is this woman?', meaning me and then gave the answer, *'Here is Ishtar and we stood at the place of the Moon'*. In ancient Assyria (modern Iraq) around 1000BC the goddess of love and war was worshipped in the form of Ishtar. The same goddess who was later to be reverenced as Aphrodite by the Greeks and Venus by the Romans, losing her martial qualities in that change process The Assyrians were the conquerors of the Sumerians and

The Clew

incorporated the qualities of the latter's Moon deity, Inanna, into their more martial goddess as well as adapting Inanna's sacred sites for their worship of Ishtar. In 1996 I had actually identified my fourth 'guide/voice' as Ishtar. On the 10 June 1996 that 'voice' had said, *'This woman and I have been parted for great time and although we have joyous reunion we are still strange to each other. Yet, I know her form and she, my voice.'* Could it be possible that once, in a far distant lifetime, I served as a priestess/oracle to Ishtar? Is this how I remembered the name? Fascinatingly, my second 'guide/voice' bore the name Assurbanipal, an actual Assyrian king. Is this the memory I was asked to reach for? Does the DNA in all of us, through its colour and patterns, connect directly with the cosmic energies for which astrology provides one tool.

Does memory live in the DNA and do I and the other group members possess, for some reason, particularly strong and unbroken DNA strands, which enable us to link to cosmic patterns of death and re-birth which stimulated us to ritualise and particularise these energies in the same way as perhaps our ancestors did in their secret enactments of 'The Mysteries'? Believing then, as, perhaps, we should consider now, that such specific ceremonies are not simply symbolic but are responses to cosmic impulses, which are energetically increased at times such as our present, when, along with other cyclical changes, our universe is experiencing a cosmic shift from the Age of Pisces to the Age of Aquarius.

Do these ceremonies occasion a physical reaction in our heavens when manifested by individuals whose birth moments give them the appropriate planetary energy correlations to the shapes needed? Are there also particular places on the Earth's surface that link with, or lock on to, particular planetary vibrations? Is this why our group were directed to specific locations to enact the patterns and movements? Indeed, immediately before the last ceremony, the great voice had said,

> *'For you see, the centre of the pulse is to be moved. It is to move from pain to light. For that which is of this place must be emitted to the world and not the pain of the 'other'.*

One of my earliest, arcane, voices had spoken, in 1990, of a new, approaching energetic influence on the Earth,

> *'She' is one who has power and will use it to form the Earth in a different way'*, it had said.

Through such ceremonies as the ones we constructed and enacted, events in which so many people willingly and hopefully took part, were the energetic foundations indeed being prepared, and finally secured, to energise this new, perhaps more peaceful, influence on our lives and our environment?

As we pass from the old, Neptunian, Age of Pisces with its memories of inquisitions, religious wars and mass suffering but also of the development of sensitivity, service and unconditional love, into the new, Uranian, Age of Aquarius (mind, freedom, communication are amongst its perceived correspondences) does the Aquarian energetic structure have to be connected to its associated energetic

The Clew

linkage points on the Earth's surface? I once found myself making the throw-away remark, "It's as if a huge marquee has been dropped over the Earth and our group has one tent peg which we have to place in the ground to secure the corner for which we are responsible, presumably others are doing the same in their places." Did Earth's oldest civilisations understand this and mark these energy attaching points with sacred structures e.g temples, pyramids? Did they also venerate natural sites, where they perceived specific planetary energies to be connecting ? Is this why they performed acts of ritual worship and ceremony, using music, tone, words, colour, gesture, to activate the impulses that they believed sustained their lives? Did, and do, the patterns they made and the group remembered, somehow concretise cosmic wave-forms and trigger both an expansion in mankind's evolution and, in some related way, the evolution of our energetic universe at the same time? Is it possible that we really are all co-creators and sustainers of life with the *Un-Named*, whatever we perceive That/Him/Her to be? Have we really forgotten so much?

Could we friends actually *ALL* have lived together before, in that ancient time in Assyria, when we held, as a group of citizens or, perhaps, temple officials, particular responsibility for the nurture and worship of the Assyrian goddess, Ishtar, the Queen of Heaven, known, in our present time, as the morning and evening star, Venus? Could we possibly also have known each other long ago in Egypt? Was it possible that we had all stood , at that time, in some star-reflecting pattern at the annual ceremony of the re-generation by his sister/wife, Isis, of Osiris, Egyptian god of Nature and the dead. Osiris, who personified within his god-form the renewing waters of the River Nile and the light of the Sun? Is this why and how we had remembered? Could some immortal part (our spiritual souls, or some remembering pulse of energy in the DNA of each of us) have lived other lives since then, together, with each other, in ones. twos, small and larger groups, and had this journey in our present lifetime been one of struggling with the personal emotional legacies (our karma) of those lives in order that we could indeed stand at an essential moment, in a particular place, as a result of the healing we had occasioned in each other and in as clear a light-filled form as we could manage? Standing 'without grudge and grievance' for a purpose!

The myth of Isis and Osiris tells us that Isis, after searching for the dismembered parts of Osiris following his murder by their brother, Set, was successful in finding all of them except one - his phallus. So she made a phallus from mud and grasses, imbued her brother/husband with the life-force, copulated with him, conceived and, subsequently, gave birth to their son, Horus - the new life. Osiris is (as was Tammuz in Assyrian legend, who, Ishtar also searched for) the Egyptian god of nature.

This myth seems to speak to us , archetypally, of some cosmic process which results in the cyclical restoration of the Earth's abundance and, therefore, is of extraordinary importance as, although our present-day science recognises natural cycles, we seem to have lost all knowledge of the restorative patterns of inter-active cosmic influences which this myth records. Could it be possible also that, throughout the past two thousand years, Christianity, at the same time as rejecting, for the most part, the 'pagan' mythology of gods and goddesses has also,

The Clew

unknowingly, retained the memory of this gnostic process of cosmic fertilisation within its doctrine of the Annunciation and the virgin birth? Events which the Gospels tell us, themselves took place as the Ages changed - at that time from Aries to Pisces.

As earlier shown in the astrological section, I was born with Chiron (my wound) conjunct Sirius, (Egyptian name, Isis) and, also, conjunct Canopus (named after the navigator of Jason's ship 'Argo') and, therefore, astrologically, the star which offers guidance on the quest. My unconscious quest to heal my 'wound' which began in 1990, certainly resulted in me 'finding' a number of men, who, apparently, I gathered together for an unconscious, energetic enactment of a sacred marriage - the coming together of Isis and Osiris. Is it possible that this symbolic union is the essential event which must be acted out, and the resulting energetic, fertilised seed or pulse locked in whenever the Earth's energy field is to experience some cosmic cyclical renewal? On the 8 July 1990 I had typed,

>*'There is a blight across the land and the Earth is dying without the prayers ... come again to the groves with those of your fellows who believe in us, we need all ... There are so few left and the work must be done.'*

So, on that November day in 1998, standing cold and bemused in a distant Cornish field, were there just enough of us to remember how to act out the strange, lonely scattering of the dismembered Osiris and, on the following day, again enough of us to recall how and where to stand to re-member this once-beloved god and how to re-create his union with Isis in order that some cyclic, cosmic potency could, at the right and proper time, be seeded upon the Earth? In the second channelling I received were the words,

>*'You are the converter, the force must pass through you into the ground.'*

Was this what we had achieved ? A purpose (our spiritual this-life dharma) that, before the final event, we could not have possibly comprehended but which, along with each one of those who had contributed to any part of the journey, we had willingly attempted. Attempted with a faith and commitment, a love and a hope that, somehow and somewhere within all of us we had reached for and found. - our *'contract'*, as Merlin had put it. In June,1990, two months after the earthquake which had begun it all, the earliest of my 'voices' had said to me,

>*'You are the people of the faith, your task is to pray and to make the journeys through the light of time'.*

Is this the explanation ? This, the contract we discharged? This, the journey which has so profoundly changed and enskilled each one of us? Changes which will lead hopefully to new beginnings and new opportunities for humanity and which will perhaps also, as we all so deeply desire, lead to a new Spring for the Earth itself.

The Astrology of The Clew

What is Astrology ?

Astrology is an interpretative tool for comprehending the energetic relationship both between Heaven and Earth and, as the ancients perceived, the gods (the planets) and mankind. It is based on, at least, four thousand years of observations of planetary movements and simultaneous human and earth experiences. Its premise is that everything that exists (everything formed at the moment of 'The Big Bang'?) interconnects and influences everything else. It is an ancient craft, an art and, many would argue, a science, in the true sense of that word. It functions not only empirically but also intuitively, using geometry and image to access deep levels of the unconscious.

THE ASTROLOGY OF THE SACRED MARRIAGE
by Avril Newey

Through studying the astrological charts generated at particular moments in my own and the group's journey, we have acquired considerable insight into the energetic nature of, and background to, those events. It is not possible, within the limitations of this book, to make available any detailed study of our research but we hope to offer such a study at a later time if there is sufficient public interest. However, in order to show the relevance of this form of investigation, simple astrological interpretations of stages in my personal journey to the energetic re-anactment of the sacred marriage (the event which was to prove to be at the very heart of my journey) and only of this one aspect of that journey, are here offered to a wider audience. For reasons of privacy, neither Jan's birth chart or any of Jan and Avril's composite charts are shown, but relevant correspondences between Jan and Avril's birth charts are detailed and the chart of the moment of their first meeting is also given.

In order that those readers unfamiliar with astrological practice may better be able to follow the correlations that will be made in the following pages, the structure of an astrological chart is presented, along with its house definitions, the symbols (sigils) of each sign and planet and an explanation of angles and aspects. An explanation of the source and application of Sabian Symbols is also given. Sabian Symbol interpretations are taken from: *'An Astrological Mandala: The Cyde of Transformations and its 360 Symbolic Phases'* by Dane Rudhyar.

The Clew

The Structure of an Astrology Chart

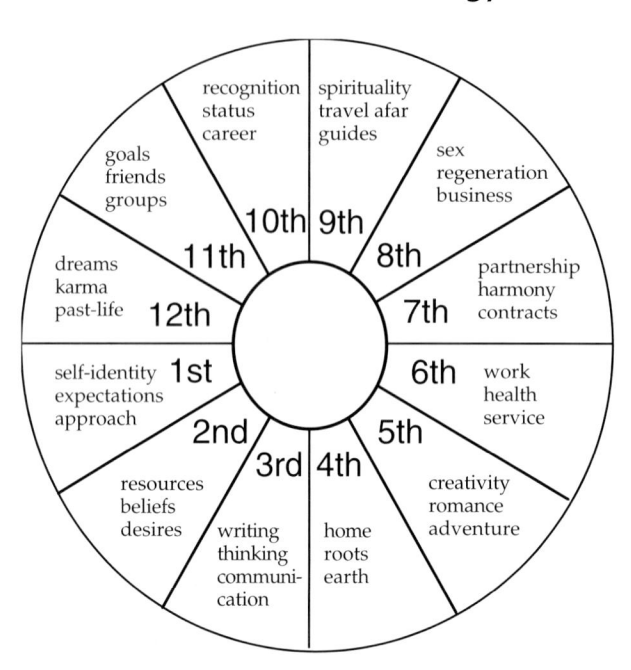

- 1st: self-identity, expectations, approach
- 2nd: resources, beliefs, desires
- 3rd: writing, thinking, communication
- 4th: home, roots, earth
- 5th: creativity, romance, adventure
- 6th: work, health, service
- 7th: partnership, harmony, contracts
- 8th: sex, regeneration, business
- 9th: spirituality, travel afar, guides
- 10th: recognition, status, career
- 11th: goals, friends, groups
- 12th: dreams, karma, past-life

Key to Astrological Symbols

Signs of the zodiac

♈	Aries	♓	Pisces	♌	Leo
♉	Taurus	♎	Libra	♑	Capricorn
♊	Gemini	♏	Scorpio	♍	Virgo
♋	Cancer	♐	Sagittarius	♒	Aquarius

Planets/Gods

☉	Sun	♀	Venus	♆	Neptune
☽	Moon	♂	Mars	♇	Pluto
☿	Mercury	♃	Jupiter	⚷	Chiron
♄	Saturn	♅	Uranus		

Other points

AS	Ascendant	☊	North node of Moon
MC	Midheaven (medium coeli)	☋	South node of Moon

Asteroids/Goddesses

⚳	Ceres	⚴	Pallas
⚵	Juno	⚶	Vesta

Planetary aspects

☌	Conjunction	0°	blends
✶	Sextile	60°	potential to harmonise
□	Square	90°	conflicts
△	Trine	120°	flows together
☍	Opposition	180°	requires balance

The Clew

The Astrological Sabian Symbols

Astrological horoscopes take the form of a circle made up (as all circles are) of 360 degrees. These degrees are themselves sub-divided into the twelve cosmic constellations from Aries to Pisces. So, anyone born on 25 December will have been born when the Sun (depending on the exact moment of birth) is on, (or adjacent to) 20 degrees Cancer and anyone with a birthday on 24 April will have a 3 degrees Taurus Sun position. It is important to point out that only the Sun has such fixed day/date positions because our calendar is based on the 360 day Sun cycle.

In our present-day world, an increasing number of people are interested in astrology and are aware that astrologers interpret someone's character and life experience from the position of the planets in the heavens at the moment of a person's birth. Particular planets in particular signs and astrological houses invite specific interpretations, which have only been arrived at after thousands of years of observation and study. However, it is not so commonly known that astrologers also believe that each one of the zodiacal 360 degrees carries a particular energy and meaning, and that it is crucial to include a study of planet tenanted degrees, as well as planet positions, when evaluating a person's birth horoscope.

In 1925, a renowned American astrologer, Marc Edmund Jones, conducted an experiment. He prepared 360 small cards, each one of these cards having, in the top right-hand corner, a small sign indicating a particular astrological sign and degree. Sitting in his car one day with a clairvoyant of Welsh extraction, Elsie Wheeler, he shuffled the cards and then, completely at random, drew a card and, without looking at it himself, asked Elsie Wheeler what picture she could clairvoyantly see. What she described, he recorded. Incredibly, in the space of a few hours on a single day, Elsie Wheeler gave Marc Edmund Jones 360 pictures. These images he subsequently named 'The Sabian Symbols'. There have been other intuitive interpretations of the energies of zodiacal degrees both before and since that day in Los Angeles but Elsie Wheeler's 'pictures' have proved to be enormously insightful and accurate when defining what energies and experiences will accompany us in our journeys through our lives.

What is so fascinating for anyone who makes a study of the 'Symbols' is to discover that aspects of the images, as well as the complete images themselves, that are delineated by the planet positions in our birth horoscopes, actually physically manifest in our lives - often at moments when a planet is transiting that degree position in our horoscope. So, the person born on Christmas Day will very likely experience during their lives Elsie Wheeler's 'Merrymakers embark in a big canoe on a lantern-lit lake', as well as feeling that their life will not be completely fulfilled unless it incorporates some kind of group participation and purpose; the person born on 13 July may well physically live a moment at some point in their lives when they give a public performance, as indicated by, 'A prima donna sings to a glittering audience'. Finally, the person with their Sun, or a planet, at 3 degrees Taurus may, one day, find themselves gazing out into their garden at the 'Natural steps leading up to a lawn of clover in bloom'. Steps which they have either constructed for themselves, or which was the feature which led them to buying the particular property that they are now so content to live in.

In every moment of existence the planets move around the heavens sounding, as the fingers of a harpist pluck and sound the strings of a harp, the energies of the cosmos. As this happens those energies become form and, in every moment, someone, somewhere on the Earth's surface sees the actual image and/or enacts the essence of the 'Sabian Symbols'.

Chart Interpretations

The particular focus (i.e. sacred marriage aspects) of the following, very limited, interpretations requires particular attention being given to the positioning and nature within the charts described, of two asteroids, Juno and Vesta.

Juno, in mythology, the wife of the Roman king of the gods, Jupiter, denotes all one-to-one contractual partnerships.

Vesta, in mythology, the goddess of the hearth fire, signifies devotion, purification and sacrifice, and is associated with religious/magical rituals and the spiritual life.

Planetary and asteroid positions are given in degrees and minutes.

The Clew

Avril's Birth Chart

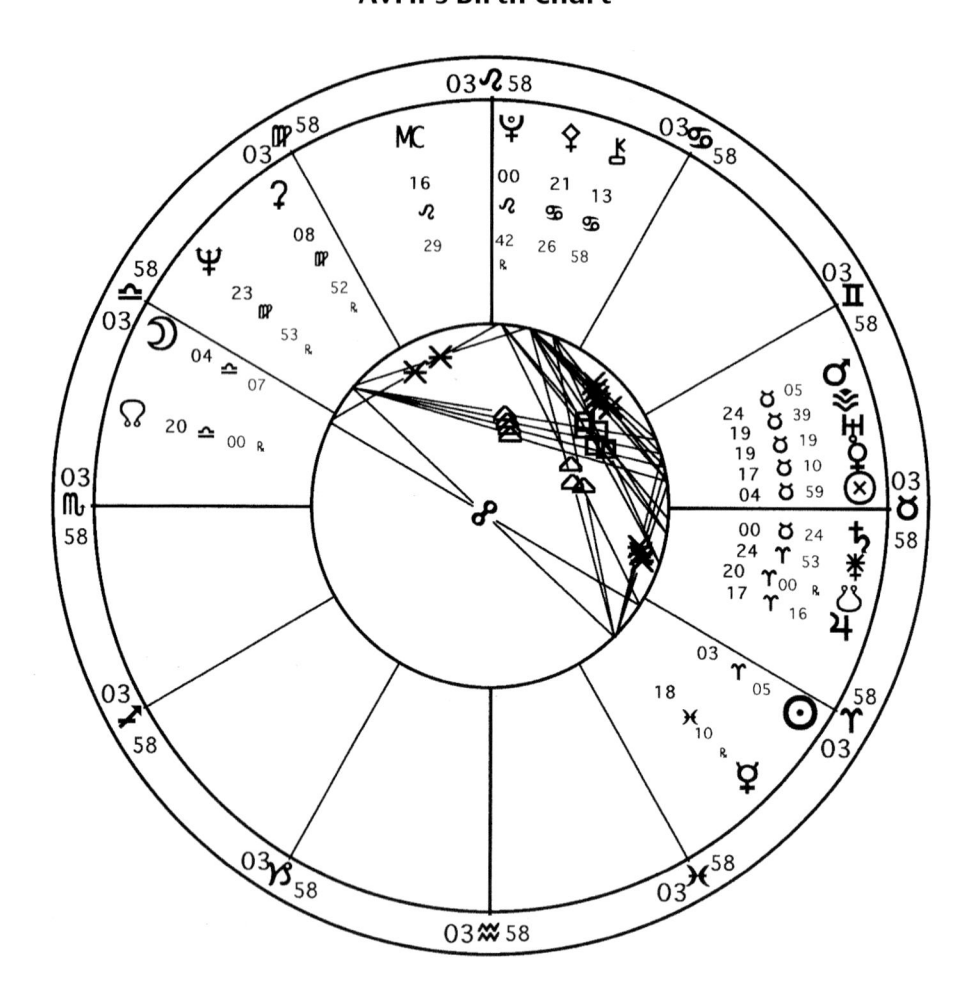

Natal Chart : Avril Newey
Saturday 23rd March 1940 21:17:00 GMT (22:17:00 GMD)
Coventry, England : 52N25 / 01W30
Tropical   Equal   True Node

VENUS 17.10 Taurus in the 7th House of contracts, marriage and one-to-one partnerships trine Neptune in the 11th House of groups/friends and goals

MEANING: Signifies the possibility of remembered love union(s) in the present lifetime, rediscovered through spiritual group activity.

The Clew

JUNO at 24.56 Aries in the 6th House of work and service

quincunx (a karmic past life aspect) Neptune

MEANING: Signifies a memory of a spiritual service, one-to-one parnership.

VESTA at 19.19 Taurus in the 7th House of contracts, marriage and one-to-one partnerships.

conjunct Venus

MEANING: Signifies the potential for a non-attached attitude towards relationship with the capacity to sublimate sexuality into spirituality.

also conjunct Uranus

MEANING: Signifies the potential for an interest in scientific and occult studies and a powerful intuitive ability.

also trine Neptune

MEANING: Signifies the potential for a devotion to spiritual or artistic ideals (These VESTA aspects are strongly suggestive of, at least, one past-life spent as a temple priestess.)

CHIRON 13.58 Cancer in the 9th house of faith and higher wisdom

Conjunct the Fixed Stars:

Sirius. Associated by the Egyptians with their gods Isis and Osiris and, also, Canopus, the navigator - signifier of the quest.

also making an exact opposition to Jan's birth Sun position

MEANING: Jan's persona relates both to Avril's karmic wound and to the potential healing of her wound ('..*and you are found and she is healed*' - Merlin).

VESTA Sabian Symbol : 'A new continent rising out of the ocean'

Interpretation: When ... light has been called upon to purify the consciousness freed from its attachment and contaminations, a new release of life can emerge.

The Clew

The Beginning

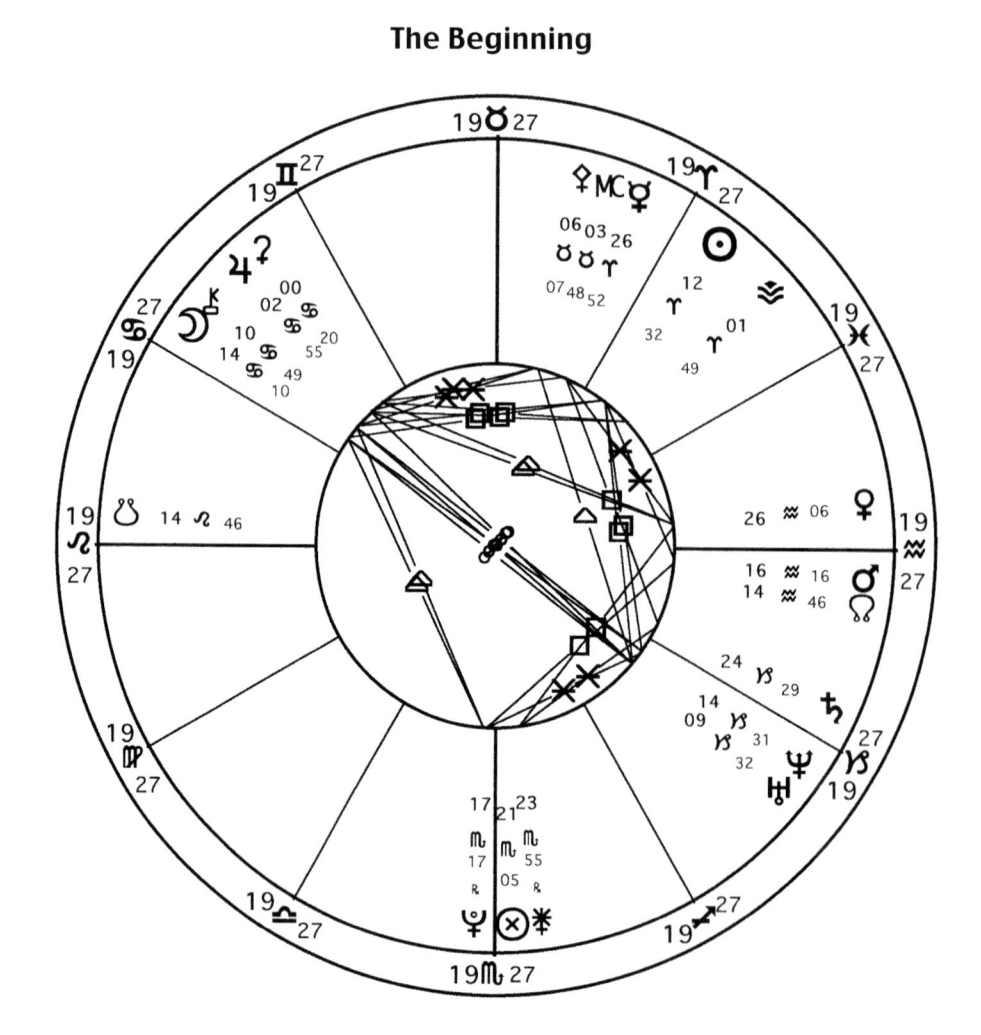

Natal Chart : The Beginning
*Monday 2nd April 1990 13:30:00 GMT (14:30:00 GMD)
Kenilworth, England 52N21 / 01W34
Tropical Equal True Node*

SUN 12:32 Aries in the 8th House of the occult, death and transformation making an exact conjunction with Jan's birth Juno placement

MEANING: The bringing to consciousness of this 'partner's' existence

square (conflict both between male/female aspects and between purpose and memory)

MOON 14.10 Cancer (Sirius/Canopus) in the 11th House of friends, groups and goals

conjunct Avril's birth Chiron (wound) position and opposite Jan's Sun birth position

MEANING: Memory of personal conflict and past-life group experience

SATURN 24.29 Capricorn in the 6th House of service square Avril's birth Juno placement

MEANING: Oppressive karmic memory, loyalty and commitment in relation to a partner

PLUTO 17.17 retrograde Scorpio conjunct the chart Nadir

MEANING: Powerful transformation potential in relation to ancestral roots and the earth.

making an exact opposition to Avril's birth Venus position

MEANING: Powerful emotion relating to a karmic past-life relationship

VESTA 1.49 Aries in the 8th House of the occult, death and transformation conjunct Avril's birth Sun placement

MEANING: The 'priestess' awakens in Avril's persona

MID-HEAVEN (MC) (direction) 3.47 Taurus in 9th house of spiritual guides/foreigners. making an exact conjunction to Avril's birth Descendant - the beginning of her 7th House

MEANING: The moment when her 'contract' with a partner/s is remembered

ZENITH 19:26 Taurus

exact conjunction with Avril's birth Vesta/Uranus conjunction in her 7th House of partnerships and contracts.

MEANING: The 'priestess' begins her contractual search for a specific partner

ZENITH Sabian Symbol: 'Wisps Of Winglike Clouds Streaming Across The Sky.'

Interpretation: '… clouds may … symbolise the presence of celestial beings … revealing the direction to take, the direction of "the wind" of destiny.'

The Clew

Avril and Jan's Meeting

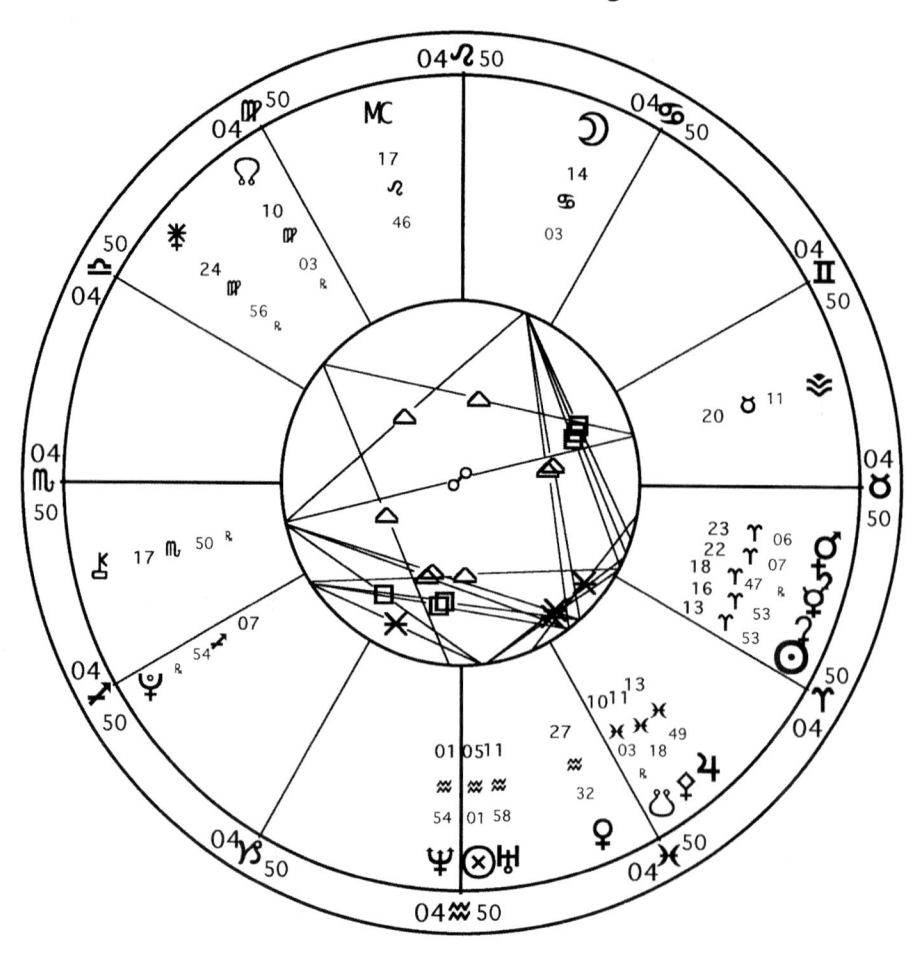

Natal Chart : Avril and Jan Meeting
Friday 3rd April 1998 20:39:00 GMT (21:39:00 BST)
Coventry, England 52N25 / 01W30
Tropical Equal True Node

NOTE: Exactly 8 years (the number anciently linked to the cycles of Saturn/karma/responsibility) from THE BEGINNING

SUN 13:53 Aries (as at THE BEGINNING) in the 6th House of service conjunct Jan's birth Juno position and

square (conflict both between male/female aspects and between purpose and memory)

206

MOON 14:07 Cancer (Sirius / Canopus) (as at THE BEGINNING) in the 9th house of spirituality / foreigners

conjunct Avril's birth Chiron position and opposite Jan's birth Sun position

MEANING: The opening of Avril's wound caused, and potentially able to be healed, by Jan.

SATURN 22:07 Aries and MARS 23:06 Aries in the 6th House of service

conjunct Avril's birth Juno position and

also quincunx her birth Neptune position

MEANING: Memory of an exacting, spiritual and, probably, cruel past-life partnership

MC 19:33 Leo in the 10th House of public recognition square Avril's birth Vesta / Uranus positions

MEANING: Potential for future public activity linked to 'priestess' role

JUNO 24:56 Virgo in the 11th House of groups and objectives conjunct Avril's birth Neptune position

MEANING: The spiritual union

VESTA 20 Taurus in the 7th House of contracts and one-to one relationships

conjunct Avril's birth Vesta / Uranus and exactly conjunct Jan's birth Vesta position. (Jan was, thereafter, to consistently insist of Avril, that ,'You have to be opposite me' - a reflection of his sensitivity to their Vesta astrological placements.)

MEANING: The 'contractual' meeting of spiritual partners The 'priest'and the 'priestess'

NADIR Sabian Symbol: 'A masked figure performs ritualistic acts in a mystery play.'

Interpretation: 'The individuals involvement in long-established patterns of activity aiming at the release of collective power ... The great Mysteries of the past ... rituals are binding, and ... the performers ... do not act as human persons but as focal points for the release of transpersonal forces.'

The Clew

Completion

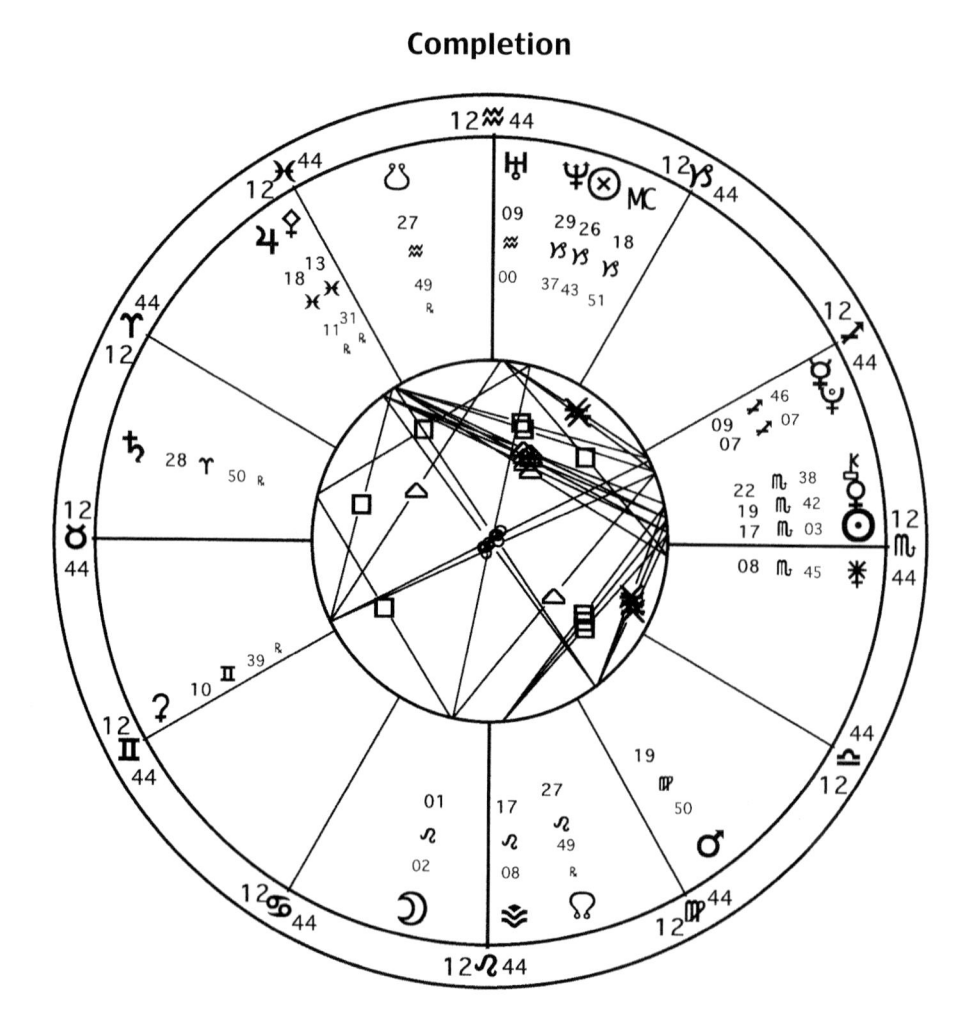

Natal Chart : Completion
*Monday 8th November 1998 16:26:00 GMT
Cornwall, England
Tropical Equal True Node*

SUN 17:03 Scorpio in the 7th House of contracts and one-to-one partnerships

MEANING: Focus on occult partnerships

(The Sun was on the exact same degree it had occupied at the Blackdown Rings ceremony and that Pluto had occupied at 'The Beginning')

conjunct Venus and Chiron

MEANING: Illumination of a wound with harmony between partners and the potential love energy to heal it

opposite Avril's birth Venus. Uranus/Vesta positions.

MEANING: The illumination of Avril's priestess relationship wound

also square

VESTA in the 4th House of the root memory and the earth

MEANING: Remembered spiritual service to the Earth.

itself conjunct Avril's birth MC and Jan's birth Pluto

MEANING: (for Avril) the potential for a future public spiritual persona. (for Jan) the focussing of personal power for social and spiritual purposes

MARS 19:50 Virgo in the fifth house of creativity and the heart trine Avril's birth Vesta and Jan's birth Vesta positions.

MEANING: The soul task to concentrate, direct and join spiritual energy from the heart

MC 18:51 Capricorn in the 9th house of higher wisdom and spiritual guides

trine

Avril's birth Venus / Vesta / Uranus

MEANING: The love of the priestess, directed for purpose

SUN Sabian Symbol: A woman fecundated by her own spirit is 'great with child'

MEANING: The nurturing and birth of new life

ZENITH Sabian Symbol: 12:44 Aquarius 'On a vast staircase stand people of different types, graduated upwards'

MEANING: The ascending evolutionary process of humanity. The image is a clear, simplistic picture of the Qabalistic diagram 'The Tree of Life' - the shape the group instinctively formed at this moment

The Clew

The Tree of Life and the Earth Healing
Ian Walker

This appendix is an attempt to use Esoteric symbology to explain the final Earth healing ritual that we did in Cornwall. In order to do this I have split it into the following sections :
Section 1 is a brief overview of the Tree of Life.
Section 2 is a description of how the group pattern formed the pattern of the Temple.
Section 3 is the ritual itself.
Section 4 is an account of how the men turned the key.

1 : The Tree of Life

Introduction

The Tree of Life, otherwise known as the Qabalah, is an ancient system said to depict the beginning and ongoing creation of the Universe. Given that 'Man' and the Earth live interdependently within the Universe then the Qabalah also depicts the 'rules' of creative evolution for both the planet and humanity. In short, it is a model of creation from both a macrocosmic perspective and a microcosmic perspective. The assumption being ' As Above so Below' (in Heaven as on Earth). The baseline metaphysical assumption is the belief in a Creator!

The Tree was said to have been given to the Hebrew race by the Archangels and, according to Jewish orthodoxy, it represents The Law. Fig.1a is a diagram of the Tree. On the face of it a cynic would probably find it absurd that a model containing 10 circles and their connecting lines can represent a complex Universe but the more one investigates the known wisdom of our ancestors relating to this system, the more profound and enriching the journey of investigation becomes. Exploration into the Tree's meaning offers the 'Apprentice' much joy in the

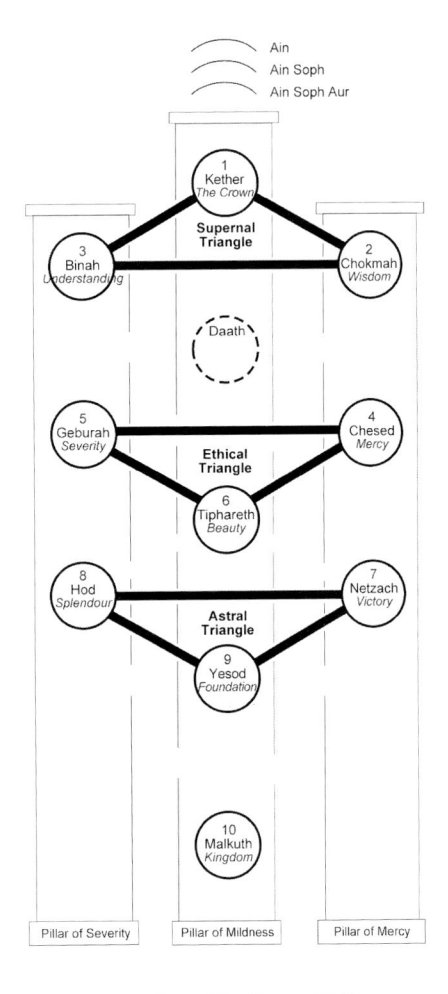

Fig. 1a : The Tree of Life

The Clew

way of revelation. As one's consciousness rises, new relationships and insights are revealed to the Seeker which, in their turn, illuminate the mind. It is beyond the scope of this appendix to give a full account of the multi-composite attributes of the Tree. There are many good books on the market which offer a comprehensive introduction to the Qabalah, two of which I have recommended in the bibliography. I will concentrate my efforts on trying to give the reader some sense of the essence of the Tree and attempt to synthesise this with the main thrust of the preceding narrative.

The ten circles are called Sephiroth and each individual sphere is called a Sephirah. The early Rabbis named these as the ten holy emanations. Although these Sephiroth were created simultaneously in space, they are, at any one point in time, in a stage of evolution. Most people have seen the 'Russian Doll' which contains a series of smaller dolls. This would be a good analogy to have in mind, because each Sephirah is evolving from it's predecessor. Imagine also that each Sephirah is a pool of water and when it fills it overflows into the lower one. Avril's spirit Guides alluded to this 'truth' when they affirmed that each Guide incrementally contained the energies of its predecessor. There does appear to be a hierarchy of consciousness in spirit, from which direction is offered to humanity and the planet which resembles this creation model. It is important to reiterate that these Sephiroth appeared simultaneously in space but developed in consciousness in time - there is a difference. Time belongs to matter made manifest, whereas the creative beginning was an instant (the Big Bang theory for example). The dotted line connecting the Sephiroth (Fig. 1b) is called the lightning flash, and shows the instantaneous directional order of the manifestation of each sphere.

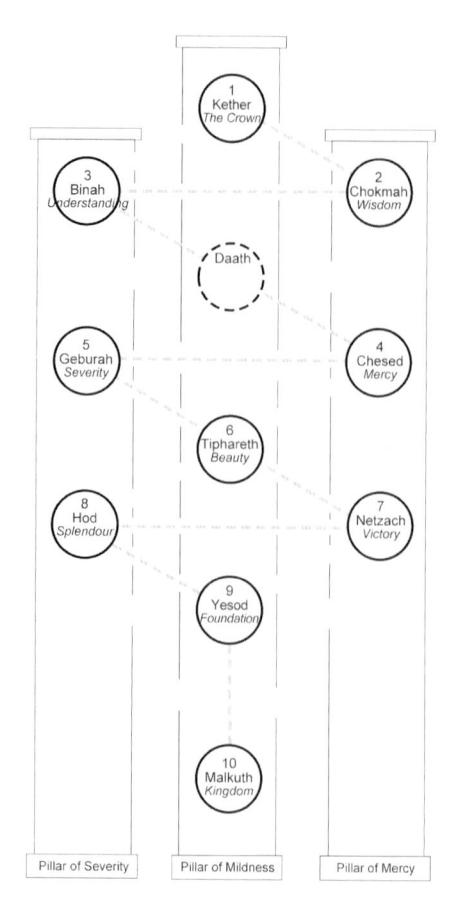

Fig. 1b : The Lightning Flash

The Main Characteristics of the Tree

The Void

Let us look first at the Tree from the perspective of the beginnings of creation. This lies above Kether in Fig. 1a. The higher one goes up the Tree the more obscure it becomes. Here one is confronted with the most profound of all questions - 'Why?' Philosophers, religious leaders and children in prams all ask the same question - 'Why?' All roads lead to Why, it seems, so don't expect an answer now! Above the Tree are both the proverbial question 'What came first, the chicken or the egg?' and the seemingly nonsensical phrase of the Zen Masters "the sound of one hand clapping." That which lies beyond creation is depicted above the Tree as the three veils of negative existence, namely - Ain, Ain Soph, and Ain Soph Aur, which represent negativity, the limitless and the limitless light.

Kether

Straight away I am faced with the paradox of the limitation of language. Kether is situated on the middle pillar at the very apex of the tree, and as such, is beyond name and symbol. However, it is recognised as a dot within a circle, and a crown above the head. The crown above the head is an attempt, amongst other things, to describe an open system. One might consider it as an intervention from a Source or Creator. A Source which, through the first swirlings of will and desire, manifests a focussed beam of creation depicted as a point; and yet the point cannot really be a point at all at this stage of creation - it is devoid of area, no matter how small. Hence the paradox ! Maybe we could call it God's desire to experience itself and to step out of being. What most people agree on is that it represents unity or wholeness, and some religions would equate that with the perfection of God. Kether then contains within it all the other nine Sephirah.

Chokmah

Chokmah is situated on the Pillar of Mercy and that of force (masculine). It is the Supernal Father within the Supernal triangle of Kether, Chokmah and Binah. The one now becomes the two, depicted by a straight line. Here we have movement from A to B, distance without a reference point. There is enough distance to look back at Kether and see itself, and vice versa. For Chokmah is the direct reflection of Kether and is represented by the circle.

I struggle with this attribution. I would personally be happier with the attribution of a spiral, or a circle within a circle, and this brings me to an important philosophical point. The tenet of this entire book and its participants is that we believe in a Creator. Religions differ in their conception of the nature of their God. The Jewish faith for example, as I understand it, believes in a perfect God, a whole God. This might explain why Chokmah is depicted as a circle in it's reflection of Kether. I personally believe in a God that is evolving. If one believes this, and that we are made in the image of God, then the evolutionary symbol of the spiral seems more fitting. Whether you believe in a circle(perfection) or a spiral (evolution) has huge philosophical implications on how you view fate, free will

The Clew

and the destiny of the planet. I leave you with that thought, for it is too big a question to go into here but a fitting metaphysical question for the Supernal triangle. Chokmah then is pure force, the phallic line but force alone is not enough in order to manifest intent - it needs a receptacle which brings me to the third Sehirah, Binah.

Binah

Binah is the Supernal Mother and completes the Supernal triangle. Binah is situated on top of the Pillar of Form and it's associated severity. Here, at the archetypal level, is the equality of the sexes, for both have equal power. Binah harnesses, contains amd organises the primal force of Chokmah. The raw, masculine, energies experience containment in form, albeit from the first principles. Remember, we are still in the abstract plane of energies here. From the perspective of the 'male' forces of Chokmah this is a death. Movement is contained and re-organised in the severe waters of Binah. The triangle is associated with this sphere by virtue of it's third emanation. We now have movement from A to B to C and a reference point in space.

The Four Worlds

I would now like to introduce you to the four worlds (see Fig. 1c). There are many ways to split up the Tree but this is a major component and cannot be ignored, especially in view of explaining the final task in Cornwall. The four worlds, in descending order, are : Atziluth, Briah, Yetzirah and Malkuth. There is some disagreement amongst commentators as to where these overlap on the Qabalah, but our experience in the final Earth healing ritual has convinced me as to where they lie.

As I understand it knowledge can come in three main ways. Common knowledge, from, for example, books, conversation and teaching; experiential knowledge from the experience of doing something, and thirdly intuitive knowledge, which can take us out of a single loop of learning into a new spiral of knowing. This can free us from conditioning and dogma. Dare to think and express the paradoxical, unthinkable, and it is in that spirit that I reveal my findings.

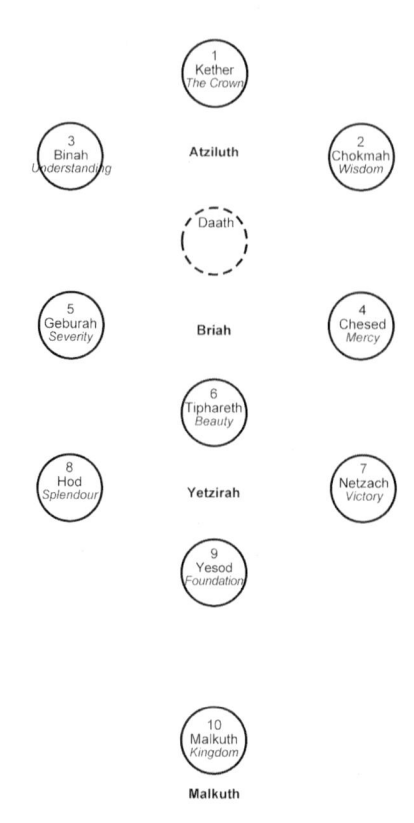

Fig. 1c : The Four Worlds

Some authors ascribe Atziluth to Kether alone but I consider it to include the entire Supernal triangle above the abyss (above Daath). These worlds are hiearchial planes or dimensions of consciousness. Each world has an energetic being that has rulership. I have taken some of the lines out of the full diagram so that the worlds can be seen more clearly. There are three flat surfaces that represent the first three worlds, below which is the Sephirah of Malkuth, a world on its own, representing form and this planet. It must be realised that the worlds exist within each individual Sephirah. One can encounter a Sephirah on different planes. As an example, humanity, or an individual, might be at a level of consciousness where they are operating in the Sephirah of Chesed on the plane of Yetzirah.

Each world has a ruling being and has associated colours. Atziluth is ruled by the God realm and has sacred God names which can be invoked. Briah is the creative world and is ruled by the Archangels. Each Archangel has responsibility for a particular Sephirah. Yetzirah is ruled by the order of Angels and each order has responsibilities for a particular Sephirah.

Daath

Both Fig.1a and Fig.1b show Daath as a dotted circle. Tradition states that it isn't a Sephirah, otherwise we would have eleven holy Sephiroth spoken of by the Rabbi's. Daath is known as the abyss. From a Christian point of view this would be the Fall from the Garden of Eden (the Supernal triangle), for Daath is said to be knowledge, and we all know what that apple represented don't we?

For reasons which I hope will soon become apparent I believe Daath to exist but in a very different way to all the other Sephiroth. The central pillar on the Tree of Life is a balancing pillar. It balances out the masculine and femine pillars. It is also the pillar of consciousness. Daath is situated on this pillar just below the Supernal triangle and represents our first gateway into the realm of matter, but at this stage it is still abstract. Metaphorically it is the eating of the apple of knowledge by Eve, but it is also symbolic of desire, consummation, and the incarnated human being on the wheel of rebirth who is prey to death and decay, as opposed to the idyllic immortal world of the Supernal garden. This is why the serpent gets a bad press!

Our experience at the final Earth healing ritual and the subsequent understanding has given me a deeper insight into this important sphere. The Aquarian era is many things but there is one important thread. Knowledge (Daath) which was once hidden by mystery schools and religions is now coming to light, either through vehicles such as this book or via direct contact with one's higher self. The days of being reliant on our priests for connection to the Divine are going. Religious dogma and attempts at keeping social control are like trying to hold back the river Danube with a sandbag. The science of D.N.A. and it's associated responsibilities is also an Aquarian example of how we are becoming more aware of our role as creators - Dolly the sheep being a famous example.

It is self empowerment at an individual level and it is collective empowerment at the level of humanity. The next era dawns and Daath comes into it's power. My insights are drawing me to the hypothesis that Daath is in fact the Star of Sirius. We may on Earth revolve around the Sun but this Solar system is, in turn, spiralling towards the star of Sirius which may be spiralling towards the Galactic centre. The Egyptians knew the importance of this star and revered it. Their civilisation was rich in knowledge, as we are discovering little by little as we uncover the mysteries of the pyramids and the Sphinx. More about Daath later when I explain the pattern that we created in Cornwall. For now we can say that Daath is the gateway between the Atziluth world and the world of Briah, and represents the descent into matter and our ascent into God consciousness. For the Tree is a two way system, evolutionary and involutionary.

Chesed

Numerology is a branch of esoteric understanding that interprets number qualitatively, and considers each number to have a unique energy which is translated into psychological patterns of behaviour. Each number has a distinct archetypal meaning and essence. The number four is always associated with matter. Within this number is the beginning and end. 1+2+3+4=10 which equates to 1. A table and a chair normally have four legs for stability. The equal-armed cross in Christian symbolism is a combination of spirit (the vertical) and matter (the horizontal) which is equivalent to the 1 contained within the 4. One could say that Chesed is the cohesive principle which begins to build matter below the abyss. Yet the matter I talk about here is still on a high vibrational arc, as it is still high up the Tree.

Metaphorically, Chesed would be the ideal smooth running country that is happy with it's ruler and whose people live in peace and abundance. It is an anabolic state which, in evolutionary terms, is trying to create a utopia, or Heaven on Earth, however one conceives that to be. However, humanity's consciousness is not at these dizzy realms yet, we often build from fear and greed, and, as a consequence, illusionary foundations are put in place. I use the term illusionary in comparison to 'truth'. Non-truth contains within it the seeds of it's own destruction. These seeds ensure that new foundations are built on a higher arc of consciousness which more closely resembles the truth that humanity strives towards. This brings me quite nicely to Geburah which administers the adjustment needed.

Geburah

This is the katabolic principle and is the Sephirah of truth and severity. From humanity's limited perspective the actions of Geburah can seem unjust, and yet one of it's virtues is justice. We on Earth are only privy to a single negative on a whole reel of film that stretches both backwards and forwards in time. This explains why we frequently express dismay on appearing to see the sword of God in it's many manifestations, such as wars and natural disasters, to name but two forms of adjustment.

The intention of this Sephirah is to make the necessary adjustment, in order that truth might reign one day in all of God's creations. Geburah breaks down and clears the decks ready for the next more evolved creative impulse to take seed. This Sephirah, more than most, suffers from many projections. Is it by chance that 1+2+3+4+5=15 which is the number of the Devil in the major arcana of the

Tarot - I think not! Another understanding of this Sephirah might be in the context of contemporary thought which mentions the mentalities of the Hawks and the Doves. The Doves would be the liberalism of Chesed. The Hawks would be, for example, those who wish to wield the sword of Geburah in order to exact change through war. In reality a balance is needed between these two opposing energies, which brings me to the next Sephirah.

Tiphareth

Fig. 1a shows this to be in the ethical triangle together with Geburah and Chesed. Tiphareth plays out the role of balancing these opposing forces through the fair witnessing mind and the compassionate heart. Tiphareth is also a gateway between the worlds of Briah and Yetzirah (Fig. 1c). From the point of view of Kether this is the child, but from the point of view of Malkuth it is the 'King'. 1+2+3+4+5+6= 21. This is the number of the Universe in the Tarot and a symbol of the high level of consciousness connected with this sphere. Indeed this is the Sephirah associated with Jesus the Son of God. Jesus exemplifies, and was a high example, of what the Pisces energies were meant to be. He was a mentor and a light for us to reflect the energies of this sphere.

Now as we enter Aquarius this possibility is in reach of us all. The phrase "No one can reach the Father except through me", was a Qabalistic fact! Tiphareth is on the central pillar of consciousness and for us to ascend and be at one with the Godhead (Kether) we have to pass through the energies of this Sephirah. Christian fundamentalism has chosen to misinterpret this and created an elitist religion. One whereby no other religion can take you to heaven, as they do not go through Jesus Christ. True from the perspective of Christ consciousness, for that is what was meant, but Christ consciousness, in my opinion, is merely a label for a state of being which is open and inclusive to all religions.

Tiphareth is at a balance point between our higher mind and our lower mind, represented by the two worlds Briah and Yetzirah respectively. This state of consciousness has access to the creative world of Briah and can transform these creative impulses into form (Yetzirah), being the world of formations. I will return to Tiphareth later when I explain Avril's role.

The World of Yetzirah

The Yetzirah world is the world of thought, and our thoughts create and crystalise into form and shape our reality. However, the astral world of images and thoughts is a potential world of deceptions and illusions. We have individual consciousness to create from, and we have collective consciousness to create from, and each influences the other.

Collective consciousness, on a day to day basis, is largely beyond our control in terms of how it impinges on our life. The only aspects within our own control are our own personal choices, based on our awareness and level of consciousness at any one point in time. We can hope to choose from our highest common denominator to influence and build our lives from. Collective consciousness has a mass momentum of it's own whereby, and often unfortunately, the lowest common denominator of consciousness creates. It often creates through the illusion of separateness and it's associated self interests, greed, pain and suffering - hence the illusions and deceptions when judged against the light of truth. Consciousness will spiral upwards when enough individuals within humanity have spiritual understanding and awareness of the connectedness of all things. This will produce a critical mass necessary for a paradigm shift. This book, amongst many others, is an attempt to raise collective awareness for this purpose.

Netzach

Netzach is situated within the world of Yetzirah and forms part of the astral triangle at the base of the Pillar of Mercy. This is principally a Sephirah of feeling. It is the dynamic force of the emotions that inspire one to love and create. This is the home of the fiery waters of passion, which allow one to focus a tremendous amount of energy upon any object of interest. Anything that is imbued by feeling, such as dance, the arts, and sex is associated with this Sephirah. Netzach is invoked by ceremonial magic by way of feeling. It ensouls the object of interest through feeling, and this gives it 'life'.

Here also we have the raw energy of nature, which elicits feelings of connectedness to the planet. Without this sephirah, love, as a feeling, could not exist, for its fiery waters inflame the heart. However, one has to be aware of the illusions of glamour, and of mistaking lust for love.

Religion has historically been less than comfortable with the natural forces of this Sephirah and has attempted to oppress elements of it in Society, hence the working out of the shadow in the collective. But without this Sephirah within the human condition we would not be able to experience empathy, compassion and ultimately live unconditional love as a race.

Hod

Hod is a sphere of form situated at the base of the Pillar of Severity. This sephirah organises and makes sense of the, often, instinctual forces which lie in Netzach. Hod is the rational, discerning, observing mind. Needless to say that all sciences come under this sphere, but so too the occult (that which is hidden). Netzach and Hod exist as the force and form of Astral Consciousness. This interdependency is crucial for the cosmic laws of manifestation whereby Hod (mind) is the Architect and Designer. Netzach ensouls the process with feeling and passion. The corresponding images of future projection upon the astral plane are translated, moulded and woven into the etheric mesh of Yesod, the next sephirah. The manifestation process is then ready to convert the original intent and design into the pre-sent realm of Malkuth. Here we experience the results of our earlier creative intent through the various 'worlds' previously described.

Yesod

Yesod is positioned on the central pillar within the astral triangle and is a gateway between the world of Yetzirah and the world of Malkuth. Yesod is called the foundation and for good reason. Ether and the collective unconscious come under this sphere. The etheric body is that which vitalises the physical body, and ailments in the physical body have to pass through the etheric body first over a period of time. This is why the power of thought is so important - a healthy mind equals a healthy body. If our thoughts and feelings are positive then the etheric charge of Yesod in the astral triangle will translate this positivity into our physical condition in Malkuth.

Avril received a channeling which talked about the nature of this sphere (see Chapter 3). *"All life is surrounded by a mist of colour* [Ether]. *This colour contains all the codes from which all forms are developed. Each level has it's own colour which gives the signal for cells to develop."* She also received a channelling which said that *"each group has it's own colour and symbol."* This means that not only does an individual have an aura but that each group of souls has a composite aura too. At some level this is what Avril was tuning into when she tried to find each individual member of the group. One could also say that, given that sound and colour are one and the same thing - a range of vibrational frequencies - then actually we may have found her via her group signal transmitter on the ether. Each soul group will have a fundamental note. We will look again at Yesod when I try and explain the group pattern.

Malkuth

This is Malkuth in the world of Malkuth, this is Kether on a lower arc, this is the densest part of the Tree. Surely the nature of the exercise is to experience heaven on Earth ? By helping to raise the vibration of ourselves and the Earth maybe we can experience love, wisdom and abundance on a continual basis. Surely it is possible to experience unconditional love as a matter of instinct made conscious, live in harmony with the planet, and honour it's place in the greater scheme of the universe and our being ? This has been our motivational wish, along with that of many others at this time, and our group has played a small part in trying to effect this intention in our Earth healing.

Malkuth and humanity's journey are inextricably linked. Hurt the Earth, rape the Earth and we hurt and rape ourselves as we are one (Kether on a lower arc). The reader has probably gathered by now that the Tree is both downward in terms of manifesting the cosmic forces and upwards in terms of raising our consciousness. It is a composite symbol for describing the workings of the universe (macrocosmic) and describing the evolutionary intent of humanity (microcosmic).

There were many clues in Avril's channellings that alluded to the importance and use of the Qabalistic structure although, at the time, she didn't have the mental concepts to interpret the coded meaning. Ashad said *"Our voices spiralled along the circles of power."* This was a direct reference to the Sephiroth. The words joy, beauty and avarice were used. The first two are positive attributes of Tiphareth and the third is the vice of Binah. These words are used quite routinely in Qabalistic circles to describe the virtues and vices of the Sephiroth. Ishtar once said *" You are come to task, for the light must seed again and fruit as before."* This again fits in with the analogy of the Tree of Life - Tree (light) Seed, Fruit and so it goes on, in never ending spirals of death and rebirth. Ashad once said that Avril *" was on the path that leads to knowledge."*

Each Sephirah is connected by a path (lines between Sephiroth in the diagrams). These paths are subjective journeys, reconciling the energies between

The Clew

any two linked Sephirah within one's psyche. They are initiatory life experiences that one needs to develop in order to move towards wholeness. The 'Masters' in the mystery schools graded the initiates as they ascended the Tree via the paths. Once a particular test or virtue was learnt and internalised on a particular path then the initiate was free to begin another. The reality is that we are all on one path or another right now, which is why it is called the Tree of Life! The Soul guides us through the experiences associated with the correspondences of a path. People will live each path differently, depending on their level of consciousness but it will be what that individual needs. The path that Ashad referred to is the path from Tiphareth to Daath (knowledge) on the central pillar. Each path is assigned a Major Arcana Tarot card which reflects that particular journey. There are twenty two paths, which correspond to the twenty two Major Arcana. The path to Daath was the path of the High Priestess - what a surprise!

2 : The Group Pattern that formed the Temple

Now that we have a general overview of the Qabalah we are in a position to contextualise the group experience and the pattern generated. Most people will be familiar with the pattern created in Fig 2. It is indeed the Star of David so coveted by the Hebrew race. For our purposes we can concentrate our attention at, and below, the abyss of Daath, for, although the Supernal triangle would have been ever-present during the Earth healing it played no part in the pattern generated by our incarnate bodies.

The seven Sephiroth in Fig. 2 have planetary correspondences. Beginning at Daath we have Saturn, at Chesed we have Jupiter, at Geburah we have Mars, at Tiphareth we have the Sun, at Netzach we have Venus, at Hod we have Mercury and finally at Yesod we have the Moon.

Each of these Planets reflects the qualities of the associated Sephirah. For example, Jupiter is the benevolent ruler, the law giver, it is also the planet of mercy and idealism, which are Chesed qualities. Mars is the warrior, the action planet, the swiftness of movement, which are Geburah qualities.

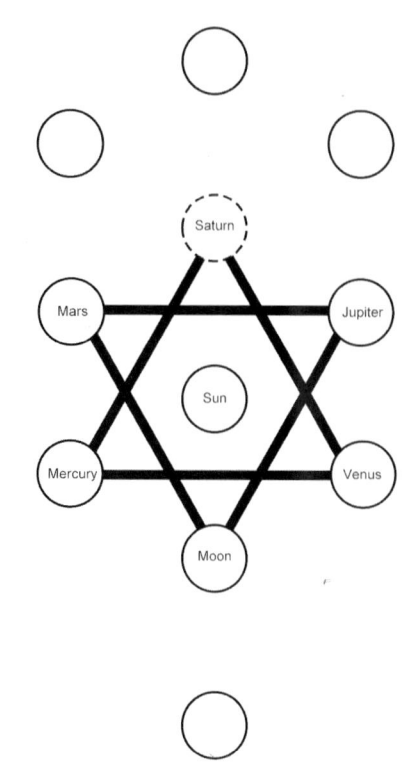

Fig. 2 : Planetary Attributions

The Sun represents wholeness, astrologically, and it is the physical heart and is located at the heart of the Tree. Venus is a planet associated with desire, feelings,

The Clew

love, lust and Nature, which are some of the attributes of Netzach. Mercury rules the mind and how we think, which links into Hod. The Moon is the unconscious and is affiliated with the waters of reflection from which pictures emerge, which is the Yesod domain.

Saturn is normally associated with Binah in the Supernal triangle but that is because it most closely resembles the limitation within form that at a human level we experience. It's position at Daath is a controversial one for commentators on the Qabalah. It is my belief that it's association here is because Saturn rules time and time begins in an incarnation sense when the abyss is crossed between the two worlds. I believe also that the energies of Sirius have to pass through the net of Saturn, for he is the Lord of Karma and therefore must administer our new creative realities as a race, based upon our previous choices made from free will, which may or may not correlate with 'truth'.

Esoterically, these planets are in the order of the ladder of the planets which have a sequential rulership of time, approximately every hour beginning at dawn. It is a continuous cycle of becoming, as the energies cascade through each Sephirah on a daily basis. Saturn is at the apex of the upward pointing triangle. This is no coincidence, as these planets correspond to each day of the week, and Saturday is ruled by Saturn which is the Jewish sabbath. It is therefore probable that Saturn rules the Jewish race, as many of their qualities match Saturn's correspondences. In occult terms the upward pointing triangle is fire and the downward pointing triangle is water. One of Avril's channellings said that *"we must bring the fire and water together like never before."* There is a very important relationship that exists between Daath and Yesod, via their respective planets, that I will attempt to explain when I refer to the ritual that we created.

Merlin said *"how might the light enter if there is no Temple to receive it, and so you must build the Temple. You lay the red carpet"* Fig. 3a. shows the same Sephiroth depicted minus some of the paths in order not to obscure the sighting of the cube. Each of the men is positioned on one of the Sephirah in the diagram. These are the positions which made up the pattern which formed the Temple. Merlin also said "for you place and turn the key to begin anew, to restore the pattern - we stand in our places."

If one looks at the pattern from a plan view, one might be able to see the shape of a Marquee. One of the insights Avril had was that of a peg holding a Marquee down. You may be able to see the shape of a peg in Fig 1c in the world of Yetzirah. The Marquee has six panels with its top sited at Tiphareth. The flexibility of this construction means that it is transportable to any place. Another quote from Merlin was *"the shapes must be restored, renewed and adjusted."* At the time, as we found and stood in our places, we restored these shapes - the first part of the mission. The cube in the centre of the Temple is an archetypal shape for matter, called Metatron's Cube. Metatron is the Archangel of Kether. Within this cube we have the five platonic solids. Add these to the sphere in the centre and we have the six prime universal shapes. I have only mentioned in detail the triangles (Star of David), the cube and the sphere, for these will suffice to explain the story but just for the record the other shapes are the Octhedron, the Dodecahedron and the Icosahedron.

3 : The Ritual

Introduction

It is important to realise that at the time of the event we were not conscious of these shapes and that we must therefore have been operating from unconscious memory. It was only many months later that we began to decode what we had done. Let's remind ourselves of what Ashad had said back in April 1991 *"Your task and those of many like you will not only be with comunication but also in locking in the correct frequencies that will be needed to move the generator pulse of the prime energy to your land and then to secure it in place."*

In other quotes he said " *It is our task to retune the Earth's energy band in order that the interactions can be revitalised. If all is to be well you must become versed in the sounds that will tune the new vibration ... All of life is light and is disseminated through particles of sound ... Love is the key ... Stand in pattern and turn the key."*

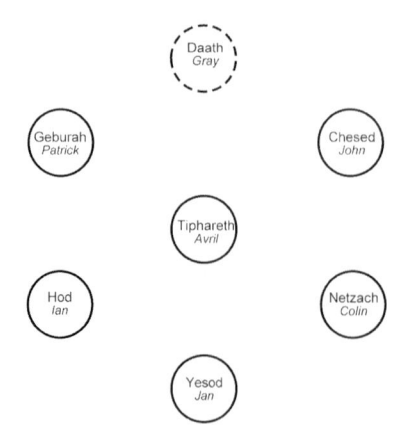

Fig. 3a : The Pattern within the Temple

In astrology every event according to its time and place, as with every birth, creates its own astrological signature. Equally, each soul at birth is specifically incarnating at that time and place because the heavens are lined up in such a way that will give that soul the experience it needs. Our event was no different. We had a time and a place and the heavens were lined up at that moment in a way that matched each of our developmental needs. We all, individually, had an Astrological relationship with that event and place and we all energetically took from that place that which we each needed for our future personal development. It was not by coincidence, we were later to discover, that each of our individual experiences subsequent to the event would mirror the archetypal psychological pattern of the Sephirah we had moved to at the end of the ritual.

The Enactment

Once the men had positioned themselves in the pattern depicted in Fig. 3a the women then formed a diamond shape on the outside for protection. This process has already been described within the story so I do not need to repeat it here, I will instead attempt to explain the meaning behind the ritual. Merlin had said " *We must lay the foundation."*

I have already stated that Yesod represents foundation. This foundation is the ether where *"all the codes are stored."* These colours/sounds in the ether are the building blocks where all forms are developed. These forms are the six primal shapes. Merlin had also said, *"you lay the red carpet."* This was not just a throw-away line, this was a literal reference to the nature of the Mars energy of the group. The colour associated with Mars is red and each of the men placed themselves in the pattern by virtue of their individual Mars positions in their birth horoscopes. You might, by referring back to Fig.3a, imagine a red hexagonal carpet with Avril standing at the centre. The Mars of each of the men who stood on the two outer pillars of the Tree is in a fixed sign of the zodiac. Patrick's is in Taurus, John's is in Leo, Colin's is in Scorpio and Ian's is in Aquarius.

These four placements are a denser version of the first swirlings at Kether. In the Bible these are the four beasts mentioned in Revelations. The Eagle (Scorpio), The Calf (Taurus), The Lion (Leo) and Man (Aquarius). The composite form of the Sphinx also corresponds to these four figures. On the middle pillar at the positions of Daath and Yesod respectively we have Gray's Mars in Cancer and Jan's Mars in Capricorn. No wonder the group experienced so much conflict, for we were each drawn to the group through the resonance of Mars. This Mars connection also explains our Knights Templar pasts which gave us much knowledge but also much turbulence.

The first part of the ritual was orchestrated by Jan and Gray who walked a figure-of-eight around Avril in the centre, passing each other and then returning to their original positions (see Fig. 3b). This is remarkably like the double helix of the D.N.A. code, and Mars, in astrological terms, rules the blood.

Now if I can take you back to Fig.2, I have mentioned the special relationship that exists between Daath and Yesod. Here we have a mirroring, or reversing, of polarity. The Moon rules Cancer which is situated at Yesod and yet Jan stood here with his Mars in Capricorn, which is ruled by Saturn. Gray stood at Daath with his Mars in Cancer which has it's connection to Saturn. They also had the added factors of Jan being a Capricorn Sun sign in the Moon Sphere, Yesod, and Gray being a Cancerian Sun sign at the place of Saturn. I am not sure what this means at this stage but I know this is not just coincidence and that there is a deep meaning behind this occurence.

Avril's role at Tiphareth was to send loving energy out towards Jan, both before and during the sounding of the note. This was via her natal Venus in Taurus position. These two were playing out a cosmic archetype. In Assyria in the second century B.C. the kings of that country would, at the annual spring festival, make love with their High Priestess (the sacred marriage) in order to ensure the fertilisation of the land. Energetically, Avril's Venus and Jan's Mars were mirroring this phenomenon. The path leading up from Yesod to Tiphareth is the path of the Tarot card Temperance. This is an alchemical card whereby fire and water are mixed together, a process which births the new seed. *"You must bring the fire and water together like never before"*. I also know through my own channelling that the Lovers card in the Tarot is assigned to Tiphareth. Hence the coming together of these two energies, the yin and the yang, through love. So whilst we were all spared the literal physical enactment of these energies they were being played out

Fig. 3b : The Helix

The Clew

by virtue of our intention and position in the pattern of the Temple.

The next stage of the ritual was Jan sounding the note which resonated with the place, time and group members of the Temple, in the ethers of Yesod. Once Jan had found the note, he held this harmonic for an intuitive amount of time. A silence then prevailed on the three dimensional level but, I am certain, continued on the other planes. After a brief pause we went on to the final part of the ritual.

4 : The Turning of the Key

The turning of the key was enacted by the movement of the men. I believe that this movement marked the starting up of what we created and also the locking in and protection of it, let me explain.

Fig. 4 shows the direction of the men's movement and the new stations that they took up from the original positions set in Fig. 3a. It will be noticed that Avril and Jan did not move. At the time and for a while afterwards we had doubts as to whether we had done this part of the ritual correctly. We thought Jan should have moved with the rest of the men but he was right to remain in position. It can be seen that our movement mapped out a five sided figure, and by joining the lines up inside this figure it made up the the shape of a pentacle. This pentagram is associated with the fifth harmonic which, in medieval times,

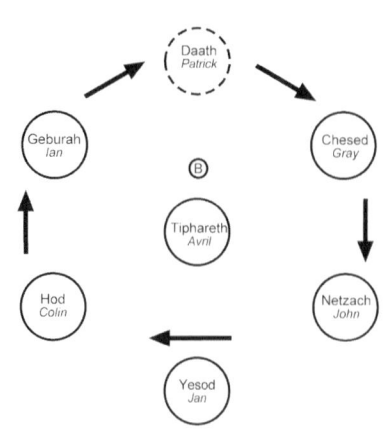

Fig. 4 : The Turning of the Key

was forbidden to be musically played in some churches as it was considered 'evil'. As I mentioned earlier the five is arrived at by 1+2+3+4+5=15 - the number of the Devil in the Tarot.

What is this all about ? In astrology the fifth harmonic is considered to be the creative harmonic - bringing creativity into form. This is exactly the role of the so-called Devil, which was demonised by the medieval Church. The Tarot card in fact pictures a Goat, which is one of the primary correspondences of the planet Saturn, the builder of form. This is the energy of the "Lord of one power" whose voice was channeled by Avril, just prior to our final ritual, bringing love into form by way of the archetypal connection of the High Priestess and the King. There is white magic and there is black magic and both use the pentagram. The only difference is the energy of the intention which lies behind it, not in the pentagram itself. Merlin had earlier stated the intention was to create from love when he said *"All you are asked is to stand without grudge or grievance for one second."* I believe that the movement of Colin from Netzach to Hod disconnected or uncoupled the energetic connection between Jan and Avril and enabled us to seal and lock in the energies.

224

The diagram also looks like an envelope, does it not, which has the same effect. But there is another reason for this pentagram. The pentagram, or quintile of seventy two degrees, is said to be instrumental in turning the spindle of the D.N.A. from which the double helix sends into motion the renewal and adjustment of the shapes. This movement, once activated, gathers a new centre from where Avril stood (at the 'genitalia' of the pentacle) to the point B at the centre of the pentagram. *"The pulse is to be moved."* Although this movement was small within the Temple itself, its projection over distance into the infinity of space and the possible new stellar alignment it may have made was, and is, beyond our comprehension.

The mission was accomplished. We had restored, renewed and adjusted the shapes and moved the pulse.

Ian's Bibliography

Fortune, Dion, *The Mystical Qabalah* Pub. Aquarian Press
Knight, Gareth, *A Practical Guide to Qabalistic Symbolism* Pub. Khan and Averill

The Clew

The Clew

The Story Told, The Challenge Made
Colin Pope

I met Avril in January 1998. In those days I was " Colin, the healer." A colleague had asked me to distant-view a cottage in Cornwall for a client. It was one of many routine tasks. I sent him a drawing of the place as I "saw" it, and forgot about it. Then Avril phoned. Something in her voice was very familiar. I was moved to find out, and so became one of the "men who must walk."

There had been nothing in my upbringing to suggest this strange way of behaving. After a 'guid' Scots grammar school education, I entered a profession and worked my way up from tying parcels and making tea. By the 70s I was a man with a mortgage, hoping for promotion, expecting to get married and settle down. Settle I did not.

For, one night in March 1973 a crackling ball entered and lit up my bedroom, flipped me onto my back, and pierced me with penetrating bolts of light. I felt so loved, and so connected with all living forms that it was almost unbearable. It was ecstasy.

In the days that followed I began to see things differently. I began to see energy fields, as auras around people, and as flows and swirls of energy through the landscape. My painfully small, semi-scientific shell of belief was broken. What followed was that journey of self-transformation that many healers will be familiar with. My professional practice began with people. Then I saw that people need healthy homes, so I went into space clearing. Then the old, sacred places began to call out.

Joining Avril's group was like coming home, being in a family. There was instant recognition, support - and a purpose, a structure. We also had squabbles and feuds that rampaged around until someone recognised what was happening, and they were "processed". I found myself engaged in something strange and silly, that I could not explain or prove to anyone, yet that something was also familiar, important and incontestable.

My aim is to begin to tease out some of the implications of Avril's discoveries. And to initiate debate about how her findings can help us to bring about changes that can start to make our world more the way we all, surely, must wish it could become.

For this is an important narrative. Let there be no hesitation about that. It deserves wide readership and discussion of the issues it raises. The corpus of source material it is based on invites serious and innovative scientific research into the mechanisms of the living landscape, and asks to be brought into a public debate about land use policies and practices. It informs and enlightens, amongst many things, the "genetic modification" controversy, and national health and economic policies across the whole developed world.

This material stands as being both important and challenging, because of the timing of its first publication, and the severity of the problems confronting our civilisation.

In orthodox terms we have just begun "The New Millenium." To those

The Clew

familiar with the concept of Archetypes, we are now in "The Age of Aquarius." Aquarius is as androgynous as a shell-suit, the 'child beyond parental control' of the Internet, as humanitarian as a pop star raging to cease the never-ending indebtedness of poor nations to states so rich they can't afford to give back even a hundredth part of what they make.

We enter an era, and we find that all the old certainties have gone. We have to learn to live with uncertainty, to find constancy within ourselves. It is a time when an unseen enemy may strike at any moment. It is a time when our children have to grow up faster than ever before, and have to know more about how corruption stalks the streets than we dare think about. It is time when it dawns on us there may not be enough to go round, when we are older or get sick, - and we are the rich, the smart and the good.

The challenge of the book is directly to us, the rich, the smart and the good. To our assumptions about "what the real world is like", "how things are." And ultimately to what is, and what it means to be, a human being. And, it must follow, whether continuing to boldly go by these assumptions about "how things are" – that ours is the best and only sensible way of doing things - actually does what it says on the tin, really will deliver a world of increasing freedom, prosperity and justice, really will bring us each health, happiness and an abiding sense of personal fulfilment.

Let me therefore begin the debate by rehearsing some of the assumptions that seem to underpin the way we hold things to be – that is, Life as seen through a 'Western-style, developed economy' prism.

We are born, we live, and, one day, we will die. We, equals our physical body, should hopefully live through to an age of dignity. If our body is not functioning well, through inheritance, accident or disease, we will expect medical science to treat the problem, and we will not enjoy waiting, or paying.

As we realise our time has come, we will hope to have lived decently enough to qualify to see our family and friends again in the next place. We will be blessed with their company for an eternity. It sounds like Heaven.

If we have failed, are faulty, we will be banished for ever. God gave us our life, we blew it, - and we get no second chance.

Maybe religion is no longer so much what we worship. Science has probably taken centre stage. It says we are extinguished, become extinct as an individual person. But we pass on a genetic likeness, maybe congealed in a test tube.

Don't talk about death, dwell on the morbid. Change the subject, put the kettle on, and get on with the next pressing thing. Let us be rational. Science and technology bring progress, do they not, and so things tend to improve. Look at the opportunities our children have, compared with us today. When I was a lad, it seemed it was only missionaries who went abroad. Then came package holidays. Now it is almost obligatory for our kids to go round the world before beginning their career.

Our free market economy and liberal democracies are superior, and are the best and only way of making things better in the world. It is evil foreigners that cause harm, hinder progress. One day, everyone will have a mobile phone with a choice of ring-tones, and the world will be saved.

The Clew

So we can dismiss Sylvia Ward's book, Avril, and her like - with ease. Channelling, dowsing, healing with invisible energies, must be some kind of delusion. It is Impressionables that buy into this stuff, you know, to compensate for what they are missing.

And, of course, Astrology is nonsense, too. It does not, can not, show or prove anything. The gravitational pull of a star thousands of light years away cannot possibly affect us, any more than the draught of air caused by a bus turning a corner in the next town does.

I have tried to represent some typical Western thinking. If it was as reasonable and coherent as it seems, we might sleep safely in our beds. As I see it, it is well-meant, but it is dangerous, because it is both incomplete and not thought through. And there is a huge failure of imagination. For imagination is, above all, the most human thing about humans. Let me explain why I see it so.

First, whether we like the implications or not, we can not deny Avril's actual experience, and its precise fit with that of her companions. For each of us, mystic, scientist, occasional reader of books of mystery and wonder, whoever and whatever we may be, our inner world, what we feel, and what it means, is ours, and is absolutely incontestable. No-one can gainsay it, tell us what we feel, and what our life means to us.

The test of an argument is its extreme. Even the experience of those who have leave of their senses has turned out to be important to our progress as a humanity. Was it not in, of all places, a mental asylum, that Jung found, and founded, his work on the Archetypes?

It is wholly unacceptable to dismiss experiences, simply because they imply possibilities that do not accord with the thinking of the time. To do so is not scientific, if science is truly about gathering knowledge. The history of science is much about those who dared to believe the unbelievable. They were marginalised or ignored, and, quite often, vilified. Such is the power of orthodoxy and of fashion in thinking, as well as in dress, and it continues to this day.

And insights, new ideas, where do they come from ? They come from the unconscious, do they not ? What of the dream of the benzene ring, or the glimpse of a spiral staircase when pondering the structure of DNA. These experiences sound so like the theme that runs through all the spiritual traditions – that of the individual seeker receiving, in the moment, according to their degree of readiness.

But there is no requirement for scientists, politicians, corporate directors or even clergy to be self-aware, to open themselves to look at the filter through which they experience, that is, to really take responsibility. Except perhaps for the Buddhist Masters, whose suffering is distilled into a smile, those who influence us, shape the conditions of our lives, the political and corporate decision-makers, project their ideas and values onto the world screen as eagerly and assuredly as Hitler did. Who dares, wins. As we try to lessen our terror, we dare not admit that one of the shadows cast over the Middle East is our own.

A way forward, I suggest, is to gather and collate the anomalous, the different, the quirky and look for themes that can be subjected to a systematic approach, to work with, rather than against. It is too easy to dismiss and diminish, and we are not elevated as a consequence.

The Clew

We need all the scientists and other professionals we can get, those who are secure in their love of truth and of new thinking, to make a bridge between the world and language of the intuitive and that of the scientific and politico-economic establishment. Such people do exist, and I invite you to approach us.

The time for this is now. Science is in Trouble. Well, not exactly Science, but the way scientific precepts are applied in practice to landscapes and populations. People are not so sure any more about the inevitable march of progress through science and technology. Here in the UK, test areas for genetically modified crops are routinely despoiled. Parents confound our immunology regime by insisting on vaccinations being done on their terms. This is surely part of a wider unease I have already hinted at. Please be clear that I am not saying science is bad, or that we are not immeasurably the better for it. Of course we are. It is the way it is deployed by government agencies and, chiefly, by multi-national corporations, that is worrying folk. They feel something has got out of control, become a monster that might turn on us at any moment. And they make accusations of greed, cynicism and hypocrisy.

So, we are in double trouble – our future is uncertain, and we feel out of control, cannot trust the means we rely on to take us towards that future.

What then are we asking of people of open and inquiring minds to consider?

Well, one thing we'll have to do is to be careful about what we mean by words like body, memory, star and so on, because there are huge conceptual differences in the way these terms are understood, and this hinders constructive exchange.

Let me offer one example. As I have already indicated, astrology is sometimes characterised as relying on gravitational forces acting on our physical bodies. Now I am not an astrologer, so I have no position to defend. However I suggest that mystics and scientists might be able to start a dialogue on a proposition that in space there are points emitting energy at a speed above that of light. Their wave/particles do not lose their charge over distance. These wave/particles could be received systematically within the partitions of the body's own energy field.

Now this personal energy field is known to science, and is the subject of serious and continuing international enquiry. The reception within the field of these charges would be experienced psychologically, like any other influences on the psyche, and induce alterations of mood and behaviour.

The position of these dark points would, of course, have to correspond sufficiently with those of the visible spectrum to explain the night-sky associations of the ancients with their mythology. The mood, and behavioural tendencies induced by these emanations would have to be observed, in longitudinal research, as behaviour consistent with those of the mythical characters, the archetypes and planetary attributes of astrology.

Maybe, like me, you have camped in a deserted landscape. As night approached you gathered round the fire, for companionship and comfort, to share food and story. Above, the stars were so bright and full, they could almost be reached, almost plucked. These times remind us that, as a species, we have spent most of our time on earth living and working outdoors. It was only as recently as my grandparent's generation that most of us came in to our little artificial environment. Now we gaze at screens for hours on end, hoping for first-rate enlightenment from second-hand experiences. They could tell you the time, with no watch, by glancing up at the sky.

I do not accept that our forebears were less observant and intelligent than we are. I do accept that they formed sound judgements about the problems of their communities, and took as much care as we do, maybe more, to pass to their children the wisdom of the family, and the culture of the clan.

The themes of human striving are common, and they are familiar :

Favoured or ignored child. Falling in, and out of, love. Doing a competent job. Living up to expectations. Loving more than one, or more than once. Losing someone you love.

Reclaiming power and keeping it. Ensuring the lineage, the inheritance. Worrying about our own children. Dowries and legacies, making, and breaking, kings and queens. Losing the gods, finding and keeping the gods… making sense of it all.

These, and others you can probably think of, play out generation after generation, like a soap opera, only real. Our sharp-eyed, smart, thoughtful, folks saw the patterns, drew the lessons. They saw the correspondences, and they troubled to bequeath their wisdom to us with the means they had – folk tales and myths, cards and games, ritual marks and movements, mounds and stones, paths and pyramids. They took great care to do this, as if it were a matter of life and death. And, it turns out, it is ! It is only our preconceptions and prejudices, our need to feel superior because, deep down, we are unsure of ourselves, that prevent us seeing the brilliance of their science and their engineering.

The resolution is not to see astrology and sacred landforms as bad astronomy misapplied by the ignorant and muddle-headed, but as a rich legacy of superb psychology that can simplify our decisions at every level of abstraction.

What of the guidance that speaks through sensitives, that they experience as guides existing outside of them in a different realm, where time is less obvious ? These voices, are outside, yet are heard quietly, in quietness, inside, and speak a timeless tongue. In Avril's case we know that, for example, those teachings that were for individual clients, sometimes produced a degree of relief from dis-ease that could not be achieved or explained by medicine. Avril is not alone in having done this type of work. In my lifetime the NHS has accepted healers do something valid and useful, and there is organic growth in the collaboration between medical and complementary practice. The debate then is not about validity and usefulness, but about how to find ways of bringing all these healing modalities to bear, ethically and effectively, on the crushing demand for health care. Central to that is ownership by the individual for their own health.

The voices continually talk about remembering, urge Avril and the others to remember. And her companions continually used their intuition to sense and reach decisions about what steps to take. Maybe intuition – knowing something, what to do, without knowing how or why, is memory.

How works, and where lies, this memory, a memory that seems to span plural lifetimes ?

We have known from the 1950s that, under certain conditions, people can be

The Clew

induced to recollect memories, often from their childhood. These are not dim snapshots, like a dusty album from Nan's attic, but a vivid re-experiencing, full of intense, forgotten, details and emotions that may have shaped a marriage or a career. It was this advance in understanding through brain surgery that showed there is a real, physiological basis for psycho-dynamic therapies.

It seems we have a memory of everything that happened to us. It is just that we cannot recall all of it, just like that. That would be too much.

So where are these memories, these wide-band records of astonishing details and convulsive emotions stored.? It seems highly likely, does it not, that some of the bandwidth of the personal energy field is allocated to memory, our brain being a bio-computer whose primary functionality is recall.

And is this memory personal, or do we plug in, energetically, to collective memory, held in some dimensional domain. Is that how this group of friends found each other, found picture, recalled name, took up their place in the land, as did their feet in ancient times? We could say that we re-membered. Each of us, each member, held, holds, a piece that makes a pattern when fitted with the others.

Now I know there are energy field practitioners who bring relief to their clients by adjusting what they understand to be the outer, universal layer of their patient's individual energy field. This seems reasonable. Such a universal field would give access to the memory of the landscape, or perhaps of its guardians, a la Avril, another segment might be that body of universal information that dowsers draw on for their geographic and health-related work, like finding running water or testing for allergies.

Independent verification of mystic or psychic phenomena is known to be difficult, because, (as the Koran points out), the universe is renewed in every micro-moment, and we are complex beings, but consistency of data and cross-checking by others working blind can surely bring confidence in the phenomena observed. I have participated in such experiments, and do not know of anyone working in the fields of dowsing, healing and the transcription of apparent guidance from other realms who would not welcome a proper investigation of "the field." The genuine have nothing to fear, and we can all only gain through fuller understanding.

And then there is the matter of re-incarnation. A World survey, of course, would show reincarnation to be normal, unquestionably, for millions of people follow the great religions of the East. It only seems unfamiliar to us, huddled in our little Western conceptual island, with its modest presumption of superior beliefs and values.

" It is absolutely necessary that the soul should be healed and purified, and if this does not take place during its life in earth it must be accomplished in future lives." These are not my words. These are not the words of a Buddhist Master, or of a Hindu Guru. These are the words of a greatly revered Church Father, Gregory of Nyssa, in 350CE. They could not be more clear and unequivocal. Bishop Origen is known to have upheld the prevailing understanding of reincarnation at the Council of Nicea, whose decisions to alter church doctrine to a one-life format patently helped Constantine the Great's dynastic ambitions, and those of many in power since.

The Clew

It seems to be very clear that the teaching that was eventually fashioned into Orthodox Christianity was originally of the Journey of the Soul, just as in all the other major traditions. A little scholarship does rather suggest that the original teaching has been amended for reasons of political expediency and control. What monarchs, and probably the Church in its times of excess, wanted was a docile and compliant flock. One shot, in or out, heaven or hell, would certainly do that. Complain, question, and I will pull the excommunication cord.

And then, as Jung saw, the Reformation almost threw out the baby with the bath-water, so more of the rich symbolism, the geomancy, the inner knowledge of the rituals was lost. Worship became focussed on the external and the transcendent. Inner inquiry became focussed on finding the known, and becoming more attached to it, - that "deepening of faith." The clergy were rather left finding they had to learn how to become social workers.

The temper of our time is different. The children of Aquarius question, question the authority, question the word. They look outside the boundaries. They also look within, and the focus of inner inquiry is freedom from the attachment to, enslavement by, the known. They may sometimes be mistaken, wildly so. They may never be able to replace religious observance, its familiarity, its comfort, its hope. But they will not see this as error, or mortal sin, or limitation, and they will not be stopped in their quest. Questioned, challenged, they will simply say " The problem is that Religion is not spiritual enough!" and go on seeking that new myth to enclose our reality.

And Time - what of that ? Is it a fourth dimension, as we were told as children, after height, width and depth ? As you probably know, there is currently a great ongoing debate about time. I will not take up more of your time cataloguing the possibilities. The point I would make is that we often refer to time when we mean sequence. The law of sequence places cause before effect. Only when the cause is acknowledged – and dealt with – does the effect leave. Time is not, at all, a great healer. We are - especially when we can stop and listen, and take responsibility for ourselves.

The One Life Illusion, interpreted into a Western model, naturally makes us think of our life as being singular and linear. What the re-incarnation factor adds is a realisation that we may be simultaneously processing events and distresses held in the past, that is in a domain within the universal field where our experiences are stored until they can be progressed.

It may be this domain, this perspective, through which our guides see us, overviewing us as a multi-faceted organism that sends learning from different exposures, back to its central soul, like a security guard monitoring a CCTV system. And did not the ancients, Plutarch and the others, hold that our soul resides in the stars ? So far and yet so near. If this is the perspective of Avril's, and our, voices, it is no wonder their sense of time and place is expressed so quaintly.

These then are just some of the theories about our nature and how we may relate to our cosmic environment that are suggested by Avril's work with our group. You may already be thinking of others. And we have not even begun to look at the wider economic implications of our relationship with the land that the voices warn and tell about.

The Clew

Here I am squaring up to the realisation that our whole advanced civilisation, our whole world economy, relies on the unabated consumption of fuel reserves that are finite, and causes the destruction of forests and habitats that create our atmosphere and regulate our climate. It is now many years since Schumacher published " Small is Beautiful" and warned a previous generation of the pinch-point that we would inevitably reach. The time when demand for non-renewables will be greater than the planet can supply - The Time of No Turning Back. It must be terribly close.

I have seen very little done in my lifetime to damage our consumptionist mind-set. The 1979 oil price-hike should have been taken as a warning to start weaning our whole economy onto a renewable, sustainable basis. In one, narrow sector of this comprehensive and inevitable problem we find, over twenty years on, people clamouring for more road capacity, and seeing themselves hard done by, because of the inhibitive price of fuel. We simply do not seem to have registered that our way of life is unsustainable. We exceed our resources as casually as we exceed the speed limit. Nothing exceeds like excess.

Part of this problem is a confusion between customer and consumer. The customer is always right : the consumer is almost always part of something wrong.

As I write these words, the Brazilian Congress is about to consider a proposal to turn an area of rain-forest the size of a European country into wood chip. You do not need me to spell out the consequences of this molestation of our environment, the quick relief, the lasting, irreversible damage. But they have mouths to feed and debts to pay. Hunger cannot wait.

It therefore comes as a profound relief to read the guidance that Avril was given. Enough has been done energetically, metaphysically, by many people working intuitively by themselves or in groups around the world to stabilise the earth, and our place in it, just for now. We have a sporting chance of pulling through. There is everything to play for, and we will play the game of our lives.

As I draw to a close there is one more observation I must make. It is simply this. We have all been very fortunate to have Sylvia Ward as the narrator of this tale. The hallmark of her skill is that she stands back to let Avril and the story shine through. She is a rare translucence.

So the word has been heard, heeded, the companions gathered. The steps have been taken to make it safe, just for today, and now the story is told. It is therefore to the readers of this book that comes the challenge, a supreme challenge of our time.

Final Wish

It is the sincere wish of all those who have participated in the presentation of this story that its publication will :

1. offer some rationale for the work of so many others who have also been working intuitively during these past years, either alone or in groups, with the concepts of personal and Earth healing;
2. encourage increasing debate between the mystic and scientific communities;
3. increase awareness of the power and memory we are all individually able to access, and the responsibility for correct use that such knowledge places on us;
4. encourages a greater understanding of and care for the amazing universe we inhabit, and an awareness of our inter-connections with it;
5. allow us to lay aside arrogance when reflecting upon the ancient world and its beliefs and practices.

* * * * *

The Clew

Bibliography

ASTROLOGY

Baigent, Michael, *From the Omens of Babylon: Astrology and Ancient Babylon*
(Arkana/Penguin 1994)

Brady, Bernadette, *Brady's Book of Fixed Stars*
(Samuel Weiser Inc 1998 ISBN 1-57863-105-X)

Clow, Barbara Hand, *Chiron*
(Llewellyn Publications 1995 ISBN 0-87542-094-X)

Devlin, Mary, *Astrology and Past Lives*
(Whitford Press 1987 ISBN 0-914918-71-0)

Ebertin, Reinhold, *The Combination of Stellar Influences*
(American Federation of Astrologers. Inc 1972 ISBN 0-86690-087-X)

George, Demetra, *Asteroid Goddesses*
(ACS Publications 1986 ISBN 0-935127-15-1)

Gettings, Fred, *The Secret Zodiac: The Hidden Art in Medieval Astrology*
(Arkana Press 1987 ISBN 0-14-019215-8)

Hand, Robert, *Planets in Composite*
(Whitford Press 1975 ISBN 0-914918-22-2)

Hand, Robert, *Planets in Transit*
(Whitford Press 1976 ISBN 0-914918-24-9)

Hickey, Isabel M., *Astrology: A Cosmic Science*
(CRCS Publications 1992 ISBN 916360-52-0)

Michelson, Neil F., *The American Ephemeris for the 20th Century*
(ACS Publications ISBN 0-935127-19-4)

Morse, Eric, *The Living Stars*
(Amethyst Books 1988 ISBN 0-944256-02-3)

Nolle, Richard, *Chiron*
(American Federation of Astrologers, Inc 1983 ISBN 0-86690-236-8)

Oken, Alan, *Soul-Centred Astrology*
(The Crossing Press 1990 ISBN 0-89594-811-7)

Rudhyar, Dane, *An Astrological Mandala: The Cycle of Transformation and its 360 Symbolic Phases*
(Vintage Books 1974 ISBN 0-394-71992-1)

Sakoian & Acker, *The Astrologers Handbook*
(HarperPerennial 1973 ISBN 0-06-272004X)

Sakoian & Acker, *The Astrology of Human Relations*
(HarperPerennial 1989 ISBN 0-06-2720309)

Spiller & McCoy, *Spiritual Astrology*
(Simon & Schuster Inc 1988 ISBN 0-671-66041-1)

ASTRONOMY

Krupp, E.C., *Skywatchers, Shamans and Kings*
(John Wiley & Sons. Inc 1997 ISBN 0-471-04863-1)

CHANNELLING

Andrews, Ted, *How to meet and work with Spirit Guides*
Llewellyn Publications 1995 ISBN 0-87542-008-7

Hastings, Arthur, *With the Tongues of Men and Angels*
(Holt, Rinehart & Winston, Inc. 1991 ISBN 0-03-047164-8)

Klimo, Jon, *Psychics, Prophets and Mystics*
(Aquarian Press 1991 ISBN 1-85538-082-X)

LeShan, Lawrence Ph.D, *The Medium, The Mystic and the Physicist*
(Penguin/Arkana 1974 ISBN 0-14-01-9499-1)

Loewe & Blacker, *Oracles and Divination*
(Shambhala Publications Inc 1981 ISBN 0-394-74880-8)

White, Ruth, *A Question of Guidance*
(C. W. Daniel Co. Ltd. 1988 ISBN 0-85207-193-0)

White, Ruth, *Working with Guides and Angels*
(Piatkus 1996 ISBN 0-7499-1605-2)

White, Ruth & Swainson, Mary, *Gildas Communicates*
((Hillman Printers (Somerset) Ltd. 1971 ISBN 85435-141-8))

EARTH MYSTERIES

Heselton, Philip, *Earth Mysteries*
(Element Books Ltd 1995 ISBN 1-85230-714-5)

Miller, Hamish & Broadhurst, Paul, *The Sun and The Serpent*
(Pendragon Press 1989 ISBN 0-9515183-1-3)

The Clew

Pennick, Nigel, *Mazes and Labyrinths*
(Robert Hale 1994   ISBN 0-7090-5508-0)

Purce, Jill, *The Mystic Spiral: Journey of The Soul*
(Thames and Hudson 1974   ISBN 0-500-81005-2)

Screeton, Paul, *Quicksilver Heritage: The Mystic Leys - Their Legacy of Ancient Wisdom*
(Thorsons Publishers Ltd 1974   ISBN 0-7225-0282-6)

HISTORY

Kramer, Samuel Noah, *The Sumerians*
(University of Chicago Press 1971   ISBN 0-226-45238-7)

Lehmann, Johannes, *The Hittites: People of a Thousand Gods*
(Collins 1977   ISBN 0-00-216314-4)

MYSTICISM

The Shrine of Wisdom Quarterly
(The Shrine of Wisdom 1925-1928)

Bailey, Alice, *The Seven Rays of Life*
(Lucis Press Ltd. 1995   ISBN 0-85330-142-5)

MYTHOLOGY

Branston, Brian, *The Lost Gods of England*
(Thames & Hudson 1974)

Graves, Robert, *The White Goddess*
(Faber and Faber 1961   ISBN 0-571-06961-4)

Guerber, H.A., *Myths of the Norsemen: From the Eddas and Sagas*
(George G. Harrap & Co 1909)

Hamlyn, Paul, *Larousse Encyclopaedia of Mythology*
(Batchworth Press Ltd 1960)

QABALAH

Parfitt, Will, *The Complete Guide to the Kabbalah*
(Rider Books 1998 ISBN 0-7126-1418-4)

REINCARNATION

Andrews, Ted,   *How To Uncover Your Past Lives*
(Llewellyn Publications   1995   ISBN 0-87542-022-2)

Christie-Murray, David,   *Reincarnation: Ancient Beliefs and Modern Evidence*
(Prism Press   1988   ISBN 1-85327-012-1)

Cranston, Sylvia,   *Reincarnation: The Phoenix Fire Mystery*
(Theosophical University Press   1994   ISBN 1-55700-026-3)

RELIGION

Eliade, Mircea,   *A History of Religious Ideas*
(Collins   1979   ISBN 0-00-215311-4)

King, John,   *The Celtic Druids Year*
(Blandford   1995   ISBN 0-7137-24633)

Nichols, Ross,   *The Book of Druidry*
(Aquarian Press   1975   ISBN 0-85030-900-X)

Ozaniec, Naomi,   *Daughter of the Goddess: The Sacred Priestess*
(Aquarian/Thorsons   1993   ISBN 1-85538-280-6)

Pollack, Rachel,   *The Body of the Goddess: Sacred wisdom in myth, landscape and culture*
(Element   1997   ISBN 1-85230-871-0)

Shepsut, Asia,   *Journey of the Priestess*
(Aquarian/Thorsons   1993   ISBN 1-85538-282-2)

Acknowledgement

Many thanks to 'The Lucis Trust' for its permission to quote from 'The Seventh Ray: Revealer of the New Age'

Notes

Chapter 1 :

1. Extracts from some of these early channellings have already appeared in David Icke's book *The Truth Vibrations* (Aquarian Press, 1991, 1-85538-136-2)

The Authors

Sylvia Ward

While sitting in a pub listening to this journey, Sylvia responded to Avril's comment that she had been told to write a book about it with four dangerous words. "I can do that." Thus began her two year involvement with Avril's story. Her own in-depth research into many channelled sources, the Knights Templar and astrology gave her the background she needed to understand the concepts in Avril's narrative. Her work as a college composition instructor and a technical writer gave her the skills she needed for the work. And her sojourn with her British husband to live in the south west of England for two years provided both the introduction and access to Avril's material and the proximity needed for the project.

Following completion of her part of the project, Sylvia returned to her native United States, and now lives in Charlottesville, Virginia, where her husband publishes an alternative press newspaper.

Avril Newey

Avril's family has lived within the Heart of England for over six hundred years, where she still lives. Her childhood in Kenilworth was a constant reminder of an intuitive connection to the land and to her family line, and instilled a vague, but insistent, sense of duty and responsibility. This journey has clarified and drawn together these seemingly disparate elements into a cohesive understanding of her own life's meaning and purpose.

By bringing this story to a wider audience Avril's desire is to point out that we have become disconnected from our roots and a care and understanding of the very land on which we stand. She asks that we look again at ancient knowledge that our modern society has sought to disparage, for the many answers it contains that our scientists, politicians and other leaders cannot supply, but which are vital for our survival. She hopes to encourage and empower others in their own journeys to realise their potential for contributing to all our futures.

PLEASE NOTE

Due to a file translation error the diagrams included in the 'Tree of Life' section have been reproduced with insufficient clarity. They are repeated here and should be read in conjunction with the appropriate text.